2008 engage
Super League Review

Mike 'Stevo' Stephenson

As the face of rugby league, Sky Sports' Mike 'Stevo' Stephenson has been appearing on UK TV screens twice a week for nearly two decades. Co-commentating with his on-screen partner, Eddie Hemmings, Stevo has developed a reputation for straight talking in the game without pulling punches. However, many viewers little realise that in this earlier days, Stevo was one of the star players in rugby league. Born in Dewsbury West Yorkshire in 1947 Stevo signed for his home town rugby league club and also gained honours with the Yorkshire county side. In 1972 he represented Great Britain in the Rugby League World Cup and scored a vital try that enabled the team to defeat favourites Australia in the final.

In 1973 he signed for Australian club Penrith Panthers for a then world record transfer fee. Stevo then entered the world of journalism and spent 15 years with the *Sydney Sun* before working on radio and TV. He has had many articles published in the UK and Australia on rugby league, food, wine and travel. He has worked on a number of books including his biography, *Stevo: Looking Back*, published by Vertical Editions.

Stevo has worked for Sky Sports as a rugby league commentator for the past 16 years. He is one of the world's leading collectors of rugby league memorabilia and established the Gillette Rugby League Heritage Centre at the famous George Hotel in Huddersfield in 2005. He now resides in Sydney and London.

Peter Morley

Peter Morley was born in 1948 and has been interested in photography for over 40 years. Whilst living in Salisbury he supplied photographs for the *Salisbury Journal* as well as national newspapers including the *Daily Express*. When his son began playing rugby, he became interested in sport photography especially rugby league photography supplying photographs for *League Weekly* and covering amateur matches, Super League matches, Grand Finals and international matches. He has also contributed to a number of books including three editions of the *Gillette Rugby League Yearbook* and has supplied pictures to rugby league clubs for their match day programmes. Currently Peter lives in Rothwell, Leeds and works as a freelance photographer supplying the *Rugby League Express* and *Rugby League World*. His current portfolio can be seen on his web site at www.rlaimages.com

2008 engage
Super League Review

Mike 'Stevo' Stephenson

Photography by Peter Morley

VERTICAL EDITIONS

www.verticaleditions.com

First published in the United Kingdom in 2008 by
Vertical Editions, Unit 4a, Snaygill Industrial Estate, Skipton, North Yorkshire BD23 2QR

www.verticaleditions.com

ISBN 978-1-904091-28-8

Cover design and typeset by HBA, York

Printed and bound by Printhaus, Northampton

CONTENTS

FOREWORD

It is with great pleasure that I welcome you to this review of engage Super League XIII. The season provided us, once again, with some tremendous on field action resulting in record breaking crowds and making it the best supported season in the competition's history.

With each round we see outstanding demonstrations of sporting talent, packaged with the family entertainment that makes rugby league such a great experience for the whole family.

Capturing special moments from throughout the season cannot have been easy, as each weekend was full of unpredictable and exciting games. A particular highlight for engage as title sponsor, was the Magic Weekend in Cardiff. This carnival of rugby league demonstrates the strengths of the game, with fans from every club coming together to appreciate the matches and spread the word to new fans.

Newly promoted Castleford proved just how close the competition was, as despite finishing at the foot of the table, they delivered some outstanding performances, most memorably beating both Leeds Rhinos and St Helens. St Helens responded to this defeat by putting together an unbeaten run of 23 games only to be halted at the final hurdle by Leeds Rhinos who retained their engage Super League title with a spectacular Grand Final performance.

This book is a great record of a wonderful season. I would like to thank Mike Stephenson for his support of the game and for sharing his thoughts in this book. A thank you must also go to Peter Morley for providing the superb images.

Andrew Haigh
Chief Executive
engage Mutual Assurance

INTRODUCTION

The *2008 engage Super League Review* rounds up a fantastically competitive season for Super League that saw Leeds Rhinos and St Helens lock horns in a thrilling battle to be Grand Final winners. The book's match reports reveal a wet and injury strewn season overall for the teams involved but despite the weather and injuries, Super League's awesome standard of play is evident throughout. Catalans Dragons surprised everyone by finishing third in the table—a great result for departing coach Mick Potter.

Over the season there were some sad and notable losses to rugby league. These include former Great Britain international, David Topliss who died suddenly aged 58 and rugby league legend Don Fox who died after a long illness aged 73. Sadly 2008 also saw the sudden and premature deaths of Adam Watene aged 31 of Wakefield Wildcats and David Myers the ex Great Britain international at age 37. All will be greatly missed.

The *2008 engage Super League Review*, written in Sky Sports presenter Mike 'Stevo' Stephenson's inimitable style, provides a blow-by-blow account of every game played in Super League. All games are written in round order including the two games played out of round order, Leeds versus Hull KR in Round 4 and Wigan versus Huddersfield in Round 16 (these have been added to their respective rounds but show different dates). Each round includes match specifics, photographs, player of the round, results and squads as well as Stevo's expert write up. The book covers all 27 rounds, play-offs and the Grand Final as well as Leeds Rhinos' victory over Melbourne Storm in the Carnegie World Club Challenge 2008. For easy access to match statistics, the back of the book includes the Super League table round-by-round.

We hope you enjoy reviewing the 2008 Super League season and reliving the action courtesy of Stevo and hope this book helps fuel your excitement for the 2009 season ahead!

The Editor

2008 engage Super League Review

engage
Mutual Assurance

Kick off: 19.30, Venue: Halliwell Jones Stadium, Att: 11,026,
Match official: A Klein

Warrington (20) 32
T: C Bridge 2, C Hicks 1, M King 1,
B Westwood 1, V Anderson 1
G: L Briers 4

Hull FC (14) 20
T: C Hall 2, G Horne 1 **G:** D Tickle 4

Warrington squad
Bridge, Hicks, Martin Gleeson, King,
Penny, Briers, Monaghan, Morley, Clarke,
Rauhihi, L Anderson, Westwood,
V Anderson
Replacements: Mark Gleeson, Parker,
Johnson, Pickersgill

Hull FC squad
Tony, Byrne, Hall, Berrigan, Williams,
Washbrook, Lee, Cusack, Houghton,
Carvell, Dowes, Manu, Tickle
Replacements: King, G Horne, Dale,
Briscoe

A side that have splashed out big bucks are Warrington. They opened their account with a solid win over a Hull side so decimated by injuries they were playing without seven major stars! Hull coach Peter Sharp knew it was going to be a tough night at the Halliwell Jones Stadium without the likes of Richard Horne, Gareth Raynor, Lee Radford, Kirk Yeaman, Richard Whiting, Matt Sing and Adam Dykes. It forced Sharp to bring in young Tom Briscoe from the junior ranks who late in the second half had the tough task of marking the big Aussie international Matt King who was making his debut alongside Michael

Monaghan. Warrington coach Paul Cullen tried to keep the lid on press speculation that this was going to be Wolves' year as the Super League fans looked forward to seeing the Australian Test stars show their skills (and in this first game of the season they sure did).

Monaghan was superb and controlled the action. Any doubts about how he would fit in with the style of Lee Briers were quickly dispelled by his tactics of keeping the ball alive and spreading it wide as often as possible. The half back combination soon clicked as they combined time and time again to breach the Hull defence. One could sense the power that Warrington were going to show this term. If Cullen could keep these two big stars fully fit for the entire season then the fans might be able to look forward to making Old Trafford. Cullen was happy with the win but realised there was still work to be done, especially in defence where Hull found a few gaps in the second half. He looked a happy man after the 32–20 victory.

The highlight of the night came about when Monaghan spotted an opening for winger Kevin Penny just five metres from his own line. A superb pass, one of many from him on the night, sent the winger racing downfield where he slipped the inside ball to King who raced away for a sensational try with just nine minutes remaining of the first half. At 20–8 it looked all over for Hull but they showed amazing fortitude to fight back and snare a neat try from Craig Hall after good work from Aussie Shaun Berrigan and Todd Byrne. Berrigan, who had finally moved into his more familiar role of running from dummy-half, had lifted the visitor's spirits and at 20–14 at the break the Wolves fans were a bit uneasy.

Tries from Ben Westwood and Chris Bridge midway through the second half calmed the nerves and sealed the match but Hull, showing such great spirit, snatched a consolation try with seconds remaining. Monaghan was outstanding, having a hand in five of the six tries and finished with 27 tackles! Adrian Morley also shone and produced a huge game of tough, fair tackling and carted up the ball repeatedly to ensure they had a wonderful springboard for unleashing Monaghan's talents. Jon Clarke also played well and controlled the dummy-half position with guile and speed. This must have made coach Cullen a happy man. Would it really be their year this time?

Player of Round 1

Michael Monaghan, Warrington
Monaghan had a hand in five tries and defended well. Looked like a great signing.

Jon Clarke controlled the dummy-half position.

Kick off: 15.00, Venue: Twickenham Stoop, Att: 8,041,
Match official: G. Hewer

Harlequins (16) 28
T: M McLinden 1, M Gafa 2, S Hill 1, H Paul 1 **G:** H Paul 4

Wigan (16) 47
T: R Mathers 1, D Goulding 2, I Palea'aesina 1, H Hansen 1, M McIlorum 2 **G:** P Richards 9
DG: T Barrett 1

Harlequins squad
McLinden, Wells, Howell, Gafa, Sheriffe, Orr, Hill, Temata, Randall, McCarthy-Scarsbrook, Purdham, Grayshon, Paul
Replacements: Rinaldi, Ward, Haggerty, Mbu

Wigan squad
Mathers, Calderwood, Goulding, Carmont, Richards, Barrett, Leuluai, Coley, Higham, Palea'aesina, Bailey, Hansen, O'Loughlin
Replacements: McIlorum, Prescott, J Tomkins, O'Carroll

Expected to struggle in Super League, Harlequins, stunned Wigan for most of the match and at one point a shock was on the cards. This was when Matt Gafa crossed to put the London outfit 28–16 in front after 50 minutes leaving the Warriors confused. Not many, including the large Wigan following, would have expected a 31 point blitz that followed and blew the Quins away. Harlequins' coach Brian McDermott refused to blame the lack of fitness for the collapse and praised his side for being a lot more inventive than last season. 'I don't think we ran out of juice, we just didn't handle a few areas well, I saw enough out there to tell me we will challenge anybody, beat anybody.' The surging runs from prop Iafeta Palea'aesina and the guile from Mickey Higham turned Wigan around. Brian Noble, the Wigan boss, was relieved that his decision to bring both back on from the bench changed the game.

Kick off: 18.00, Venue: The Jungle, Att: 7,060, Match official: P Bentham

Castleford (12) 14
T: M Shenton 1, S Donlan 1
G: J Westerman 3

Catalans (2) 21
T: T Bosc 1, J Croker 1, G Mounis 1
G: T Bosc 4 **DG:** T Bosc 1

Castleford squad
Dorn, Wainwright, Shenton, McGoldrick, Donlan, Thackeray, Sherwin, Leafa, Henderson, Korkidas, Guttenbeil, Lupton, Westerman
Replacements: Moore, Huby, Haberecht, Boyle

Catalans squad
Greenshields, Stacul, Jean-Baile, Wilson, Khattabi, Bosc, McGuire, Chan, Gorrell, Ferriol, Gossard, Croker, Carlaw
Replacements: Guisset, Raguin, Mounis, Casty

It proved to be a great first round and fans were flocking to the grounds in thousands, even Castleford packed in over 7,000 for the visit of Catalans. Both sides were tipped to struggle this term with the hope it would be a season of consolidation. The atmosphere at The Jungle was cracking and most hoped for an entertaining game. Sadly, new season nerves affected both sides as they squandered chances early and looked off key for long periods of the match.

The Tigers did finally click when Donlan scored out wide after good work from

Michael Korkidas is hauled to the ground.

Luke Dorn who looked the sharpest out on the field. When Shenton took a neat inside pass from Sherwin to cross just before the break, the home side looked in command at 12–2. Sadly for Castleford they dropped off in the second stanza allowing the French outfit to get back into the game. Aaron Gorrell, back after a long injury, started taking control and combined with McGuire and Bosc allowed the Catalans to surge back into the game. Thomas Bosc proved to be the difference with a try and a field goal to add to his four two pointers which left their coach Mick Potter happy at achieving a somewhat rare away win.

Castleford coach Terry Matterson was confused over the way his men had dropped away late in the match. 'We had enough opportunities to win the game, but we shouldn't have to work so hard and we need to be a bit smarter.' Maybe the ploy of engaging three and sometimes four players into the tackle kept Catalans at bay in the first 40 but left the players tired later on. Either way it was going to be a tough season for the Tigers.

Kick off: 15.00, Venue: The Galpharm
Stadium, Att: 15,629,
Match official: Ian Smith

Huddersfield (4) 10
T: R Jensen 1, L Robinson 1
G: C Thorman 1

Leeds (22) 30
T: B Webb 2, R Hall 2,
J Jones-Buchanan 1
G: R Burrow 1, K Sinfield 4

Huddersfield squad
Thorman, Elford, Whatuira, Wild, Jensen,
Brown, Robinson, Crabtree, Hudson,
Griffin, Lolesi, Snitch, Raleigh
Replacements: Gatis, Skandalis, Mason,
Cudjoe

Leeds squad
Webb, Donald, Toopi, Senior, Hall,
McGuire, Burrow, Leuluai, Diskin,
Peacock, Jones-Buchanan, Ellis, Sinfield
Replacements: Lauitiiti, Bailey, Kirke,
Ablett

Huddersfield seemed to be victims of a
cruel streak when champions Leeds put
them to the sword. No new signings from
the Rhinos indicated a settled team and
they didn't disappoint their new coach
Brian McClennan when they 'bashed'
one of the league's bigger packs with
some tough no nonsense defence. Leeds
looked the business, were in good shape
and must have been confident about
taking on the Aussie champions
Melbourne Storm. It was a solid showing
with both forwards and three quarters
sharing the workload.

New signing Luke Robinson tried hard for
the Giants on his club debut but behind a
beaten pack the result was never in
doubt and the Giants must realise they
need to work harder in the forwards. A
record crowd at the Galpharm Stadium of
over 15,000 set the scene for hopefully
the best campaign for quite some time
for the home side. It became clear when
Webb, who had an outstanding match,
crossed after just three minutes and
when Ryan Hall crossed just before the
break to make it 22–4 that it wasn't to be
the claret and gold's day. Centre Paul
Whatuira showed touches of class and
effort, and Luke Robinson's individual try
showed merit but it was surprising that
Leeds didn't tag on more points to a 30–
10 victory. Coach McClennan was happy
with the first 40 minutes as he knew the
Giants would come at them hard in front
of a huge crowd. 'Our ruck defence was
excellent, but we are going to have to be
more disciplined.' Giants' boss Sharp was
in no mood to look for excuses, 'We
didn't build pressure, pushed passes, we
got too excited and overplayed.' It
certainly didn't give much encouragement
to the Huddersfield fans who knew the
trip to Odsal next weekend against
Bradford was not going to be easy or
pleasant. They needed to improve.

Kick off: 15.00, Venue: New Craven
Park, Att: 8,713, Match official: B Thaler

Hull KR (16) 24
T: S Briscoe 1, Jake Webster 1,
D Fitzhenry 1, C Newton 1
G: Jake Webster 1, S Murrell 3

St Helens (6) 22
T: S Tyrer 1, C Flannery 1,
K Cunningham 1, P Clough 1
G: S Tyrer 3

Hull KR squad
Briscoe, Fox, Walker, Jake Webster,
Fitzhenry, Chester, James Webster, Vella,
K Netherton, Mills, Newton, Galea,
Murrell
Replacements: Crossman, Aizue, Gene,
Cockayne

15

Luke Robinson makes his debut against Leeds.

St Helens squad

Wellens, Gardner, Gidley, Tyrer, Meli, Pryce, Long, Fozzard, Roby, Graham, Gilmour, Wilkin, Flannery
Replacements: Bennett, Cunningham, Clough, Fa'asavalu

'When the red, red robin...'

'When the red, red robin comes bob, bob, bobbing along ...' was the tune on most East Hull fans' lips after Hull KR put high flyers St Helens to the sword. The result was clouded in controversy due to the fact referee Ben Thaler turned down a try scored by Saints in the last play of the game. It was all hands to the pumps by the Rovers as they tried in vain to stop a rampant Saints from keeping the ball alive after the hooter had sounded. Fourteen passes and a never say die attitude from the visitors looked to have pinched the match when Gidley dived over. A deathly silence surrounded the ground whilst the Saints players danced around with glee at pulling off what they thought was another great escape. To be fair to Rovers they deserved to win after leading 16–6 at half time through tries from Webster, Newton and Fitzhenry to a Cunningham reply for the Saints. They showed tremendous courage after St Helens dragged themselves back into the game and squared the score line at 22–22 with just 13 minutes remaining.

Rovers were out of the blocks early and stunned the visitors with some enterprising play. Scott Murrell led the way with an impressive performance, and when Jake Webster kicked a penalty to stretch the lead to 24–22 with six minutes to go the home fans were confident of hanging on. Steve Tyrer had a chance to snatch a draw two minutes from time but his kick went astray and the majority of the crowd breathed a sigh of relief until the dramatic end. This was when the touch judge informed the referee that he felt Lee Gilmour was tackled before passing the ball from the floor.

Saints coach Daniel Anderson was far from despondent after the game saying he thought the Rovers were awesome and hardly put a foot wrong in the first half, 'They didn't make an error and had plenty of possession and they punished us.' Shaun Briscoe once again starred both in attack and defence but Murrell took the honours with a fine all round effort. Rovers boss Justin Morgan didn't get carried away with the win. He admitted that they beat Leeds at the same time last year and finished 11th. Rovers seemed a different outfit this term and the fans had more than a touch of respect for Morgan. Although early in the season, he must have been confident about making the play-offs and after this showing even the bookies were cutting their odds.

Sunday 10 February 2008

Kick off: 15.30, Venue: Belle Vue Stadium, Att: 9,851,
Match official: R Silverwood

Wakefield (10) 26
T: P Reilly 1, R Atkins 1, L George 2
G: T Martin 1, D Brough 4

Bradford (6) 24
T: M Platt 1, P Sykes 1, T Newton 2
G: P Deacon 4

Wakefield squad
Blaymire, Reilly, Martin, Atkins, George, Brough, Obst, Bibey, Drew, Moore, Ferguson, Ferres, Demetriou
Replacements: Henderson, Leo-Latu, Sculthorpe, Wilkes

Bradford squad
Platt, Evans, Sykes, Hape, Tupou, Harris, Deacon, Vagana, Newton, Lynch, Nero, Langley, Burgess
Replacements: Morrison, James, Godwin, Jeffries

The debut of two Wakefield players, Brad Drew (the former Giants star) and Danny Brough, was going to be the key to Wakefield's efforts this term. According to their coach John Kear they didn't let him or the fans down. The Wildcats trained well in the off season and trial games indicated they could be a huge threat. Trial performances don't win anything and when it came to the big stuff, could they compete this term with the big boys? On this showing against the Bulls, yes was the answer.

Many Wakefield fans were wondering if the loss of Ben Jeffries would leave the side a bit short on talent and creativity but Brough's showing soon wiped away any fear. Brough is a talented player and his vision proved the key to an upset against strong favourites Bradford. His kicks frequently pinned the Bulls back leaving them frustrated and when he slotted over the conversion of the Luke George try to make it 18–6 the home win looked secure. Despite a late charge from Bradford the Wildcats held out to a 26–24 win leaving Kear happy that his decision to leave out Jamie Rooney was spot on. 'Rooney is a little rusty and short of game time and is still nursing a shoulder injury,' said the Trinity coach and when he does come back he will give them an even bigger boost than the first round win.

Bradford were punished for a lack of fire and discipline and coach McNamara knew there was room for improvement. As expected, the home fans gave former star Ben Jeffries the bird when McNamara finally brought him into the fray. Sadly for Bradford it proved a turning point in the game as it was Jeffries' wayward pass that allowed winger Luke George to race away 50 metres for a score. This delighted the home fans who last year praised the same player to the rooftops! Rugby League can be a cruel sport at times.

Danny Brough plays his first Super League game for Wakefield.

engage
Mutual Assurance

Friday 15 February 2008

Kick off: 19.30, Knowsley Road,
Att: 13,396, Match official: R Silverwood

St Helens (8) 30
T: A Gardner 2, S Tyrer 1, F Meli 1,
J Roby 1, P Clough 1 **G:** S Tyrer 3

Warrington (14) 22
T: C Hicks 1, Martin Gleeson 1, K Penny 1,
L Briers 1, P Johnson 1 **G:** L Briers 1

St Helens squad
Wellens, Gardner, Gidley, Tyrer, Meli,
Pryce, Long, Fozzard, Roby, Graham,
Gilmour, Bennett, Flannery

Replacements: Cunningham,
Hargreaves, Clough, Frodsham

Warrington squad
Bridge, Hicks, Martin Gleeson, King,
Penny, Briers, Monaghan, Morley,
Clarke, Rauhihi, L Anderson, Westwood,
V Anderson
Replacements: Mark Gleeson, Parker,
Johnson, Bracek

It was a bridge too far. Sadly, the hoodoo
that hangs over Warrington each time
they travel to St Helens conspired to slap
down Paul Cullen's side yet again. With
five top stars missing from the St Helens

Ali Lauitiiti scores against Wakefield.

line-up, it appeared this was going to be the night the Wolves took Saints apart. After leading 14–8 at half time, the away fans were confident. Again, the injury jinx hit the side. Unlucky for some, and especially for Chris Bridge, the 13th minute proved to be a tragic time for the Warrington fullback who, after a traumatic 2007 season, was carried off with a ruptured Achilles tendon. As with so many of these bad injuries, the tackle he was involved in looked harmless, yet it looked likely to be the end of the season for the talented fullback.

Warrington's scrum-half Michael Monaghan started the game heavily strapped and looked a far cry from his impressive debut the week before. Despite his problems, he still showed enough skills to steer the Wolves back into the game after Roby gave the home side the lead early on. Matt King also showed some nice touches despite suffering a calf strain after one minute from the kick off and struggled gamely to continue until midway through the first half before he limped off. Despite this Warrington shook the Saints with tries from Hicks and Martin Gleeson to look in command at the break.

What happened to Warrington in the first minutes of the restart will be printed forever in the mind of coach Cullen who watched in horror as three tries in seven minutes blew the game away from them. With King off, Cullen moved sub Bracek to centre to partner

Penny on their left hand side. Not surprisingly, the Saints played towards the inexperienced partnership and blasted them away through sheer brilliance from Matt Gidley who created tries for Gardner (2) and Clough to put them in a commanding lead at 22–14.

Despite a late comeback from a Johnson touchdown Warrington were struggling and expectedly Saints pulled away for a 30–22 victory. James Graham was outstanding in taking the ball up time and time again and predictably, his coach Anderson was more than pleased with the effort. 'Graham was phenomenal tonight and kept us going, we earned that win and took advantage of Matt King not coming back out. It's difficult when your opposition puts someone in a position when they are not a recognised centre and we took advantage of that,' said Daniel Anderson.

Friday 15 February 2008

Kick off: 20.00, Belle Vue, Att: 9,863, Match official: P Bentham

Wakefield (0) 8
T: L George 1, R Atkins 1

Leeds (38) 44
T: K Senior 1, S Donald 2, D McGuire 1 M Diskin 2, K Sinfield 1, A Lauitiiti 1
G: K Sinfield 6

Wakefield squad
Blaymire, George, Martin, Atkins, Reilly, Obst, Brough, Bibey, Drew, Moore, Ferres, Ferguson, Demetriou
Replacements: Rooney, Sculthorpe, Henderson, Wilkes

Leeds squad
Webb, Smith, Toopi, Senior, Donald, McGuire, Burrow, Scruton, Diskin, Peacock, Jones-Buchanan, Ellis, Sinfield
Replacements: Lauitiiti, Bailey, Ablett, Kirke

The Wakefield fans' faces betray their disappointment.

Eighty minutes can be a long time on a football pitch when your defence can find no answer to a rampaging side. It was like this for Wakefield as Leeds prepared for their upcoming World Club Champions' battle with the Melbourne Storm by blowing the Wildcats away on their home ground to the tune of 44–8.

It took a bewildered Trinity coach John Kear a long time to recover from a 17-minute period where the Rhinos were unstoppable. Six tries in such a short period that produced 32 points left no doubt to the Melbourne spies who attended the match that beating the Champions of Super League would be no easy task.

Wakefield were stunned and never got out of the blocks as Jamie Peacock and Gareth Ellis (bound for Wests Tigers at the close of the season) took them apart. A 'warm' dressing room awaited the stunned players as they trudged off at half time. Coach Kear's words of wisdom, given at a high volume one suspects, certainly did the trick and they produced a much better showing for the next 40 minutes. In fact they won the second half 8–6 but it was all over at half time when the scoreboard was showing 38–0 at the break.

This was not only a warning just to the Storm but also to all in Super League.

Rhinos boss Brian McClennan was delighted. 'To be able to do that to Wakefield! Jeez, if we could play like that for 80 minutes we would be a hard side to play against,' he said Wildcats coach John Kear was pleased with the way they stemmed the tide but was left confused as to why the energy was not on show as it was against Bradford the week before. 'We will have to look at the video and find out if it was us that stemmed the tide in the second half or if Leeds just let their foot off the gas.'

Kick off: 20.00, JJB Stadium,
Att: 16,667, Match official: I Smith

Wigan (8) 28
T: L Colbon 1, P Richards 1. T Leuluai 2
G: P Richards 6

Castleford (6) 16
T: M Leafa 1, P Lupton 1, T Haberecht 1
G: J Westerman 2

Wigan squad
Mathers, Colbon, Goulding, Carmont, Richards, Barrett, Leuluai, Coley, Higham, Palea'aesina, Hansen, Bailey, O'Loughlin
Replacements: Hock, Prescott, McIlorum, O'Carroll

Castleford squad
Dorn, Owen, Shenton, McGoldrick, Wainwright, Thackeray, Sherwin, Leafa, Henderson, Korkidas, Guttenbeil, Lupton, Westerman
Replacements: Higgins, Huby, Haberecht, Fletcher

Wigan, with new chairman Ian Lenagan watching his first home game at the JJB, would have expected better things from the team. Wigan were playing a Castleford side that struggled last week against Catalans. It would have upset Lenagan greatly when his side allowed the Tigers to take control early on and score through Peter Lupton to take a lead. With just seconds remaining of the first half, Castleford coach Terry Matterson would have been smiling at the thought of going to the break at 6–2 in front, only for Pat Richards to spoil things just before the break.

Trent Barrett's high bomb allowed the tall winger to grab the ball and score under the posts. It was a redeeming piece of skill from the former Australian stand off because he had blown a certain try by not passing to Leuluai after a clean break just minutes before. Brian Noble was not happy with his side's execution in the first half. 'We failed to control the ball; we were the better team in everything but the scoreboard. We tried to play too much football.'

Like St Helens, Wigan produced the killer blow soon after the restart with some good solid work from Andy Coley creating the position for chances to come. And come the chances did. Within five minutes, Liam Colbon and Thomas Leuluai had crossed the line and at 20–6 the Tigers were out of it. Full credit goes to Castleford for not throwing in the towel. They tried hard to get back into the match with Haberecht and Leafa crossing the line but the early two try blitz never left the 28–16 result in doubt.

Terry Matterson was not too despondent after the game and praised his side's effort but was critical over the penalty count against them. 'The try just before half time didn't help, nor did the penalty count, but we've got a real good group of people who are working their butts off for each other and I'm really proud of them.' Despite a great effort, the Tigers' season looked set to be a tough one but they could still take some scalps down at The Jungle throughout the year.

Thomas Leuluai added two tries in the defeat of Castleford.

Saturday 16 February 2008

Kick off: 18.00, Grattan Stadium,
Att: 10,124, Match official: B Thaler

Bradford (24) 38
T: J Evans 1, P Sykes 1, T Newton 1
G Morrison 1, S Finnigan 2
G: P Deacon 7

Huddersfield (6) 12
T: P Whatuira 1, L Robinson 1
G: C Thorman 2

Bradford squad
Platt, Evans, Sykes, Nero, Hape, Harris,
Deacon, Vagana, Newton, Lynch,
Langley, Morrison, Burgess
Replacements: Halley, Godwin, Finnigan,
James

Huddersfield squad
Thorman, Elford, Whatuira, Wild, Jensen,
Brown, Robinson, Griffin, Hudson,
Skandalis, Lolesi, Snitch, Raleigh
Replacements: Crabtree, Gatis, Jones,
Jackson

The last time Huddersfield beat Bradford on their home soil a couple of blokes started walking on the moon! The odds of the Giants overcoming a 39-year loss record were not in their favour, especially not when playing against a side that lost against Wakefield the week before in a shock result. Bradford coach Steve McNamara knew his forward pack were muscled out of that game and knew the Giants would see a different pack take on the huge set of Huddersfield forwards. This proved to be the case.

With Burgess, Lynch and Morrison running riot it was no surprise when the Odsal boys took a 12–0 lead through Terry Newton and Simon Finnigan who crossed within 17 minutes, with the latter scoring with his first touch of the ball! The try was a slap in the eye for Huddersfield who tried to snare Finnigan

Terry Newton added to the score line for Bradford against Huddersfield.

from Salford at the end of last season. There was more to come from the debut boy when he scored his second try just before the break. Huddersfield's lack of cohesion was evident with stand off Kevin Brown playing out wide and the combination with half back Luke Robinson was non-existent. The simple fact was that they lacked leadership and were battered up front.

The Giants tried hard after the restart and raised their hopes when Paul Whatuira, one of the few to impress for the away side, scored in the 47th minute but, the runaway intercept try by Paul Sykes sealed the victory. Surprisingly, coach Jon Sharp was not too upset with the loss and suggested it was an improvement on their poor showing against Leeds in round one. 'We have to play for 80 minutes and we give away too many points,' he added. Whilst Jon may have seen the light at the end of the tunnel many of the claret and gold fans trudged out of the Odsal Grattan Stadium somewhat confused and far from happy. More than one shouted 'Rubbish!' Bradford played well at times yet they too had moments of switching off. More than the odd supporter was left wondering why new signing Jeffries was not selected and why top class centre Shontayne Hape was playing on the wing. I wondered too!

Kick off: 18.30, Stade Gilbert Brutus, Att: 8,350, Match official: G Hewer

Catalans (14) 20
T: C Greenshields 1, J Wilson 1
A Gorrell 1 **G:** T Bosc 4

Hull KR (6) 24
T: P Fox 2, B Galea 1, S Gene 1
G: Jake Webster 4

Catalans squad
Greenshields, Stacul, Wilson, Mogg, Pelo, Bosc, McGuire, Ferriol, Gorrell, Guisset, Gossard, Carlaw, Chan
Replacements: Mounis, Griffi, Casty, Raguin

Hull KR squad
Briscoe, Fox, Jake Webster, Welham, Fitzhenry, Chester, James Webster, Vella, K Netherton, J Netherton, Newton, Galea, Gene
Replacements: Cockayne, Aizue, Mills, Crossman

Flying down to the deep South of France was going to be a huge problem for teams when the hot Mediterranean summer kicked in. Hull KR were relieved to find the weather much cooler when they took on Catalans at the Stade Gilbert Brutus. The French were confident after a good second half showing against the Tigers the previous week and Rovers coach Justin Morgan knew it would be tough. So much so that he had three prop forwards on the bench in an effort to match the massive Catalans pack but it was the boot of Thomas Bosc that proved the difference in the first half. His three goals to add to the Aaron Gorrell and John Wilson four pointers gave the home side a 14–6 advantage.

The French side showed the previous week they can come home strong. Rovers knew they would need something special to change the game and this came in the shape of Peter Fox. The winger does not have the same skills as his famous namesakes Neil and Don from the sixties but in terms of finishing, he is a hero for the Robins. Two tries in six minutes took Hull KR into the lead.

Catalans were not to be outdone, Bosc again coming to the fore with a lovely break to send fullback Greenshields in

Old stager Stanley Gene came to the rescue against Catalans.

for a converted try to lead 20–18. With 15 minutes to go, a thriller was on the cards. The old stager Stanley Gene came to the rescue with four minutes remaining when his grubber kick towards the posts saw a melee of players dive over the in goal area. How the video ref could sort it out was anyone's guess but he gave the PNG star the nod, Webster's conversion made it 24–20 and Rovers held out a last gasp effort from the Catalans to hang on to what coach Morgan said was a great effort. Morgan stated afterwards, 'We were poor in the first half yet turned it about in the second, we wanted to come and get the points here and we did just that'. Mick Potter's feelings about the Robins side were, 'I tip them to finish in the top six for sure, they played well despite having a few key players out, we didn't control the ruck and they deserved their win.'

Sunday 17 February 2008

Kick off: 15.15, The KC Stadium, Att: 13,313, Match official: A Klein

Hull FC (0) 6
T: S Berrigan 1, **G:** D Tickle 1

Harlequins (14) 24
T: M Gafa 2, D Howell 1, C Randall 1
G: R Purdham 2

Hull FC squad
Tony, Williams, Byrne, Hall, Raynor, Washbrook, Lee, Dowes, Berrigan, Cusack, Manu, Tickle, G Horne
Replacements: Houghton, King, Wheeldon, Dale

Harlequins squad
McLinden, Wells, Gafa, Howell, Sheriffe, Hill, Orr, Temata, Randall, Ward, Purdham, Grayshon, Paul
Replacements: Rinaldi, McCarthy-Scarsbrook, Haggerty, Mbu

To most pundits the Harlequins were going to be just a nuisance factor in 2008 and despite them driving to Hull full of confidence many fans expected the black and whites to bounce back on home soil even though they still had injury problems. Again, the Harlequins had a flying start and a burst of tries in a short time proved a winner, three tries in the opening 15 minutes were enough to see the London side take command of the game. With Chad Randall steering things here, there and everywhere the Hull outfit never got back into the match. Quins' coach Brian McDermott stated the week before that he thought his side did not lack fitness after they had fallen apart late in the game against Wigan. He claimed just a few bad defensive options allowed the Warriors to fight back, but the Hull fans were hoping they would capitulate yet again and allow their team to find some sort of form.

Sadly, the home fans were not impressed and jeered their players and coach both at half time and full time. Hundreds left the stadium well before the final hooter with Harlequins leading 24–0 with four minutes to go. Hull boss Peter Sharp was brave enough to take on board the flak the crowd threw at him and the players, 'The fans are loyal here and they had every right to give us some stick.'

'I'd be a liar if I wasn't happy with that performance,' said McDermott afterwards. Not many teams go to the KC stadium and win convincingly and it could have been even better if Hull had not grabbed a late consolation Berrigan try in the last minute. Concern for the Quins came when Scott Hill was stretchered off with a whiplash injury to the neck, a problem that could affect the London team's chances of keeping their high league position.

Friday 22 February 2008

Kick off: 19.30, Venue: Grattan Stadium, Att: 10,756, Match official: P Bentham

Bradford (4) 16
T: J Evans 1, P Sykes 2 **G:** P Deacon 2

St Helens (16) 22
T: A Gardner 1, K Cunningham 1, J Graham 1, L Gilmour 1 **G:** S Long 3

Bradford squad
Platt, Evans, Sykes, Nero, Hape, Harris, Deacon, Vagana, Newton, Lynch, Langley, Morrison, Burgess
Replacements: Halley, Godwin, Finnigan, James

St Helens squad
Wellens, Gardner, Gidley, Talau, Meli, Pryce, Long, Fozzard, Cunningham, Graham, Gilmour, Clough, Bennett
Replacements: Hargreaves, Sculthorpe, Frodsham, Roby

The return of Paul Sculthorpe to the Saints line-up ensured a huge crowd welcomed St Helens to the Grattan Stadium but the former GB skipper's start from the bench was overshadowed by the bad injury to prop forward Nick Fozzard. Fozzard limped off after just five minutes with a knee injury that would put him out for most of the season and added extra woe to a Saints side who were without four of their top class forwards.

Bradford must have fancied their chances when the big forward was helped from the field of play despite conceding a try to the ever enthusiastic and over worked James Graham. Sadly for the Bulls fans, the Saints bounced back with some outstanding play to send in Ade Gardner on the 10 minute mark and 10 minutes later when Lee Gilmour crossed to make it 16–0, the crowd were stunned into silence.

There were even more problems for St Helens coach Daniel Anderson when sub Gareth Frodsham was pole axed with a fair shoulder charge from young Sam Burgess. He was helped from the field of play looking dazed and wobbly on his feet. Obviously he was not played again as he was in cuckoo land until well after the game. It was one of the hits of the season! Paul Sykes did not deserve to be on the losing side for he showed some real class in scoring two tries in the second half to keep Bradford in the hunt. Yet his second four pointer left it too late for them to snatch a win. The experience of Keiron Cunningham and Leon Pryce proved to be the difference in the end as the Bulls fought back late in the match. Midway through the final half Cunningham scored yet another try from close in. This took Saints to a 22–10 lead and proved a bridge too far for the Bulls.

James Graham's 18 hit ups and 37 tackles was again a feature of the Saints play. It is a matter of how long this guy can keep going throughout the season at this pace. With so many injured forwards the tyro realises he will have to play the full 80 minutes for a long time to come. Coach Anderson was full of high praise for Graham and the steadiness of Cunningham and Pryce. 'We were under the cosh for a while but Long, Cunningham and Pryce were exceptional.' Bulls' boss McNamara knew they had thrown away any chance of a win by conceding 16 points early. 'Saints scored from the errors we made and they scored from the penalties we gave.'

Kick off: 20.00, Venue: The KC Stadium, Att: 13,226, Match official: G Hewer

Hull FC (8) 24
T: S Berrigan 1, L Radford 1, D Tickle 1, D Houghton 1 **G:** D Tickle 4

Wigan (16) 22
T: G Carmont 1, P Richards 1, P Bailey 1, G Hock 1 **G:** P Richards 3

Hull FC squad
Tony, Williams, Byrne, Hall, Raynor, Washbrook, Berrigan, Dowes, Lee, Cusack, Manu, Radford, Tickle
Replacements: Houghton, King, Wheeldon, G Horne

Wigan squad
Mathers, Colbon, Goulding, Carmont, Richards, Barrett, Leuluai, Coley, Higham, Palea'aesina, Hansen, Bailey, O'Loughlin
Replacements: Hock, McIlorum, Prescott, O'Carroll

It was only a Tickle but enough to inflict pain on a Wigan side expected to beat a depleted Hull FC side. Hull snapped back and twice overcame an eight points' deficit to take the spoils 24–22 in a thriller. Trailing 16–8 at the break and 22–14 going into the last quarter it looked all over for Peter Sharp's side but a Lee Radford try made it just four points adrift with a quarter of an hour remaining and set the game up for a nervous finish. Radford's return from injury made the Airlie Birds a far better proposition and was a marked

Peter Sharp ex Hull FC '...we still have a lot of improving to do.'

improvement from the previous week according to coach Sharp. 'It's nice to get on the scoreboard, a win makes it easier but we still have a lot of improving to do.'

With nine minutes remaining, Tickle grabbed the ball from his high kick to score under the posts and his conversion took Hull into the lead for the first time in the second half. Wigan threw everything at them for the remainder of the game but the Hull side hung on for their first win of the year. Wigan boss Brian Noble was upset at not taking the two points. 'I think we should have won but we lacked patience in the second half.'

Player of Round 3
Lee Radford, Hull
An excellent all round game with some huge hits that turned the tide against Wigan. Radford led by example.

Kick off: 20.00, Venue: Headingley,
Att: 14,083, Match official: B Thaler

Leeds (14) 34
T: K Senior 2, S Donald 2, D McGuire 1,
A Lauitiiti 1, I Kirke 1
G: R Burrow 1, K Sinfield 2

Catalans (6) 6
T: D Pelo 1 **G:** T Bosc 1

Leeds squad
Webb, Smith, Toopi, Senior, Donald,
McGuire, Burrow, Leuluai, Diskin,
Peacock, Jones-Buchanan, Ellis, Sinfield
Replacements: Lauitiiti, Bailey, Kirke,
Ablett

Catalans squad
Greenshields, Stacul, Wilson, Mogg,
Pelo, Bosc, McGuire, Ferrio, Gorrell,
Guisset, Carlaw, Chan, Raguin
Replacements: Mounis, Griffi, Casty,
Baile

This was the week that the Leeds Rhinos
could fine tune for their big test against
the Melbourne Storm. The Catalans
Dragons were expecting a tough contest
as they flew into Leeds. The Super
League champions did not let the home
fans down with a 34–6 demolition of
the French side. It was a convincing
performance and coach Brian
McClennan was happy to escape any
injury worries but admitted the game
was scratchy at times.

Catalans failed to find any sort of form
with passes going astray and weak
defence at times. Not that Leeds worried
over such issues as they went in at the
break 14–6 up thanks to tries from
Donald, Senior and Kirke, Sinfield
finding difficulties with the boot and
landing just one conversion whilst
playing against a strong wind.

The French outfit failed to use the wind

Keith Senior dashes down the wing for a 50 metre try.

advantage in the first 40 and
understandably, coach Mick Potter was
far from impressed. Leeds on the other
hand went into kicking action early from
the restart, repeatedly hoofing the ball
deep down into Catalans territory,
sometimes on the first and second

tackles. This ploy brought them dividends with a further four tries in the second stanza.

Keith Senior was the pick of the bunch and showed some of his international form, scoring two tries and cropping up everywhere in a wonderful performance. Unsurprisingly the Headingley club snapped him up for another season when it appeared the huge centre was going to retire at the end of this term. This boost was all Leeds needed to take on the Aussie champions the following week. They had no losses and riding high on the table was a huge lift for their confidence. The team seemed able to score tries at will and the big question was whether they had been tested enough in defence to take on the tough guys from down under. Coach McClennan was happy things had worked out. 'I can't wait for next Friday; it's been a long time coming.' Dragons boss Potter was upset with the 15–7 penalty count, 'It didn't help us especially in the first half when it was 10–3 against us. We can't play a quality team and be on the wrong end of the penalty count.'

Senior created the biggest roar from the crowd whilst charging away for a dramatic try that must have convinced Leeds to sign him up for the 2009 season. He showed shades of his international best with a solid defensive stint and some barnstorming runs.

Saturday 23 February 2008

Kick off: 18.00, Venue: Twickenham Stoop, Att: 3,176, Match official: I Smith

Harlequins (10) 34
T: M Gafa 1, R Sheriffe 1, S Hill 1, C Randall 1, H Paul 1, L McCarthy-Scarsbrook 1 **G:** R Purdham 5

Wakefield (12) 18
T: S Grix 1, B Ferres 1, S Obst 1
G: D Brough 3

Harlequins squad
McLinden, Wells, Gafa, Howell, Sheriffe, Hill, Orr, Temata, Randall, Ward, Purdham, Mbu, Paul
Replacements: Rinaldi, Haggerty, McCarthy-Scarsbrook, Walsh

Wakefield squad
Grix, Martin, Gleeson, Atkins, George, Rooney, Brough, Watene, Drew, Moore, Ferres, MacGillivray, Demetriou
Replacements: Sculthorpe, Obst, Henderson, Wilkes

It was only round three but who would have thought the Quins would be up in third position? Not even the media brigade could hold up their hands and say, 'I told you so!' Most had pencilled Harlequins in for a wooden spoon struggle with the likes of Castleford and Catalans but try telling that to coach Brian McDermott who praised his side after taking Wakefield apart with a second half blitz and running out 34–18 winners. With no star signings this term the London outfit worked hard on fitness and developing the junior ranks. They gave their youth a chance and it paid off for them with the likes of McCarthy-Scarsbrook putting in a fine showing. The Wildcats suffered with bad injuries to Drew, Martin and Demetriou in the first half but appeared to have the game in their grasp within the first half hour where they were splitting Harlequins apart. Only amazing defence stopped a riot as Wakefield showed real class and led at half time 12–10. It was a different side that came out for the second half.

It was obvious that the Wildcats would miss the scheming of Drew and the enthusiasm of their skipper Demetriou but the team's error count cost them

Henry Paul was outstanding for Quins against Wakefield.

dearly. This was despite stretching their lead to 16–10 with a Brett Ferres try only minutes after Tony Martin limped off with hamstring problems. Chad Randall got the home side back on track with a neat converted try to drag them within two points. When Rikki Sheriffe scored after yet another Wakefield mistake the writing was on the wall. Henry Paul crossed soon after to sound the death knell of his former club where he made his name in the game 15 years previously.

Louie McCarthy-Scarsbrook topped off a fine win when he crossed with 10 minutes remaining to put them in such a high league position. Chad Randall and Henry Paul were outstanding but the error count from Wakefield allowed them plenty of possession to play with. Randall's distribution at dummy-half was outstanding whilst the old stager Paul was back to his best in both attack and defence. John Kear would not accept that his trio of injuries was the reason for the loss. 'We had 13 players out on the field and leading 18–10, we should have closed the game down but tried to play our way to victory when we should have dug deep and ground it out.'

Kick off: 15.00, Venue: The Galpharm Stadium, Att: 7,184
Match official: R Silverwood

Huddersfield (28) 64
T: C Thorman 1, S Elford 1, P Whatuira 1, J Lolesi 2, R Jensen 1, K Brown 1, L Robinson 2, K Mason 1, S Snitch 1, A Raleigh 1 **G:** C Thorman 8

Castleford (6) 12
T: M Wainwright 1, P Lupton 1
G: J Westerman 2

Huddersfield squad
Thorman, Elford, Whatuira, Lolesi, Jensen, Brown, Robinson, Mason, Hudson, Skandalis, Crabtree, Snitch, Wild
Replacements: Gatis, Raleigh, Jackson, Griffin

Castleford squad
Dorn, Owen, Dixon, McGoldrick, Wainwright, Thackeray, Lupton, Leafa, Henderson, Huby, Guttenbeil, Haberecht, Westerman
Replacements: Higgins, Korkidas, Boyle, Fletcher

Huddersfield finally hit the high spots to take apart poor Castleford 64–12 in a match that did little to help Tigers coach

Matterson's sleeping patterns must have been affected.

Terry Matterson's sleeping pattern! Predictably, he blasted his players. 'We didn't do justice to the supporters who travelled here today; our performance isn't good enough at the moment. I could roll out the excuses but I won't even though we only had 17 players available we should have done better.'

Kevin Brown was the star man as he guided the Giants about the field with aplomb and helped create three tries in 10 minutes after the break to give Castleford no hope of getting back into the game. With injuries mounting for the Tigers, it was hard to see where their first win would come from. It was set to be a hard season for the club and one could only expect the odd upset from time to time, maybe on home soil, for the fans to cheer about.

Sunday 24 February 2008

Kick off: 15.00, Venue: New Craven Park, Att: 8,704, Match official: A Klein

Hull KR (4) 28
T: K Welham 1, Jake Webster 1, D Fitzhenry 1, B Fisher 1, E Cockayne 1
G: S Murrell 4

Warrington (28) 29
T: C Hicks 2, P Johnson 1, Martin Gleeson 1, B Westwood 1
G: L Briers 4 **DG:** M Monaghan 1

Hull KR squad
Briscoe, Fox, Welham, Jake Webster, Steel, Fitzhenry, James Webster, Vella, Fisher, Aizue, Newton, Galea, Murrell
Replacements: Crossman, Mills, Gene, Cockayne

Warrington squad
Hicks, Johnson, Martin Gleeson, V Anderson, Penny, Briers, Monaghan, Morley, Clarke, Rauhihi, Westwood, L Anderson, Grix
Replacements: Mark Gleeson, Bracek, Parker, Harrison

With their home side trailing 28–0 and 15 minutes still remaining of the first half, it was understandable that many Rovers' fans headed for the exits. Unfortunately those fans that left missed a weird and exciting finish that left both coaches dumbfounded! Hull KR coach Justin Morgan was pulling his hair out at the shoddy performance in the first half despite Hull scoring a late try from Jake Webster to go in at the break 20–4 down. To say the Robins boss tore a few strips off his players was an understatement and his charges came out firing for the second stanza.

Paul Cullen must have been a happy man as he witnessed some scintillating skills from the Wolves in the first 40 minutes. But not even he could have expected such a fight-back from the home side. With 20 minutes remaining Warrington still held their 24 point lead and two league points surely were in the bag, but the Robins came fighting back to score four tries in just 13 minutes! Eight minutes from time, Michael Monaghan slotted over a field goal that eventually turned out to be the winning point and Warrington's only score in the second half. Hull KR threw everything at Warrington in the final minutes to no avail as a relieved visiting side hung on to take the spoils.

'You can't give up 28 points and expect to win—we played some footy in the second half but it wasn't meant to be,' was Justin Morgan's comment after the game. Paul Cullen was baffled at the penalty count. 'Seven against us in the first half and six against us in the second, to say I'm not happy is an understatement.' Again, Michael Monaghan claimed the man of the match award and looked set to challenge for player of the year if his form continued in the same vein.

Ben Westwood scores in Warrington's clash with Hull KR.

engage
Mutual Assurance

Kick off: 18.00, Venue: Headingley, Att: 18,467, Match official: R Silverwood

Leeds (4) 20
T: S Donald 1, L Smith 2, D McGuire 1
G: K Sinfield 2

Hull KR (6) 12
T: Jake Webster 2 **G:** Jake Webster 1, S Murrell 1

Leeds squad
Webb, Donald, Toopi, Senior, Smith, McGuire, Burrow, Leuluai, Diskin, Peacock, Kirke, Ellis, Sinfield
Replacements: Lauitiiti, Bailey, Scruton, Ablett

Hull KR squad
Briscoe, Fox, Walker, Jake Webster, Fitzhenry, Chester, James Webster, Vella, K Netherton, Mills, Newton, Galea, Murrell
Replacements: Gene, Crossman, Aizue, Cockayne

The dark clouds were still hovering over Headingley Carnegie on 2 February but at least the gloom and doom of relegation was swept away for the start of Super League 13. Again, the season had an early start to allow Leeds a free weekend to play Melbourne Storm in the World Club Championship decider later in the month. As anticipated the venue was a near sell-out as Champions Leeds took on the new look Hull Kingston Rovers.

Despite the chill in the air, most fans knew it would be a 'warm' and stern test for the Rhinos and their new coach Brian

McClennan as the 'Robins' had bought up big time in the off season, leaving them a formidable outfit on paper at least. The question was simple; could the Rovers gel quickly and give Leeds a tough game? The answer was yes.

Justin Morgan is no mug and has proved over the few years in the Northern hemisphere what a talented coach he is. Out went a huge lump of last year's players, replaced by some worldwide talent which showed that coaches have to be ruthless to survive. Sentiment plays no part in modern day rugby league. Morgan shipped out or retired no less than 15 players from last season. This move sent out the message that Mr Morgan was intent on snaring a play-off spot this term and that last season 11th spot on the table was a sad memory.

Leading the charge was Shaun Briscoe (from neighbour Hull), Ben Galea, (Wests), Jake Webster (Gold Coast), Peter Fox (Wakefield), Daniel Fitzhenry (Wests), David Mills (Harlequins), Clint Newton (Melbourne), Garrett Crossman (Melbourne), Luke Menzies (Batley), Liam Watts (Castleford) and star centre Chev Walker from Bath Rugby Union. All this was in addition to the mid-season controversial signing of Paul Cooke last year. The red and whites from Hull looked threatening. Cooke was out through suspension but no Leeds fan turned up that night feeling confident. It was also ironic that the former Leeds star Chev Walker would be making his debut on the ground where he learned his trade before switching to the 15-a-side code.

The Rhinos had just flown back from

Florida, America where they played a trial game against their Australian 'Sister' club South Sydney (part owned by film star Russell Crowe) where they scraped a two point win after leading 22–0 at half time. Amazingly, to overcome jet-lag the Rhinos were told to eat up big on hamburgers and drink milk shakes! So with 'junk' food in their bellies and a 10-hour flight behind them, the away side could have caught the Champions off guard. It proved to be the case as Leeds started out rusty to be bashed about by a more than eager Rovers outfit that crashed into the fray with no fear.

Leeds were stunned and couldn't get their game into full swing. Maybe the quarter pounders with gherkins were slowing the team's reactions. Either way, Big Macs' outfit was being crunched and munched! Briscoe was everywhere, both in attack and defence and with Walker and Webster creating havoc out wide a shock result was on the cards.

The Rhinos couldn't find their rhythm as the Rovers' pack surged into the fray

The Hull KR defence put the brakes on Kylie Leuluai.

with Rovers controlling the ruck area and keeping Leeds on the back foot. Hooker Ben Fisher failed a fitness test before the game and was replaced by Netherton who did a fine job in controlling the play the ball area but Rovers lacked that bit extra go forward and spark at dummy-half to get them good field position. They soon found it when Morgan replaced the hooker with Ben Cockayne, a fiery character with a never say die attitude.

His running from dummy-half split Leeds and allowed Rovers control over field position and he combined in a simple but effective run-around that saw New Zealand centre Webster crash over for a try that left the home side rocking. It lifted Rovers' spirits and left McClennan's men subdued and struggling to find cohesion. Skipper Kevin Sinfield looked relieved when he heard the hooter go for half time giving Leeds a chance to regroup.

The Headingley crowd were deathly quiet at half time for they knew a shock loss was on the cards. This was not so at the scoreboard end where the red and white clan were singing and chanting. A few ignored the cold and displayed upper bodies that indicated they knew what Big Macs were all about.

Typically, Leeds came out with more confidence and didn't panic. Slowly they fought back and started to win the kicking game and the territory that comes with it. Sadly the boys from East Hull found it hard to get anywhere near the Leeds goal line and when they did they started to give away silly penalties. This allowed the Rhinos the upper hand, with Cockayne spoiling his good work by messing about at the play the ball area and letting Leeds off the hook.

Rob Burrow at last started to dictate the game, and his weaving runs took their toll on the Rovers defence. But still the red and whites stood firm with a swarming defence that somehow denied the home side rushes. Leeds had winger Lee Smith to thank for swinging the game, his speed and finishing lifted his side back into the match when it looked likely the sluggish Rhinos were done. Smith gave them the green light to advance and helped shock his team mates into action.

Onlookers felt that with all the ball and added pressure the dam would break. It did break late in the game when the individual skills of McGuire sealed a desperate win in the dying minutes. Justin Morgan was disappointed and indicated that perhaps Leeds had had a run of luck. It was true that a few decisions went Leeds' way especially in the second half when the official did not see a foul on winger Peter Fox. The away side should have had a penalty and this had a huge bearing on the result because it allowed Leeds no less than three sets of six on the trot and a tired Rovers outfit buckled under the pressure.

The 20–12 score line flattered Leeds. The team knew they had to improve heaps to hold onto the Super League trophy. The old saying that good teams can play a bit under par and still snatch a win was relayed around the ground whilst a dejected set of East Hull fans left the stadium. They at least knew their season was full of hope, and so it will be if they play with the same courage and intensity throughout the campaign. All Super League fans realised early on Jake Webster was going to be a sensation for his two tries were top class.

Paul Deacon receives medical attention in the game against Wigan

Saturday 1 March 2008

Kick off: 18.00, Venue: JJB Stadium,
Att: 15,444, Match official: R Silverwood

Wigan (12) 28
T: D Goulding 1, G Carmont 1,
P Richards 1, H Hansen 1, J Tomkins 1
G: P Richards 4

Bradford (8) 14
T: W Godwin 1, C Feather 1
G: P Deacon 3

Wigan squad

Mathers, Colbon, Goulding, Carmont,
Richards, Barrett, Leuluai, Coley,
Higham, Palea'aesina, Hock, Hansen,
O'Loughlin
Replacements: Fielden, Prescott,
McIlorum, J Tomkins

Bradford squad

Platt, Evans, Sykes, Hape, Tadulala,
Jeffries, Deacon, Vagana, Godwin,
Lynch, Morrison, Langley, Burgess
Replacements: Feather, Nero, Harris,
Finnigan

Harrison Hansen scores a spectacular try.

Leon Pryce scored in Saints close win over Wakefield.

Former Bradford coach Brian Noble could be excused for forcing a smile after beating his old club 28–14 at the JJB stadium but even he admitted the Warriors were still a long way from being the real deal. 'We improved on last week's performance but we have plenty to brush up on before we can feel confident at taking on the big boys.'

Bradford were of course one of those big boys a couple of years back and their display hardly excited their coach Steve McNamara who was critical of his side throwing away an early eight point lead. Wigan stormed back with some classy tries from Carmont and Goulding to go in at lemons 12–8.

Big Joe Vagana lasted barely seconds in the second half and left the field with a broken arm that left Bradford light in the pack. Wigan took full advantage despite the cold, wet and slippery conditions. The return of Stuart Fielden was another high for Noble and once the big bloke gets into match shape the Warriors will start to trouble plenty of sides. Three tries from Richards, Tomkins and Hansen sealed Bradford's fate and left the Bulls with just one win in four games, their worst ever start to a Super League campaign.

Sunday 2 March 2008

Kick off: 15.00, Venue: Knowsley Road, Att: 10,777, Match official: I Smith

St Helens (18) 34
T: P Wellens 2, A Gardner 2, L Pryce 1, J Graham 1 **G:** S Long 5

Wakefield (18) 30
T: S Gleeson 1, J Rooney 1, A Watene 1, S Obst 1, B Ferres 1 **G:** D Brough 5

St Helens squad
Wellens, Gardner, Gidley, Talau, Meli, Pryce, Long, Hargreaves, Cunningham, Graham, Gilmour, Clough, Sculthorpe
Replacements: Roby, Bennett, Eastmond, Frodsham

Wakefield squad
Grix, Reilly, Gleeson, Atkins, George, Rooney, Brough, Watene, Obst, Wilkes, Ferres, Ferguson, Moore
Replacements: Sculthorpe, MacGillivray, Bibey, Henderson

How do they do it? St Helens yet again amazed themselves by snatching a win when it looked all over. Struggling to find fit players in the forwards, the boys from Knowsley Road stunned a Wakefield side that looked to be coasting towards a memorable victory after leading 30–18 with just 13 minutes remaining.

Despite scoring early, Saints looked sluggish, lacked coordination and were thankful that the Wildcats also were finding it hard to control the ball. Pryce and Wellens crossed to hold a 12–0 lead within the first 10 minutes but when Watene scored after Gardner failed to take a high bomb and then Pryce produced a high shot that allowed Wakefield the possession for Sam Obst to stroll over and square things up. The hard working James Graham again gave Saints the lead in a scrappy contest that failed to hit the high spots and left the home crowd far from confident, especially when Paul Sculthorpe once again suffered an injury, leaving the field after just 32 minutes.

Rooney's pass allowed Brett Ferres to score with just seconds remaining of the first half to draw level at 18–18. Wakefield were good value for taking the lead 10 minutes after the restart when Rooney crossed. When Sean Gleeson crossed to make it 18–30 the Wildcats were looking at pulling off an upset. Danny Brough's running, passing, tackling and shouting was amazing. His kicking game appeared to mesmerise the Saints yet a team cannot go to sleep against a top side like St Helens, who clawed their way back to score three late tries to snatch a win they did not really deserve.

Sunday 2 March 2008

Kick off: 15.00, Venue: Halliwell Jones Stadium, Att: 9,060,
Match official: P Bentham

Warrington (14) 38
T: C Hicks 2, P Johnson 1,
M Monaghan 1, J Clarke 1,
V Anderson 1, A Bracek 1

G: L Briers 5

Catalans (12) 18
T: C Greenshields 1, J Murphy 1,
S Raguin 1 G: T Bosc 3

Warrington squad
Reardon, Hicks, Martin Gleeson, Johnson, Penny, Briers, Monaghan, Morley, Clarke, Rauhihi, L Anderson, Westwood, V Anderson
Replacements: Mark Gleeson, Parker, Wood, Bracek

Catalans squad
Greenshields, Murphy, Stacul, Wilson, Pelo, Mogg, Bosc, Chan, Gorrell, Guisset, Raguin, Croker, Mounis
Replacements: Casty, Gossard, Baile, Touxagas

Michael Monaghan once again took the plaudits from the Warrington fans as the Wolves coasted to a 38–18 victory over a disjointed Catalans outfit at the Halliwell Jones Stadium. The classy Aussie half back scored early and set up plenty of chances for his side and the fans were surprised they hadn't a lead bigger than 14–12 at the break. At 10–0 after 10 minutes, the Wolves slackened off and seemed to feel this was going to be a walk in the park but the French side fought back leaving Warrington coach Paul Cullen bemused.

Things got worse for the coach when Paul Wood suffered another injury to the shoulder soon after the break, a sad blow to a man who has worked hard to regain fitness after shoulder surgery. Hooker Jon Clarke cemented the win after 50 minutes taking a neat pass from Martin Gleeson to cross under the posts to stretch the lead to 20–12. Referee Phil Bentham hardly endeared himself to the French side by slamming the team 13–3 in the penalty count and sending three Catalans players to the sin-bin.

Paul Cullen was pleased to see his side take the points against Catalans.

© Warrington Wolves

Kick off: 15.00, Venue: The Galpharm Stadium, Att: 8,012,
Match official: S Ganson

Huddersfield (12) 28

T: S Elford 1, P Whatuira 1, K Brown 1, L Robinson 1, E Crabtree 1
G: C Thorman 4

Hull FC (8) 8

T: C Hall 1 **G:** D Tickle 2

Huddersfield squad

Thorman, Elford, Whatuira, Lolesi, Jensen, Brown, Robinson, Mason, Hudson, Skandalis, Crabtree, Snitch, Wild
Replacements: Gatis, Raleigh, Jackson, Griffin

Hull FC squad

Tony, Sing, Byrne, Hall, Raynor, Washbrook, Dykes, Dowes, Lee, Cusack, Radford, Tickle, G Horne
Replacements: King, Wheeldon, Houghton, Dale

Hull FC could not seem to take a trick as they lost yet another of their top players during a 28–8 thrashing at the hands of the Huddersfield Giants. Ewan Dowes went off with knee damage to add to coach Peter Sharp's woes. He had no option but to throw in to the fray yet more youngsters. Sharp wasn't too downhearted, 'We'll certainly get better, and we must not be too despondent, it's tough now but we'll get through it.'

Kevin Brown is unable to stop Hull's Craig Hall from scoring.

Eorl Crabtree celebrates a try for Huddersfield

For once Kevin Brown and Luke Robinson hit the high spots as they schemed the Giants' success but Hull made it hard for them in the first 40 minutes. Giants coach Jon Sharp wasn't too concerned about only leading 12–8 at half time. 'We started to win the energy battle late on in that first half and knew we had the power to get on top.' And so it proved as Huddersfield ran in three classy tries after good solid work from their huge pack of forwards.

Player of Round 4
Kevin Brown, Huddersfield
Strong, decisive and creative, Brown composed all sorts of problems for Hull.

Kick off: 15.30, Venue: The Jungle, Att: 6,268, Match official: B Thaler
Castleford (12) 16
T: L Dorn 1, K Dixon 1, R McGoldrick 1
G: J Westerman 2

Harlequins (12) 22
T: J Wells 1, D Orr 1, L McCarthy-Scarsbrook 1, R Purdham 1
G: R Purdham 2, H Paul 1

Castleford squad
Dorn, Owen, Dixon, McGoldrick, Wainwright, Lupton, Sherwin, Huby, Moore, Korkidas, Guttenbeil, Haberecht, Westerman
Replacements: Leafa, Henderson, Higgins, Fletcher

Harlequins squad
McLinden, Wells, Gafa, Howell, Sheriffe, Orr, Randall, McCarthy-Scarsbrook, Rinaldi, Ward, Purdham, Temata, Paul
Replacements: Barker, Clubb, Heckenburg, Haggerty

The Tigers were left wondering where their first win of the season would come from after seeing the Quins strike back in the dying seconds to score not just one, but two tries and sink Terry Matterson's side 22–16. Holding onto a 16–12 lead within the final minute, one would have expected Castleford to close up shop and defend for their lives to snare that elusive win. Yet Harlequins took advantage of some poor decision making from talented youngster Joe Westerman who dived for glory two minutes from time and lost the ball when a more intelligent kick into the in goal area would have sufficed. Harlequins took possession and scored 10 points in the remaining seconds thanks to former Tigers star Danny Orr who produced two tactical kicks for Wells and Purdham to score and snatch a win from nowhere.

WORLD CLUB CHALLENGE

Friday 29 February 2008

Kick off 19.30, Venue: Elland Road, Att: 33,204, Match official: A Klein

Leeds (8) 11
T: S Donald **G:** K Sinfield 3
DG: K Sinfield 1

Melbourne (4) 4
T: R Hoffman 1

Leeds squad
Webb, Smith, Toopi, Senior, Donald, McGuire, Burrow, Leu uai, Diskin, Peacock, Jones-Buchanan, Ellis, Sinfield
Replacements: Lauitiiti, Bailey, Scruton, Ablett

Melbourne squad
Slater, Turner, Chambers, Folau, Quinn, Geyer, Cronk, Lima, Smith, White, Hoffman, Kaufusi, Johnson
Replacements:
Aitken, Blair, Tagataese, Manu

Friday night is all right for fighting! That is exactly what the Leeds Rhinos did when they beat Australian champions the Melbourne Storm in a rousing 11–4 contest at Elland Road. Last year's engage Champions displayed the same tough defence that snuffed out St Helens on Grand Final day at Old Trafford last year but the Melbourne side made them fight all the way.

It was not exactly the best of weather that greeted the Aussie side as strong winds and rain bounced down throughout the game, yet despite such conditions, both sides played some amazing rugby. Intensity was a key factor as both teams opted for a close no-nonsense approach. Both teams

Scott Donald touches down for the only Leeds try in the game.

Ali Lauitiiti drives through the Melbourne defence.

Lee Smith leaps to take the ball.

displayed fine defence with some cruel tackling at times.

The Rhinos had been in top form and scored plenty of tries in the opening games of the Super League season. Nobody doubted their attitude to open play but could they knuckle down and handle a tough assignment under immense pressure from the boys down under? The answer was yes as the Rhinos showed amazing fortitude to keep out the Storm.

Sinfield opened the scoring with a good range penalty yet Melbourne crossed for a great try out wide after 15 minutes. Handling proved difficult and a rare fumble from Rob Burrow allowed the Storm a scrum win and the chance to set up camp for an all out attack. Melbourne captain Cooper Cronk

elected to run on the last and the power play allowed him to send second rower Ryan Hoffman into the corner for an unconverted try to stun the pro Leeds crowd.

When Danny McGuire left the field with a shoulder injury soon after it looked as though the Aussies would take control. Some magic play from Sinfield and Burrow settled the ship and set the scene for some torrid tackling, none more so than Jamie Jones-Buchanan's shoulder charge on Steve Turner that stunned both the ball carrier and the crowd!

The fans soon found their voices after that big episode and Leeds grew in confidence and started to take control. Two minutes from the break, Brent Webb took advantage of an open field to dance across the face of the defence and send out a great long ball to Scott Donald who dived into the corner. Sinfield's conversion was magnificent and sent Leeds into the sheds 8–4 in front.

The Storm tried hard in the second stanza to drag themselves back into the game but the conditions were getting worse and handling was becoming difficult to say the least. With little chance of McGuire returning, Leeds opted for a safety first defensive effort especially when centre Clinton Toopi also retired with a bad shoulder injury on 50 minutes. This left coach McClennan with problems with the interchange but the remaining squad held out bravely as Storm upped the tempo.

Another huge hit by Kylie Leuluai on Antonio Kaufusi shook the stadium and, like Jones-Buchanan's effort in the first half, lifted the side. Sinfield added a penalty midway through the second half to steady the ship and soon after dropped a one pointer to stretch the lead to seven points.

It was simply a wonderful effort from both sides in cyclonic conditions and the crowd cheered both sides from the field for their effort. The look on Kevin Sinfield's face said it all when he raised the silver trophy. He and his team mates had done Super League proud and sent yet another Aussie side back down under with the kangaroo tail between their legs.

Player of the Game

Kevin Sinfield
A controlled and measured performance. Sinfield was a class act in directing Leeds to victory.

The Leeds celebrations begin.

engage
Mutual Assurance

Kick off: 19.30, Venue: The Jungle,
Att: 9,459, Match official: P Bentham

Castleford (14) 38
T: R McGoldrick 1, S Donlan 1,
M Shenton 2, L Dorn 2, J Westerman 1
G: J Westerman 5

Leeds (6) 20
T: S Donald 3, J Tansey 1
G: K Sinfield 2

Castleford squad
McGoldrick, Donlan, Shenton, Dixon,
Wainwright, Dorn, Sherwin, Huby,
Moore, Korkidas, Guttenbeil, Lupton,
Westerman
Replacements: Henderson, Leafa,
Higgins, Clayton

Leeds squad
Webb, Smith, Gibson, Senior, Donald,
Tansey, Burrow, Bailey, Diskin, Leuluai,
Ellis, Jones-Buchanan, Sinfield
Replacements: Lauitiiti, Scruton, Ablett,
Burgess

'From champagne to flat beer,' was
most probably what Rhinos fans thought
as they witnessed a rare turnaround of
fortunes. They went to the Jungle full of
confidence as World Club Champions
and came away with a sour taste after a
good hiding.

It had been a long time since the black
and gold's could claim to be 'Classy
Cas'. Not many of their supporters
packed into the small ground expected a
top class effort from a side yet to win a
game in Super League. How they were
wrong and with a 38–20 winning score
the pubs in Castleford were doing plenty

of business!

Maybe the Rhinos had celebrated a
touch too much after defeating
Melbourne storm the week before. Not
according to coach Brian McClennan,
'There are no excuses, we were
disappointing and I don't want to
disrespect the way Castleford played.
They were probably unlucky not to have
won by more.' The crowd of just over
9,000 will remember this match for
years to come and no doubt the, 'I was
there that night,' claims will swell the
attendance to well over 20,000 in the
years ahead. Tigers coach Terry
Matterson was not shocked and
suggested it was a good time to get
Leeds. 'I was confident we were going to
win, I felt something brewing after we
just lost on the bell against Harlequins
the week before.' To say he was proud
was an understatement when the likes
of Ryan McGoldrick, Brent Sherwin and
Luke Dorn combined in great fashion to
rip the Leeds defence apart.

Until this game, the Rhinos had
conceded just seven tries for the season
yet conceded the same number of tries
in one game against a newly promoted
outfit struggling to find form. Castleford
had the right tactics and got into the
faces of the Rhinos early. They never
allowed them space to weave their
magic although when Scott Donald
scored after just a quarter of an hour
there was a sense that Leeds would have
another victory.

Joe Westerman, a villain in coughing up
possession to allow Harlequins a win the

week before turned hero with a try and five goals to eclipse his opposite Kevin Sinfield. This was no fluke, Castleford played some outstanding rugby league and the support was second to none. Leeds tried everything to get back into a game that the Tigers were bossing for most of the time. Not even a hat trick

from Leeds winger Scott Donald could take away the glory the home side deserved. It was understandable that the fans were still milling about the ground late into the night after the final whistle, one happy supporter shouting out, 'It's like the old days down the Lane.' It was indeed.

Castleford played some outstanding rugby league to overcome World Club Champs Leeds.

Friday 7 March 2008

Kick off: 19.30, Venue: Knowsley Road, Att: 10,204, Match official: R Silverwood

St Helens (22) 30
T: A Gardner 1, W Talau 1, M Smith 1, J Roby 1, K Eastmond 1 **G:** M Smith 5

Hull FC (14) 29
T: K Yeaman 1, D Washbrook 1, A Dykes 1, D Houghton 1, C Hall 1
G: D Tickle 4 **DG:** A Dykes 1

St Helens squad
Wellens, Gardner, Gidley, Talau, Meli, Pryce, Smith, Hargreaves, Cunningham, Graham, Gilmour, Clough, Roby
Replacements: Bennett, Tyrer, Eastmond, Frodsham

Hull FC squad
Tony, Sing, Byrne, Yeaman, Raynor, Washbrook, Dykes, Cusack, Houghton, King, G Horne, Tickle, Lee
Replacements: Briscoe, Hall, Wheeldon, Burnett

Another top side to struggle in this round was St Helens who yet again snatched a victory in the dying moments. Hull FC stunned Saints with two tries in just seven minutes as Dykes and Houghton crossed to lead 12–0 and silence the home crowd who knew only too well the red hot red and whites were a long way from top form.

After their last gasp winner against Wakefield, the Saints were hoping their ability to fight back yet again would save the day, and so it proved but not without a huge fright. Both sides were hit by injuries and considering so many major stars were missing, the game was exciting and skilful.

Lady luck hardly paid a visit to the boys from the KC stadium. With the scores locked at 28–28, the drop goal from Adam Dykes appeared to have swung the game to the visitors with just three minutes remaining. Dykes went from hero to zero after giving away a penalty when a fly kick from fullback Tony bounced into the retreating half back giving referee Silverwood no option but to award the penalty.

The crowd of over 10,000 stood in silence as Matty Smith lined up the goal attempt to snatch the win for St Helens in dramatic circumstances. Smith's cool head and boot sent the ball over the bar to send the home crowd wild and drive another nail into Peter Sharp's coffin. Despite the loss, officials at the Hull club should surely have seen the hardship Sharp was enduring and one felt sorry for his predicament for the players gave their all and deserved to get a draw at least. Sharpe was reluctant to comment though finally admitted, 'To come so close is very disappointing.'

Saturday 8 March 2008

Kick off: 15.00, Venue: Twickenham Stoop, Att: 3,284, Match official: I Smith

Harlequins (12) 24
T: D Howell 1, R Sheriffe 1, C Randall 1, L McCarthy-Scarsbrook 1
G: H Paul 2, R Purdham 2

Huddersfield (0) 0

Harlequins squad
McLinden, Wells, Gafa, Howell, Sheriffe, Paul, Orr, Temata, Randall, Ward, Mbu, Barker, Purdham
Replacements: Rinaldi, Clubb, Heckenburg, McCarthy-Scarsbrook

Huddersfield squad
Thorman, Elford, Whaturia, Lolesi, Jensen, Brown, Robinson, Mason, Hudson, Skandalis, Crabtree, Snitch, Wild
Replacements: Gatis, Raleigh, Jackson, Griffin

Harlequins, like Leeds and Warrington, were sharing the leadership role in Super

Rikki Sheriffe added his name to the score sheet in Harlequins' defeat of the Giants.

League. No league fan outside the capital city would have given the London side a chance of being in such a high position come the end of round five. This prompted coach Brian McDermott's tongue in cheek declaration, 'If the season lasted just six weeks we would be in the Grand Final.' He would not normally consider his team's position in the league table until round eight or nine but it surely felt nice that the team was flying so high with a squad that was hardly bursting at the seams with depth.

Full credit went to Harlequins for a fine win against a side tipped to make the play-offs again. Huddersfield must have left London wondering how they failed to score a point against a side tipped to battle for the wooden spoon. The 24–0 score line was convincing and Giants' boss Jon Sharp had little praise for his outfit admitting, 'We were outplayed, out enthused and their kicking game was better. If you don't rock up here with enthusiasm you're going to come out second best.'

Danny Orr continued to hit the high points and control the game as he had done all season, and with solid work from the forwards, the Quins were a tough side to get on top of. Chad Randall and David Howell crossed for tries in the first stanza and at 12–0 with a solid defence, it looked safe for McDermott's boys. An injury to Henry Paul left them down at the break and the Giants tried hard to unsettle the home side defence. Ryan Hudson went close to scoring but passed forward. This decision lifted Quins but deflated the Giants, and when winger Rikki Sheriffe scored out wide after some outstanding jinking from Mark McLinden the points were in the bag. The London outfit were set to play Leeds the following week where the true value of

their position would be realised and McDermott knew only too well Rhinos' loss to Castleford ensured the boys from Headingley would be fired up.

Saturday 8 March 2008

Kick off: 18.00, Venue: Halliwell Jones Stadium, Att: 13,024,
Match official: S Ganson

Warrington (16) 32
T: C Hicks 1, Martin Gleeson 1, M King 1, P Johnson 1, V Anderson 1, R Parker 1
G: L Briers 4

Wigan (4) 20
T: L Colbon 1, D Goulding 1, A Coley 1, H Hansen 1 **G:** P Richards 2

Warrington squad
Reardon, Hicks, Martin Gleeson, King Johnson, Briers, Monaghan, Morley, Clarke, Rauhihi, L Anderson, Westwood, V Anderson
Replacements: Mark Gleeson, Parker, Pickersgill, Bracek

Wigan squad
Mathers, Colbon, Goulding, Carmont, Richards, Barrett, Leuluai, Palea'aesina Higham, Coley, Hock, Bailey, O'Loughlin
Replacements: Fielden, Hansen, McIlorum, O'Carroll

Many in the media, including me, thought this would be Warrington's year. The team's solid 32–20 win over Wigan gave substance to the prediction. Yet the Wolves had to tough this one out and hang on in the end to secure a win that took them to equal top of the league table.

Warrington were in top form and scored three tries in the first half, thanks once again to the skills of Michael Monaghan who quickly became the 'gun' player of the season. The game had two sin-bins, one sending off, 10 tries and a record penalty count that upset the crowd, players and fans alike. The fact that rugby league continues to have periods of clampdowns on certain rules irritates everybody. Why referee Steve Ganson insisted on grabbing the limelight with his whistle left people baffled. At one point, I thought I was at a rugby union match as the merry whistle blower decided to allow so much advantage and then bring the players back for a penalty!

Our game needs flowing football and referees that allow it. Wigan boss Brian Noble was disappointed the game was a stop-start affair and Warrington coach Paul Cullen was bemused, 'There was a lot of talent on show and I'm not sure a game should be stopped that much.' To be fair to Ganson he had no hesitation in sending off Wigan fullback Richie Mathers for a high shot on centre Matt King who received attention for well over six minutes before being stretchered off the park. It looked a bad shot and will surely earn the Warrior a few games and

add extra problems to a Wigan side that looked disjointed at times. The team needed to fire up Trent Barrett. The Aussie star usually kick starts his season when the dry grounds come around and the cherry and white mob needed the sun to shine quickly to provide them with more direction than was on show in this game.

Not that Warrington cared as Wigan had yet to win at their new stadium. Their healthy position riding high alongside Leeds at the top of the table must have fuelled the hope that the off-season signings were doing their job. Maybe it was not just hysteria sweeping around the Halliwell Jones Stadium this term.

Player of Round 5

Michael Monaghan, Warrington
Quick hands and great distribution proved far too much for Wigan in an outstanding display.

Referee Ganson dismisses Wigan's Richie Mathers.

Michael Monaghan played an excellent game against Wigan.

Kick off: 18.30, Venue: Stade Gilbert Brutus, Att: 7,485,
Match official: A Klein

Catalans (6) 18
T: C Greenshields 1, T Bosc 1, A Chan 1
G: T Bosc 3

Bradford (6) 20
T: S Hape 1, G Morrison 1, S Finnigan 1
G: P Deacon 4

Catalans squad
Greenshields, Murphy, Wilson, Stacul, Pelo, Mogg, Bosc, Chan, Gorrell, Guisset, Raguin, Croker, Gossard
Replacements: Mounis, Fakir, Casty, Khattabi

Bradford squad
Platt, Evans, Sykes, Hape, Tadulala, Jeffries, Deacon, Lynch, Newton, Burgess, Nero, Langley, Morrison
Replacements: Tupou, Feather, Finnigan, Godwin

No team enjoys the flight to Perpignan and a worried Bulls outfit knew the welcome would be tough as they trotted out onto the Stade Gilbert Brutus ground. Not even Bradford guru Steve McNamara could have envisaged such a frantic struggle for league points. Two points in the table and sitting in the bottom three hardly encouraged the Bulls fans to fork out hard-earned cash to fly down to the South of France. Was it not for the chance to enjoy nice weather, support would have been thin on the ground. Like Harlequins, Catalans Dragons had been heavily tipped to finish bottom of the league and realised a win, especially at home, would help keep spirits high in the land of frog's legs!

The first half was scrappy with neither side eager to risk much open play as the 6–6 score line at the break proved. When Shontayne Hape crossed for a converted try midway through the second half it looked like Bradford would run away with it. The Dragons could thank the return of prop Jamal Fakir for lifting the spirits when he crunched Wayne Godwin with a heavy tackle, which aroused the French camp. Catalans have some classy players and predictably, Thomas Bosc and Adam Mogg started to hit top gear. When Alex Chan and Thomas Bosc scored, the home side found themselves in front 18–14 for the first time with hardly six minutes remaining. The Catalans coach Mick Potter felt they

A touch of magic from Deacon turned the tide for Bradford.

could just hang on and with the defence looking strong, it took a touch of magic from Paul Deacon to turn the tide the Bulls' way. Deacon found it hard to break down the swarming defence and opted for a cross kick with just two minutes left that found the hands of Tame Tupou who quickly off loaded to James Evans to send in Simon Finnigan for the try to tie the game at 18–18. Deacon coolly kicked the conversion and broke the hearts of a gallant French effort giving the Bulls a 20–18 win.

Potter was distraught, 'It was a fantastic comeback, I'm proud of the boys but that's the second time we have been beaten on the bell, Hull KR did the same, it's frustrating.' Bulls' boss Steve McNamara was happy the way his side fought back despite having so many players injured, 'I'm delighted, there was some heroic defence out there.'

Sunday 9 March 2008

Kick off: 15.30, Venue: Belle Vue, Att: 8,822, Match official: B Thaler

Wakefield (16) 22
T: R Atkins 2, S Obst 1 **G:** D Brough 5

Hull KR (8) 20
T: Jake Webster 1, M Vella 1, S Murrell 1
G: Jake Webster 1, S Murrell 3

Wakefield squad
Grix, Gleeson, Henderson, Atkins, George, Rooney, Brough, Watene, Obst, Moore, Ferres, MacGillivray, Ferguson
Replacements: Sculthorpe, Bibey, Wilkes, Murphy

Hull KR squad
Briscoe, Fitzhenry, Jake Webster, Walker, Steel, I'Anson, James Webster, Vella, Cockayne, Aizue, Newton, Galea, Murrell
Replacements: Crossman, Mills, J Netherton, K Netherton

Belle Vue saw another thriller played out where the Wildcats held off a late surge from Hull Kingston Rovers to earn their second win of the season and drag themselves off the bottom of the table. Trinity looked in charge for most of the game with Danny Brough again leading the way and a fine display from hooker Sam Obst. This ensured a win was on the cards but Rovers just would not lie down.

The home side dominated for an amazing 25 minutes as the Robins had little possession and field position, but Wakefield could still only boast an 8–0 lead. When Scott Murrell converted his own try, the home side looked nervous. They could thank a disputed penalty try awarded to Sam Obst just before the break to go in for lemons 16–8 to the good. Rovers' coach Justin Morgan was far from convinced the try should have been given, 'You have to be good to see it,' he claimed after the game, although he didn't just claim that was the reason for the loss. 'We played poorly— brainlessly at times.'

Rovers did have their chances and there was some neat play from Michael Vella who chased his own little kick through to score. This left the Wildcats confused and when Jake Webster scored on 61 minutes the visitors took the lead 20–16. Thankfully, talented centre Ryan Atkins saved the day when he broke clear from a tackle and crossed for his second try allowing Danny Brough the conversion to seal the victory 22–20. Trinity coach John Kear was relieved his team had held out Rovers over the last 10 minutes or so and suggested, 'We must have gone via Huddersfield to get to Pontefract to get the win.' He was right, it was hardly a straightforward performance but winners are grinners.

engage
Mutual Assurance

Kick off: 19.30, Venue: KC Stadium, Att: 12,124, Match official: A Klein

Hull FC (18)
T: T Byrne 2 **G:** D Tickle 5

Wakefield (8)
T: D Ferguson **G:** D Brough 2

Hull FC squad
Tony, Sing, Byrne, Yeaman, Raynor, Berrigan, Dykes, Cusack, Lee, King, Radford, Tickle, Washbrook
Replacements:Hall, Houghton, Horne, Wheeldon

Wakefield squad
Reilly, Gleeson, Henderson, Atkins, Murphy, Grix, Brough, Watene, Leo-Latu, Moore, Ferres, MacGillivray, Ferguson
Replacements: Blaymire, Wilkes, Bibey, Sculthorpe

It doesn't matter how you win, as long as you do! Hull coach Peter Sharp was in no mood after the game to talk about classy or exciting play. This 18–8 victory over Wakefield was all about guts and determination. 'This was all about grinding out a win, it wasn't pretty but it was tough.'

You can say that again and the fact that five goals from Danny Tickle steered them to a desperate win indicated they were determined to get off the bottom of the league table. Todd Byrne bagged a brace of tries, one in each half, that helped snuff out any Trinity fight-back with only Dale Ferguson crossing for the visitors in a scrappy first half, although two goals from Danny Brough allowed

them to go into the sheds on level terms 8–8, but it was all Hull after the restart. Wakefield will rue the fact they bombed a couple of tries early when Atkins could have given them the lead but knocked on with the line at his mercy. After that escape Hull took control of the match. Scrum-half Adam Dykes started to influence the game with some neat kicks, one providing Byrne with his second try and when Tevita Leo-Latu was sent off for a high shot on Dykes it was curtains for the Wildcats. Again, two sides started the match down on troops and one wondered if the winter break had been enough to prepare the players for another intense season this year. Players were going down like ninepins each round and it was obvious the side who kept healthy this year would win the title. Cats coach John Kear came to the KC stadium with a plan of slowing the game down and only entertaining any flowing football close to their opponent's line, a factor that nearly worked as they scrambled back in defence time and time again. 'Both defences were outstanding, we had a couple of chances that we didn't take and Hull took the couple that came their way, I'm proud of the lads' effort.'

Hull just deserved the spoils in a bruising encounter, and it outlined the importance of having a good goal kicker in tight games, Tickle kicked all his five chances to steady the ship. Peter Sharp was also proud of his men who certainly rolled up their sleeves and offered some heroic defence at times. 'It wasn't pretty from the sidelines but we worked hard and ground out the victory.'

Adam Dykes again received some heavy treatment especially from the forwards and looked battered and bruised as he left the field. He showed enough skills and determination to lift Hull out of the doldrums and his combination with half Shaun Berrigan was starting to gel, although I felt both were looking forward to better weather when their skills would be appreciated more.

Friday 14 March 2008

Kick off: 20.00, Venue: Headingley, Att: 14,557, Match official: B Thaler

Leeds (24) 48
T: L Burgess, R Burrow, J Jones-Buchanan, J Peacock, N Scruton, J Tansey, B Webb, B Kaye
G: K Sinfield (8)

Harlequins (0) 0

Leeds squad
Webb, Hall, Ellis, Senior, Donald, Sinfield, Burrow, Bailey, Kaye, Leuluai, Peacock, Lauitiiti, Jones-Buchanan
Replacements: Tansey, Worrall, Burgess, Scruton

Harlequins squad
McLinden, Sheriffe, Clubb, Howell, Wells, Orr, Rinaldi, Temata, Randall, Ward, Barker, Purdham, Mbu
Replacements: Worrincy, Grayshon, McCarthy-Scarsbrook, Heckenburg

Pick yourself up, brush yourself down and start all over again! That was the message the Rhinos coach gave to his World Champs who the week before looked like World Chumps after a huge loss to Castleford. Harlequins arrived at Headingley in great spirits knowing this was a table topping clash and the victor would hold pole position. It was a nervous bunch of home fans who watched their heroes trot out on a cold windy night. To say the crowd got their money's worth depends on which team you were supporting but the Rhinos just blasted the London outfit off the park. It took only seven minutes before star forward Jamie Jones-Buchanan crossed and when Jamie Peacock charged over four minutes later the result was never in doubt as Harlequins struggled to keep pace and possession to show their wares.

The buzz in the crowd was not so much about Leeds getting back into top gear after the blip down at the Jungle but over the surprise signing of Aussie star Danny Buderus for next season. In 2009 Buderus will replace Gareth Ellis who is set to jet his way to Sydney to play with the Wests Tigers but many in the crowd were confused at Leeds buying another hooker! Matt Diskin was suspended for this game and coach Brian McClennan had no option but to throw in youngster Ben Kaye for his debut. The kid didn't let the side down, producing some neat touches and plenty of hard work, as did the other debutant Simon Worrall who gave notice that the youth policy at Headingley is in top shape. There was little doubt the Rhinos wanted to emulate the Cunningham-Roby pairing that has been such a huge success at St Helens and having two thinkers like Diskin and Buderus plotting the attack make Leeds look like a near complete team for next year.

It was hard to imagine that the Rhinos could look fitter and more eager than last term when they took the trophy at Old Trafford but on this showing it was going to take a fine outfit to stop them. Skilful, tough and a penchant for open thrilling play left the crowd in raptures and the Harlequins wondering if the scoreboard would ever stop clicking over! Tansey and Webb added tries

Luke Burgess touches down in the Rhinos rout of Harlequins.

before the break to send them into the sheds at 24–0, leaving London coach Brian McDermott with plenty of problems. 'I don't think I've seen a team play that well for over a year, it was a joy to watch, it's just a shame I was the opposition coach.'

'Bluey' McClennan was in raptures at seeing his debut boys do so well and the selection of Ali Lauitiiti to start a game for the first time in 12 months helped produce a vintage display from the huge talented second rower. Harlequins couldn't stop his charging forays through the defence and not surprisingly Leeds added another 24 points in the second half to win 48–0 in a rout that sent the message out that last week's loss was a small blip. It also threw down the gauntlet for all the other sides.

Saturday 15 March 2008

Kick off: 18.00, Venue: New Craven Park, Att: 8,083,
Match official: S Ganson

Hull KR (10) 20
T: C Walker 1, D Fitzhenry 2, B Cockayne 1 **G:** S Murrell 2

Castleford (0) 4
T: C Huby 1

Hull KR squad
Briscoe, Steel, Jake Webster, Walker, Fitzhenry, Galea, James Webster, Vella, K Netherton, Mills, Newton, Gene, Murrell
Replacements: Aizue, Crossman, Cockayne, Menzies

Castleford squad
McGoldrick, Donlan, Shenton, Dixon, Wainwright, Dorn, Sherwin, Huby, Moore, Korkidas, Guttenbeil, Lupton, Westerman
Replacements: Leafa, Higgins, Clayton, Henderson

Was it a case of after the lord mayor's show? Either way, Hull Kingston Rovers were fired up and ready to welcome the Castleford heroes who dumped the World Champs Leeds the week before. 'They played well against Leeds last week and that spurred us on to digging deep at training all week, we were more than ready,' said Justin Morgan the Rovers coach. In fact the Robins boss was disappointed they hadn't kept the Tigers pointless after conceding a Craig Huby try three minutes from the end. 'It would have been nice to have a big fat zero at the end.'

Castleford probably wished that the game had been called off as the teams had a desperate fight against a low hanging sea mist that threatened the match. Thankfully the wind cleared the mist enough to allow the home fans at least a chance to see their side crush a disappointing Tigers outfit that displayed little of the skills from the week before. Makeshift stand off Ben Galea was soon in the picture providing a super kick to the corner for Daniel Fitzhenry to score

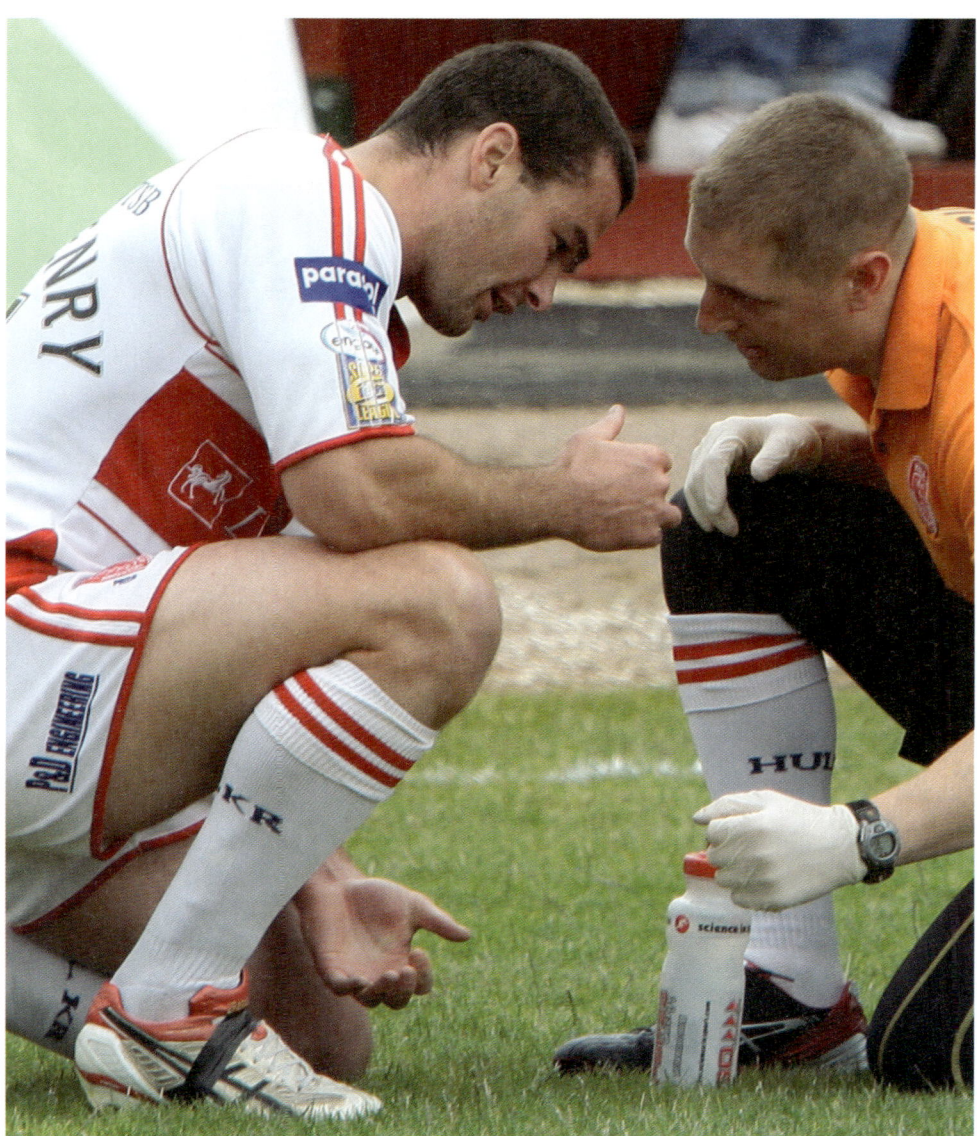

Daniel Fitzhenry scored twice in Hull KR's win over Castleford.

on just four minutes. Castleford looked lethargic and although they did tighten up their defence for a while, the plain fact was they couldn't get their hands on the ball for any long periods. When they did have a few chances the Rovers defence held strong and the Tigers defensive effort early in the match started to take its toll. When Ben Cockayne latched onto a Scott Murrell grubber the writing was on the wall at 10–0. Fitzhenry scored his second touchdown soon after the restart and Chev Walker wrapped it all up when he accepted a neat pass from James Webster six minutes later to put the result beyond doubt. Scott Murrell and James Webster were outstanding and teased the Tigers with some neat kicks and intelligent passing, whilst big centre Jake Webster showed enough to back up the home fans' cry that he's the next Mal Meninga! Praise indeed but there's no doubting the man's character, strength and ability.

Saturday 15 March 2008

Kick off: 18.30, Venue: Stade Gilbert Brutus, Att: 7,828
Match official: I Smith

Catalans (8) 24
T: D Pelo 2, A Chan 1, R Casty 1
G: T Bosc 4

St Helens (6) 10
T: F Meli 1, J Graham 1 **G:** M Smith 1

Catalans squad
Greenshields, Khattabi, Wilson, Stacul, Pelo, Mogg, Bosc, Chan, Gorrell, Guisset, Raguin, Croker, Mounis
Replacements: Ferriol, Fakir, Casty, Touxagas

St Helens squad
Wellens, Gardner, Gidley, Talau, Meli, Pryce, Smith, Hargreaves, Roby, Graham, Gilmour, Bennett, Flannery
Replacements: Wilkin, Clough, Fa'asavalu, Eastmond

Four losses on the trot were hardly a sign of confidence when Catalans welcomed the mighty Saints to the South of France. Coach Mick Potter must have been left wondering when their second win of the season was due. Potter was heavily tipped to replace St Helens coach Daniel Anderson next season and couldn't have selected a more fitting display to help his ambitions as Catalans clicked into gear after half time to go on and win 24–10. The result was no fluke even if Saints were down on forwards yet again.

Normally, teams visiting the Stade Gilbert Brutus start slowly and struggle to get into any sort of attacking pattern. So it proved with both sets of forwards crashing into each other in a fight for superiority and it took the Saints 25 minutes to breach the Dragons defences. James Graham has been a tower of strength for Saints this season and has carried the workload superbly in the absence of so many star forwards. It was no surprise when his bulk took him over for the first try of the game from a neat short pass from Roby. Catalans hit back with a converted try to Dimitri Pelo shortly before the break to lead 8–6 and it was Pelo again who struck to stretch the lead to 12–6 three minutes into the second half. Three minutes later substitute Remi Casty crashed through three defenders close to the line. Bosc's conversion gave them a 12 point lead to give coach Potter some confidence they could hang on to as they had been undone by both Bradford and Hull KR in the dying moments of the previous matches at home. Saints finally clicked into gear with fullback Wellens creating the overlap for Francis Meli midway through the half. The nerves set in for the home side when Matt Gidley went close before being tackled into touch by the corner flag. Nerves were settled when Alex Chan showed his strength to dive over near the posts with four minutes remaining to snare a vital victory in front of yet another big crowd nearing 8,000.

Sunday 16 March 2008

Kick off: 15.00, Venue: Grattan Stadium, Att: 11,838, Match official: R Silverwood

Bradford (14) 23
T: P Sykes 1, B Jeffries 1, S Burgess 1, **G:** P Deacon 5 **DG:** P Deacon 1

Warrington (6) 10
T: C Hicks 1, P Johnson 1 **G:** L Briers 1

Bradford squad
Sykes, Tadulala, Evans, Hape, Tupou, Jeffries, Deacon, Lynch, Newton, Feather, Nero, Finnigan, Burgess
Replacements: Solomona, Godwin, Cook, James

Warrington squad
Reardon, Hicks, Martin Gleeson, King, Johnson, Briers, Monaghan, Morley, Clarke, Rauhihi, L Anderson, Westwood, V Anderson
Replacements: Mark Gleeson, Parker, Pickersgill, Bracek

The excitement of being up in the top sphere of Super League could just have got to the Warrington players as they tried far too hard to win the game on every set of six against a Bradford side who started well and never really lost control. After their solid win against Wigan seven days earlier coach Paul Cullen selected the same 17 but they lacked the composure of the previous week as they tried to force the pass far too often. 'We paid the price for pushing the pass,' said Cullen. 'Their field position and kicking game was better,' added the Wolves boss.

Paul Sykes opened the scoring after 10 minutes and even though Paul Johnson pulled one back for the visitors seven minutes later it was clear that Bradford were bossing the game thanks to some fine kicking from both halves, Deacon and Jeffries. Jeffries, the off-season signing from Wakefield, was dropped after the first round loss to the Wildcats, but showed his coach that his speed, thinking and strong kicking game was the major reason for this success. In cold, wet conditions it was always going to be a hard grafting game with little frills on show. Someone forgot to tell this to Warrington who tried to play open rugby instead of taking a leaf out of Bradford's game plan of kick for position and squeeze out the mistakes from the opposition. David Solomona returned on the bench after eight weeks with an injured knee and picked up another knock to take the icing off the fine win. Paul Sykes also left the field with an elbow problem. Injuries are another cloud that has hung over nearly all clubs this season.

After the break Bradford tightened their defence even more and Warrington could find no chink in the armour until Briers' chip over found Chris Hicks to claim his eighth try of the season. This gave them a glimpse of a win, but Ben Jeffries sealed it soon after with a neat 70 metre try that made it 22–10 with three minutes remaining. When Deacon dropped a field goal it was all over.

Ben Jeffries sealed the win over Warrington with a 70 metre try.

Sunday 16 March

Kick off: 15.00, Venue: The Galpharm Stadium, Att: 8,417, Match official: P Bentham

Huddersfield (8) 19
T: K Brown 1, L Robinson 1
G: L Cudjoe 5 **DG:** K Brown 1

Wigan (8) 20
T: D Goulding 1, G Carmont 1, A Coley 1 **G:** P Richards 4

Huddersfield squad
Cudjoe, Elford, Whatuira, Lolesi, Jensen, Brown, Robinson, Mason, Gatis, Skandalis, Jones, Raleigh, Wild
Replacements: Crabtree, Jackson, Griffin, Hudson

Wigan squad
Richards, Calderwood, Goulding, Carmont, Colbon, Barrett, Leuluai, Fielden, Higham, Coley, Hock, Bailey, O'Loughlin
Replacements: Palea'aesina, Hansen, McIlorum, O'Carroll

When you lead 19–8 with just four minutes remaining you have every right to feel gutted when you go on to lose the game. That was the feeling the Giants had when Wigan amazingly snatched a win they didn't deserve. Sadly the Huddersfield players put the cue on the rack and left the Warriors a slight glimpse of success when they should have slowed the pace down and shut up shop. The fact they didn't irritated Giants coach Jon Sharp. It wasn't the only thing to upset the Huddersfield boss who left no doubt about the referee's handling of the game. 'I believe an absolute injustice has occurred, it started in minute one and finished in the 80th,' Sharp added.

To add insult to injury Darrell Griffin was sent off after dissent to the official after the full time hooter when Wigan were dancing about with glee at pulling off a sensational win. Sean O'Loughlin's two outstanding breaks in the final minutes allowed the Warriors back into the game

Harrison Hansen tackles Huddersfield's Luke Robinson as Wigan stage a fight-back.

Wigan fans are jubilant as their team snatches a last gasp victory over Huddersfield.

after the 73rd-minute field goal from Kevin Brown surely wrapped up the match, or so they thought. Poor defence allowed the Wigan skipper the chance to create tries for Andy Coley and George Carmont to set up a final conversion from Pat Richards just five metres in from touch. Richards, who was in great form with the boot, thumped the ball over the bar to make it four from four and sent the travelling fans crackers in the stands, leaving the Giants fans wondering what had happened. O'Loughlin was outstanding and so was debut boy Leroy Cudjoe who was drafted in at the last minute after Chris Thorman was ruled out with a rib injury on the morning of the game. Cudjoe kicked well, produced some nice touches and defended like his life depended upon it and pleased his coach no end. 'The kid's been playing well in the reserves and deserved his chance,' Sharp said. Most of the 8,417 crowd left the ground thinking little of the new kid on the block; the talk would go long into the night about how the Giants threw it away.

engage
Mutual Assurance

Thursday 20 March 2008

Kick off: 20.00, Venue: Headingley,
Att: 19,296, Match official: S Ganson

Leeds (26) 44
T: B Webb 3, L Smith 1, S Donald 1,
R Burrow 2, J Jones-Buchanan 1
G: R Burrow 2, K Sinfield 4

Bradford (2) 2
G: P Deacon 1

Leeds squad
Webb, Smith, Ellis, Senior, Donald,
Tansey, Burrow, Leuluai, Diskin, Peacock,
Jones-Buchanan, Lauititi, Sinfield
Replacements: Worrall, Burgess,
Scruton, Hall

Bradford squad
Halley, Tadulala, Nero, Hape, Evans,
Jeffries, Deacon, Lynch, Newton,
Feather, Solomona, Finnigan, Burgess
Replacements: Harris, Godwin, Cook,
James

Easter is a time of reflection, chocolate
eggs and sweet little bunnies bouncing
across the meadow! Try telling that to
the Bradford Bulls who arrived at
Headingley on a cold, windswept
Thursday night hoping to stop the
rampaging Rhinos from racing away
from them at the top of the league
table.

What they found was a side ready to
inflict upon them a box full of magic
tricks and a defence that bordered on
cruelty, leaving them totally shattered
both in body and mind. We all knew
Leeds had been firing on all cylinders of
late but the derby games nearly always
throw the formbook out of the window.

Not on this occasion as the Rhinos ran
rampant over a Bulls outfit that tried
everything to stop the rot. Deacon's
penalty goal early gave them a solid start
but when in-form Jamie Jones-Buchanan
crossed after seven minutes one sensed
the Rhinos were in a mood to run riot,
and that they did despite having prop
Kylie Leuluai carried off after a collision
with Chris Feather.

Not that it stopped the home side from
cutting loose as Jones-Buchanan yet
again came to the forefront with a smart
piece of thinking in taking the ball from
a quick 20 metre tap that confused the
Bulls defence. He raced downfield 60
metres before unselfishly off loading to
Lee Smith to race in out wide. Squeezed
into these two touchdowns was a four
pointer from Brent Webb and it looked
more than likely Bradford were looking
down the barrel of a big score. And so it
proved with Jones-Buchanan having the
game of his life, breaking through on no
less than five occasions in the first half
alone. Makeshift centre Gareth Ellis
turned the clock back to his early three
quarter days with a fine performance,
but the team ethic kept the Leeds fans
buzzing, and they applauded them off
the field at half time looking at a
scoreboard reading 26–2.

Bradford, again without the big forward
Joe Vagana and a with a rather subdued
David Solomona, just couldn't get into
any sort of rhythm as Leeds snuffed out
each move with solid tackling and were
losing possession under the pressure. To
be fair, Bradford were more confident in
the second half and attacked the Leeds

line from the whistle. They also set up camp to at least launch a rare attack, sadly for Bulls skipper Paul Deacon his grubber kick was snapped up by Luke Burgess who showed great composure to draw the defence. He slipped a pass to winger Scott Donald who raced away for a 70 metre try that sealed the game. To say the Bulls were frustrated was an understatement as some outstanding Leeds defence repelled each attack. Tempers were starting to flair when the referee put Terry Newton on report for a high shot. He was replaced straight away by coach Steve McNamara.

It was an outstanding performance by Leeds and the crowd were entertained royally with some incredible tries, none more so than when Rob Burrow sidestepped three times to dive under the posts. Amazingly Rhinos coach Brian McClennan expressed a little concern about the second half showing! 'We were a bit slack with the ball at times and we still have things to work on.' He did add that he thought the second half defensive effort was superb which is not to be sniffed at as for the second week running the opposition failed to score a try. Leeds threw down the gauntlet to the rest of the league in a big way and nobody was looking forward to playing them in this mood.

Player of Round 7

Jamie Jones-Buchanan, Leeds
What a game, Jones-Buchanan won the man of the match inside the first 30 minutes—explosive to say the least. Bradford had no answer to him.

Jamie Jones-Buchanan hauls down Semi Tadulala.

The weather conditions influenced the Hull derby.

Kick off: 12.15, Venue: New Craven Park, Att: 9,284, Match official: A Klein

Hull KR (6) 11
T: Jake Webster 1, D Fitzhenry 1
G: P Cooke 1 **DG:** James Webster 1

Hull FC (0) 10
T: K Yeaman 1, D Tickle 1
G: D Tickle 1

Hull KR squad
Briscoe, Steel, Walker, Jake Webster, Fitzhenry, Cooke, James Webster, Vella, Fisher, Mills, Newton, Galea, Murrell
Replacements: Crossman, K Netherton, Gene, Aizue

Hull FC squad
Tony, Sing, Yeaman, Byrne, Raynor, Berrigan, Dykes, King, Lee, Cusack, Radford, Tickle, Washbrook
Replacements: G Horne, Wheeldon, Houghton, Fellous

After a six match suspension the return of Paul Cooke added that extra spice to another tough Humberside derby. A record crowd at Craven Park witnessed an intriguing match that eventually was settled by a 'wobbly' drop goal from James Webster with just three minutes on the clock remaining to make it 11–10 in Rovers' favour.

Cooke looked more than a bit rusty and never influenced the match in the same way he's done in the past but it was a pleasing sight for coach Justin Morgan none the less. Cooke may have failed to hit the high spots but half back partner James Webster certainly did as he guided the Rovers around the park with such aplomb with the likes of Mick Vella and Clint Newton laying the platform. Hull FC, still missing the power of Garreth Carvell and Ewan Dowes in the pack, were struggling to hold the Rovers six. Yet brave defence held them out only conceding one try to Jake Webster in the first 40 and having a video call for a try from Motu Tony turned down just before the break.

This gave some hope to Peter Sharp's men and with Shaun Berrigan getting into the game it was no surprise when his pass sent in Danny Tickle half way through the second half but the try scorer failed with an easy conversion, a miss that would come back to haunt them. Tickle didn't miss though when Dykes sent in Kirk Yeaman who cut back inside to stroll in near the posts and the game was locked at 10–10 with just eight minutes remaining. Rovers looked slightly shell shocked as Hull FC started to gain momentum. The game looked destined for a draw until the visitors decided to kick on the fourth tackle down field in the hope of forcing the error and setting up for the one pointer. Sadly they didn't take into account the skills of their former fullback Shaun Briscoe who carried the ball back into

Daniel Fitzhenry scores in Hull KR's narrow victory over Hull FC.

the opposition's half with a classy break and set up the chance for James Webster who obliged with probably the most important kick of his career.

Kick off: 14.30, Venue: Knowsley Road, Att: 17,500, Match official: R Silverwood

St Helens (22) 46
T: P Wellens 1, M Gidley 1, W Talau 1, F Meli 2, L Pryce 1, S Long 1, J Graham 1, K Eastmond 1
G: S Long 4, K Eastmond 1

Wigan (0) 10
T: G Carmont 1, M McIlorum 1
G: S O'Loughlin 1

St Helens squad
Wellens, Gardner, Gidley, Talau, Meli, Pryce, Long, Hargreaves, Roby, Graham, Gilmour, Flannery, Wilkin
Replacements: Bennett, Clough, Fa'asavalu, Eastmond

Wigan squad
Richards, Calderwood, Goulding, Carmont, Colbon, Barrett, Leuluai, Fielden, Higham, Coley, Hansen, Bailey, O'Loughlin
Replacements: Palea'aesina, McIlorum, J Tomkins, O'Carroll

Despite injuries and lack of form the Saints knew they had to produce the goods if they had any chance of keeping pace with league leaders Leeds and what better way than to crunch their old rivals on a traditional Good Friday derby against Wigan. A full house at Knowsley Road ensured the atmosphere was electric. Unfortunately for the Warriors only Saints were running on full power, as Wigan had no answer to the attacking prowess of the home side.

Sadly, before the game started, there was a one minute's silence for the passing away of the great centre Eric Ashton, a stalwart to both clubs and a sad loss to the game. One hoped that his old club from his playing days could produce a fitting tribute to his name. It wasn't as though Wigan didn't try, but the fact was Saints never let them get into any stride at all as they launched wave after wave of attack that left the Warriors confused. Quick play the balls and scooting runs from Roby and then later from Jon Wilkin provided the side with plenty of momentum to chalk up four tries to lead 22–0 at the break.

The sin-binning of Wigan hooker Mickey Higham hardly helped Wigan's cause yet nobody in the crowd could use that as an excuse as Saints were scintillating especially when Maurie Fa'asavalu came off the bench to spice things up with some strong running. He did get flattened by a shoulder in the ribs tackle from Thomas Leuluai which dropped him like a sack of beans! After several minutes he recovered enough to bounce back up with a huge grin and gave the thumbs up to the Wigan half back in a 'Well done' exchange. One would have thought it would inspire Wigan to better things and for a while the introduction of prop Iafeta Palea'aesina gave them hope. But Sean Long had other ideas providing some wonderful passes and precise kicks that kept turning the opposition around Michael McIlorum's try early in the second half gave Wigan hope but only a consolation try by George Carmont 10 minutes from time gave the Warriors fans anything to shout about. 'It was an improvement on what we have been doing lately,' said a happy coach Anderson. 'It was an impressive victory,' he added.

No doubt he was pleased to see one of his youngsters show fine form when the kid they are claiming to be the next Jason Robinson raced away in spectacular fashion to score in the corner with just seconds remaining on the clock. Kyle Eastmond is one player destined to become a regular first team player in the famous red and white jersey. He thinks quickly and has plenty of pace, but most importantly he looks to have that 'cocky' air about him that all top class cheeky half backs need.

Kick off: 15.00, Venue: Twickenham Stoop, Att: 3,854,
Match official: P Bentham

Harlequins (18) 22
T: M Gafa 1, D Howell 3, H Paul 1
G: H Paul 1

Catalans (6) 24
T: D Pelo 1, A Gorrell 1, G Mounis 1, D Carlaw 1 **G:** T Bosc 4

Harlequins squad
McLinden, Clubb, Gafa, Howell, Sheriffe, Hill, Orr, Temata, Randall, Ward, Mbu, Purdham, Paul
Replacements: Rinaldi, Worrincy, Barker, Grayshon

Catalans squad
Greenshields, Stacul, Khattabi, Duport, Pelo, Wilson, Bosc, Ferriol, Gorrell, Chan, Raguin, Croker, Mounis
Replacements: Casty, Fakir, Touxagas, Carlaw

Harlequins were cruising at 14–0 up midway through the first half and appeared to have the game under control. In the end they allowed the French outfit to take the spoils with a great fight-back and a 24–22 win. Two tries from David Howell and one each for Henry Paul and Matt Gafa against a single four pointer from Aaron Gorrell

took the London outfit into the sheds with a commanding 18–6 lead against a Catalans team without Adam Mogg and Casey McGuire.

Quins coach Brian McDermott couldn't quite grasp how they enabled the French side back into the game and was upset at their defence, though praised the opposition for the way they outplayed them in the second half. 'We stopped defending and lost a lot of our structure.' Star of the show for the Catalans was Thomas Bosc who stepped up to the plate and produced some neat touches and high kicks that confused the opposition's defence. With the Twickenham Stoop boys making error after error the gate was wide open for a comeback. Dimitri Pelo got the ball rolling, and tries to Dane Carlaw, David Howell and Greg Mounis grabbed an amazing win that pleased their coach no end. 'I thought the 12 point difference wasn't a hill too hard to climb, we changed a few things and we executed better in the second half.' That they did, as a stunned Harlequins side moped off at the finish realising they'd had the game in their hands but failed to control the ball and field position. They had a final tilt at snatching the game back when Rikki Sheriffe broke through out wide but the hesitation from Dwayne Barker allowed Catalans time to scramble back.

Kick off: 15.00, Venue: Halliwell Jones Stadium, Att: 9,320,
Match official: B Thaler

Warrington (12) 30
T: C Hicks 2, Martin Gleeson 1, L Briers 1, A Bracek 1 **G:** L Briers 5

Huddersfield (8) 14
T: J Lolesi 1, E Crabtree 1

G: L Cudjoe 2, T Hemingway 1

Warrington squad

Reardon, Hicks, Martin Gleeson, King, Penny, V Anderson, Briers, Morley, Clarke, Rauhihi, Johnson, Westwood, L Anderson
Replacements: Mark Gleeson, Parker, Pickersgill, Bracek

Huddersfield squad

Cudjoe, Elford, Whatuira, Lolesi, Jensen, Brown, Robinson, Mason, Hudson, Skandalis, Jones, Raleigh, Wild
Replacements: Crabtree, Jackson, Snitch, Hemingway

The return to form of centre Martin Gleeson cheered up Warrington coach Paul Cullen no end for it was the classy three quarter's style and strength that helped steer the Wolves to a hard fought win over Huddersfield 30–14. Cullen should also be impressed with the way his outfit toughed it out and showed patience at a time when the Giants took it to them midway through the first half.

It was all Warrington in the opening 10 minutes. When Lee Briers produced some magical sidestepping to cross for a try he easily converted, one worried for Huddersfield's welfare. Yet the Giants slowly started to click and when Jamahl Lolesi crossed during the 10 minute sin-binning of Louis Anderson it was all square at 6–6. Again it was Lee Briers to the rescue when his long cut out pass found Chris Hicks that enabled them to go to the sheds with a 12–3 lead.

Briers kicked an early penalty six minutes after the restart and it was his conversion of Martin Gleeson's try on 48 minutes that looked to have wrapped it up at 20–8, only to see big prop Eorl Crabtree snatch a converted try a few minutes later to give the visitors some hope. Steady play by Warrington allowed them

to get good field position and man of the match Chris Hicks crossed for his second of the day to allow the Wolves to run away with it.

Giants coach Jon Sharp was upset with their discipline, 'We have to wise up to fact we give away too may penalties yet technically and system wise I'm happy.' Paul Cullen was more pleased with the way his side settled down and controlled the game at vital times. 'We slowly took control of field position and the completion rate increased so we could open up and score some tries.'

Eorl Crabtree snatched a try in Huddersfield's defeat against Warrington.

Friday 21 March 2008

Kick off: 20.00, Venue: Belle Vue,
Att: 9,287, Match official: I Smith

Wakefield (16) 28
T: R Atkins 1, A Murphy 1, J Rooney 1,
D Brough 1, S Obst 1
G: J Rooney 2, D Brough 2

Castleford (10) 16
T: L Dorn 2, P Lupton 1
G: C Huby 1, J Westerman 1

Wakefield squad
Blaymire, Gleeson, Demetriou, Atkins,
Murphy, Rooney, Brough, Watene, Obst,
Moore, Ferres, MacGillivray, Ferguson
Replacements: Sculthorpe, Bibey,
Henderson, Wilkes

Castleford squad
Dorn, Owen, McGoldrick, Dixon,
Fletcher, Lupton, Sherwin, Higgins,
Henderson, Korkidas, Guttenbeil, Huby,
Clayton
Replacements: Thackeray, Leafa,
Westerman, Boyle

Bragging rights feature highly on Easter weekend's derby games and the tension between Wakefield and Castleford was evident with some big hits on show in the first few minutes. Despite playing into a strong wind Wakefield secured a 16–10 lead at half time as the Tigers failed to take advantage of a gale-forcer and pin the Wildcats back, leaving the home side confident of taking the spoils.

Yet Castleford tore the script up, dug in deep and defended for their life and with more care and attention to ball control could have pushed the Wildcats much closer. Coach Terry Matterson was dumbfounded over their first half showing but was pleased at the response after the break. 'We gave ourselves a mountain to climb and were always chasing the game. It was a really dumb performance, and there are no excuses.'

Star of the show was Danny Brough, the former Tiger, whose two fine bursts

Ryan Atkins scores for Wakefield against Castleford

Danny Sculthorpe looks for the off load

brought him a solo try soon after half time. Then another burst provided Ryan Atkins with the try that sealed it soon after. Brough has been in fine form this year and the responsibility of being handed the captaincy for Scotland in the upcoming World Cup has added even extra bite to his game. He may not be the official skipper at Wakefield but there's little doubt who calls the attacking shots out on the field of play. Luke Dorn was perhaps the only highlight of a Tigers showing that played in fits and starts, loosing far too much ball early in the tackle count in the first

40 minutes. They at least completed 16 out of their 18 sets in the second stanza but the impact of Brough was enough to seal their fate. Dorn has overcome a poor season for Salford last term to find a new vim and vigour this season down at The Jungle. His two tries in this match emphasised the improvement of his game under the guidance of coach Terry Matterson who admitted Dorn and the rest of the squad showed they can play good rugby at times. 'I thought we played some good footy [in the second half] but we can do even better than that.'

engage
Mutual Assurance

Kick off: 13.00, Venue: The KC Stadium, Att: 14,113, Match official: P Bentham

Hull FC (0) 4
T: G Raynor 1

Leeds (18) 30
T: B Webb 1, L Smith 1, K Sinfield 1, R Burrow 1, C Ablett 1 **G:** K Sinfield 5

Hull FC squad
Tony, Byrne, Hall, Yeaman, Raynor, Berrigan, Dykes, Wheeldon, Lee, Cusack, Radford, Tickle, Washbrook
Replacements: R Horne, Fellous, Burnett, Briscoe

Leeds squad
Webb, Smith, Ellis, Senior, Donald, Sinfield, Burrow, Scruton, Diskin, Burgess, Peacock, Lauitiiti, Jones-Buchanan
Replacements: McGuire, Bailey, Tansey, Ablett

Snow, wind and driving rain! Boy was I sick and tired of the weather! It was hardly a Happy Easter Monday. There may have been arctic conditions but full credit to all those loyal fans who supported their team in what could hardly be described as 'Summer Rugby League'. Not that it stopped over 130,000 fans attending the full Easter programme with Sky viewers also providing huge ratings giving the sport a healthy look. Sadly the players found it tough going as the majority took to the field carrying injuries due to the tight Easter schedule. But the players gave their all in some outstanding matches, tinged with a touch of controversy, and some close encounters with only one game being a walk-over.

As anticipated, Leeds blitzed poor Hull FC who have battled through an injury crisis and had no answer to the Rhinos skill and strength. Even the return of Richard Horne failed to help when he re-injured his leg in the warm up to the match, leaving coach Peter Sharp scratching his head wondering when the tide might turn for the good. Leeds were in no mood to feel sympathetic to the black and whites' cause as they produced a master class of strong running and support play that had the crowd breathless. Even the home fans could not deny the classic play that was on show, where at times 10, 12, and on one occasion, 15 passes were produced to create tries of top quality.

Coach Sharp rued the fact the Rhinos were 'Bigger, better and stronger. We just couldn't live with them today,' and to be fair to the under-pressure Hull boss not many sides could have lived with the boys from Headingley in this mood. Jamie Peacock was a man mountain and the probing of Sinfield and Burrow never allowed Hull to get in their stride. This was not surprising as again they were missing the tough up front pair of Carvell and Dowes, allowing the Rhinos pack to run riot.

At 18–0 at the break, one feared for the home side. The only thing left for the suffering fans was the hope they at least could cross the try line as this was looking like the third game on the trot that Leeds would nil their opposition. Yet a faint cheer went up when winger

Raynor nipped into the corner for a good try just two minutes from time. The look on the Rhinos players faces gave the impression they had lost a £10 note and found a 5p piece as the Hull flyer dived over, such is the team spirit instilled into them this year by their new coach Brian McClennan. One would have thought he would be more than happy with a 30–4 win at the KC stadium. He cracked a smile when interviewed on Sky Sports but soon went into sombre mood, suggesting they dropped a few balls and that they have yet to peak! 'I don't think we're playing our best football,' which was worrying for all the other teams in the engage Super League, but who could doubt it? Could the World Champions get any better? Most fans asked themselves that after Good Friday when Leeds put Bradford to the sword in fine fashion, laid down the gauntlet and sat back to watch what the others would do. To be fair, Saints replied by ripping Wigan apart. This left us all mulling over the fact that it could be a two horse race.

Kevin Sinfield had a major influence in Leeds' win over Hull FC.

Jamahl Lolesi scores in Huddersfield's narrow win over Saints.

Kick off: 15.00, Venue: The Galpharm Stadium, Att: 7,131,
Match official: I Smith

Huddersfield (16) 28
T: P Whatuira 1, J Lolesi 1, R Jensen 1, D Griffin 2 **G:** C Thorman 4

St Helens (20) 26
T: P Wellens 1, L Pryce 1, J Roby 1, C Flannery 1 **G:** S Long 5

Huddersfield squad
Thorman, Lawrence, Whatuira, Lolesi, Jensen, Brown, Robinson, Mason, Gatis, Skandalis, Snitch, Crabtree, Jones
Replacements: Raleigh, Jackson, Griffin, Hudson

St Helens squad
Wellens, Gardner, Gidley, Talau, Meli, Pryce, Long, Fa'asavalu, Roby, Graham, Gilmour, Flannery, Wilkin
Replacements: Bennett, Clough, Eastmond, Frodsham

A two horse race for the title it might have been. Trouble was Saints fell off their horse at Huddersfield and lost 28–26 in a thriller that left coach Daniel Anderson fuming over referee Ian Smith, who he claims did his side no favours. Anderson called for video cameras at all games, not just the ones televised by Sky. He was angry over Paul Whatuira's try being awarded to the Giants on the stroke of half time, claiming the play had come after the half time hooter. The video replays show quite clearly he played the ball before the officials blew the hooter. On Smith, Anderson questioned if the official was up to standard for Super League games, 'I'm bemused by his performance in general. He's not had a TV match—which shows something. The RFL have to invest in technology because the try before half time was diabolical.' Amazing what a few weeks can do to a bloke's attitude, as Mr Anderson had called for coaches and

The St Helens fans show their disappointment.

players to support officials more at the start of March!

Despite the controversy, Saints were left wondering how they threw away a 14–0 lead and allowed Huddersfield back into the match. James Roby, Sean Long and Leon Pryce were cutting them to ribbons at will in the first quarter only to slow down and take the foot off the pedal allowing Darrell Griffin to score around 20 minutes into the game and when James Lolesi accepted a neat pass from Stuart Jones to score the game was wide open. Leon Pryce stirred Saints back into the lead by latching onto a Long kick to score and when the St Helens scrum-half converted, it looked as though the away side had regained their composure and a commanding lead. That was until the controversial touchdown before the break.

Huddersfield couldn't believe their luck as Saints fumbled a stack of chances and took control when Griffin, returning from suspension, scored his second try of the game. It's not possible to keep a team like Saints down for too long and James Roby's good work secured them the lead yet again. But the Giants were solid enough to strike back. Jensen held on to a neat pass from Lolesi to score and showed some outstanding defence as St Helens threw everything at them in a last gasp attempt to turn the game but they held on to win 28–26 and stop the rot of three losses on the trot. 'I thought we smartened our act up today, we were more disciplined and our bench proved to be the difference, we had some quality there and wore them down,' said coach Jon Sharp. The win was a huge bonus for the coach as he was due to sign a new contract the following week to keep him at the Giants for another year at least.

Kick off: 15.00, Venue: JJB Stadium, Att: 16,457, Match official: B Thaler

Wigan (4) 18
T: M Calderwood 1, L Colbon 2
G: P Richards 3

Hull KR (0) 12
T: C Walker 1, C Newton 1
G: P Cooke 2

Wigan squad
Richards, Calderwood, Goulding, Carmont, Colbon, Barrett, Leuluai, Fielden, McIlorum, Coley, Bailey, Hansen, O'Loughlin
Replacements: Higham, Palea'aesina, J Tomkins, O'Carroll

Hull KR squad
Briscoe, Steel, Walker, Jake Webster, Fitzhenry, Galea, James Webster, Vella, Cockayne, Mills, Gene, Newton, Murrell
Replacements: Aizue, Lovegrove, Cooke, Fisher

Wigan bounced back from their Good Friday mauling against Saints with a hard fought victory over Hull KR 18–12 at the

Pat Richards kicked three goals in Wigan's defeat of Hull KR.

JJB where again slippery conditions contributed to make handling a problem. The home side raced to a 10–0 lead and appeared to have crushed any advances Rovers made at them with some solid defence that pleased coach Brian Noble no end. Full credit to Hull KR who fought hard to get back into the match and two tries in the space of 10 minutes from Clint Newton and Chev Walker took them in front for the first time at 12–10. A Pat Richards' penalty squared it all up at 12–12 and the struggle began.

The final quarter proved a ding-dong battle with either side grafting for field position in the hope of going for the drop goal, but Wigan stunned the Rovers by going for the power play. Trent Barrett kept the ball alive to send centre Darrell Goulding clear who in turn supplied the final pass for Mark Calderwood to cross under the posts with just five minutes left. It was a sheer piece of magic from the Aussie Barrett who kept both his nerve and Wigan in the hunt for a top five position. It needed something outstanding to break down the hard working Rovers defence who battled tirelessly in the final 10 minutes. Justin Morgan praised Wigan's attitude, 'They deserved to win because they backed themselves when they could have gone for a field goal.'

Monday 24 March 2008

Kick off: 15.30, Venue: The Jungle, Att: 7,245, Match official: S Ganson

Castleford (12) 31
T: R Owen 1, P Lupton 1, J Westerman 3
G: J Westerman 5 **DG:** B Sherwin 1

Warrington (18) 34
T: S Reardon 1, Martin Gleeson 1, V Anderson 1, L Anderson 1, B Westwood 1, Mark Gleeson 1,
G: C Hicks 3, L Briers 2

Castleford squad
Dorn, Fletcher, McGoldrick, Dixon, Owen, Lupton, Sherwin, Leafa, Henderson, Korkidas, Huby, Clayton, Westerman
Replacements: Thackeray, Higgins, Boyle, Massey

Warrington squad
Reardon, Hicks, Martin Gleeson, King, Penny, V Anderson, Briers, Morley, Clarke, Rauhihi, L Anderson, Westwood, Johnson
Replacements: Mark Gleeson, Parker, Pickersgill, Bracek

Warrington were another side that raced into a solid early lead yet they had to produce a last gasp play to snatch a four pointer with seconds remaining to secure a hard 31–34 victory at The Jungle. It was a tough result for the Tigers after being tied at 30–30 when the boot of Brent Sherwin looked to have sealed the valuable two league points with a drop goal. But the good feeling didn't last long as Warrington fought back with a last minute effort when the two Gleeson brothers combined to send Louis Anderson in for the winner.

Castleford deserved more as they fought back from 12–0 down. A hat trick from young loose forward Joe Westerman was the highlight of a fine and exciting game, yet the plain fact was that the Tigers just couldn't seem to close the game down when the going was tight. Matterson was furious at allowing the Wolves to score so late and the troubled coach must have been wondering what to do next as he had such a small squad to choose from. Trouble was, the market was not actually flowing with talent and he was left with no option but to persevere and do his best to patch up the side. They played some attractive flowing footy that could breakdown

Martin Gleeson scored in Warrington's win at The Jungle.

most defences but it was in the tackling department and with their lack of composure where the problems occurred. Paul Cullen was a relieved Wolves coach and proud at the way his team fought back and had belief in themselves to play open football to secure the win. 'I was delighted with the way we kept our nerve and came back to win,' Cullen said.

It was a close scrape, yet kept alive the dream of silverware, although the injuries to Lee Briers (calf) and Stuart Reardon (hamstring) would have made it hardly a time for huge celebrations as they crossed back over the Pennines. Yet two wins over Easter was a huge bonus irrespective of how it was done.

Monday 24 March 2008

Kick off: 18.00, Venue: Grattan Stadium, Att: 8,428, Match official: A Klein

Bradford (30) 32
T: D Halley 1, J Evans 1, P Deacon 1, S Burgess 1, D Solomona 1
G: P Deacon 6

Harlequins (12) 24
T: H Paul 1, M Worrincy 2, D Barker 1
G: H Paul 4

Bradford squad
Halley, Evans, Sykes, Hape, Tadulala, Jeffries, Deacon, Lynch, Newton, Burgess, Solomona, Nero, Finnigan
Replacements: Kopczak, Godwin, Cook, Harris

Harlequins RL squad
Wells, Clubb, Gafa, Howell, Sheriffe, Hill, Paul, Temata, Randall, Ward, Worrincy, Purdham, Mbu
Replacements: Haggerty, Melling, Barker, Grayshon

Bradford eased away from the bottom section of the table with a first half blitz of the visiting Harlequins that left the result never in doubt, especially with such foul weather making things difficult for both sides. The Quins never got into gear until the second stanza but by that time the game had gone, and so had some of the fans that didn't take too kindly to what appeared to be a case of putting the cue on the rack.

One can't blame them, Easter takes a lot out of the players and with a score of 30–12 at the break the chance of a Harlequins fight-back was remote. Yet the London side did try hard to inject some life back into the match and won the second half 12–2 but those at the ground knew the Bulls were never in danger after Dave Halley, Sam Burgess and David Solomona scored tries in the first half against a tired looking Harlequins. Paul Deacon was in fine form picking up 16 points and seems to have recovered from a bad patch to again steer the team around the park with authority and ensure the Bulls start their battle to climb the table.

Monday 24 March 2008

Kick off: 18.00, Venue: Stade Gilbert Brutus, Att: 8,120,
Match official: R Silverwood

Catalans (16) 28
T: C Greenshields 1, C Stacul 1, D Ferriol 1, A Chan 1, D Carlaw 1
G: T Bosc 4

Wakefield (0) 20
T: M Blaymire 1, R Moore 1, R Bibey 1, S Grix 1 **G:** J Rooney 2

Catalans squad
Greenshields, Stacul, Wilson, Duport, Pelo, Mogg, Bosc, Ferriol, Gorrell, Chan, Raguin, Croker, Mounis
Replacements: Carlaw, Fakir, Casty, Touxagas

Wakefield squad

Blaymire, Gleeson, Martin, Demetriou, Murphy, Rooney, Brough, Watene, Golden, Wilkes, Moore, MacGillivray, Ferguson
Replacements: Bibey, Henderson, Grix, Sculthorpe

Catalans continued with their run of wins by being too strong for a Wakefield side who started badly, recovered in the second half and just failed to snatch a win late in the game. I don't know what state coach Mick Potter's nerves were in this year but no one could blame him if he became a nut case before the end of the season as his outfit always appeared to collapse late in their games. It may have been thrilling for Catalans' opponents to watch, but devastating if you were a Catalans fan or coach and after scoring three good tries from David Ferriol, Cyril Stacul and Clint Greenshields in the first 40 minutes one would have expected an easy ride for the last 40. But it wasn't.

It took a strong effort from Rickey Bibey to turn the tide shortly after the restart to wake the Wildcats out of their stupor and with coach John Kear's words of wisdom ringing in their ears the visitors made a game of it. With Wakefield looking hungry the French side started to make mistakes and were thankful of a breakaway try from Dane Carlaw to steady the ship. This forced the hand of the Wildcats who threw caution to the wind and opened out their attacking play.

Three tries in the space of about 20 minutes from Richard Moore, Matt Blaymire and Scott Grix left the result on a knife edge and the home side were thankful of a storming effort from prop Alex Chan only minutes from time to keep their winning ways intact. The paying public sure get their money's worth down in the south of France (as well as nice weather) as each home game becomes a thriller where the heart beat races faster than the turnstiles do!

Another crowd over 8,000 indicates things are on the up and up in the Perpignan area where the fans are becoming concerned at the rumours about their coach going to take over at St Helens next year. It was bad enough to have lost the influential Stacey Jones last season without them having to change another key person come the season's end.

Thomas Bosc added four goals in Catalans' defeat of Wakefield.

engage
Mutual Assurance

Friday 28 March 2008

Kick off: 19.30, Venue: Knowsley Road, Att: 11,188, Match official: A Klein

St Helens (6) 10
T: P Wellens 1 **G:** S Long 3

Leeds (8) 14
T: A Lauitiiti 1 L Burgess 1
G: K Sinfield 3

St Helens squad
Wellens, Gardner, Gidley, Talau, Meli, Pryce, Long, Hargreaves, Roby, Graham, Gilmour, Flannery, Bennett
Replacements: Cayless, Wilkin, Clough, Fa'asavalu

Leeds squad
Webb, Hall, Ellis, Senior, Donald, McGuire, Burrow, Leuluai, Diskin, Peacock, Jones-Buchanan, Lauitiiti, Sinfield
Replacements: Bailey, Scruton, Burgess, Worrall

It was the game we had all been looking forward to, a repeat of last year's Grand Final, a showdown to see if the Rhinos were going to be unstoppable this season was on the cards. So too were bragging rights as both the Leeds coach, Brian McClennan, and Saints coach, Daniel Anderson, traded a few comments in the press in the week's build up. McClennan was Anderson's number two when they both ran the New Zealand side a fact that added extra bite to a contest that sadly the weather spoiled.

Again the rain and wind presented the players with tough conditions but it didn't stop the contest from being fierce. Nor did it stop both sides trying to force the ball early. To say there was a buzz about the ground was an understatement as the talk was over Castleford announcing a new signing that would shock the sporting world! Secrets are hard to keep in our game as the fans and journalists wracked their brains to suggest who the 'big signing' was. At first Paul Sculthorpe was named, then Iestyn Harris did the rounds, even Craig Gower (playing Union in France) got a run, so who was it?

Not that the players were worried over such matters as Leeds stamped their class with some fine play from Brent Webb to provide a neat inside pass to Ali Lauitiiti to score out wide after Saints had taken a 4–2 lead from two Long penalties. It was a sign of respect that both sides took any chance for a goal with glee. It was against the run of play as Leeds were left defending for most of the first half as the home side had a huge wind advantage behind their backs and long raking kicks downfield kept the Rhinos for most part in their own quarter. Lauitiiti's converted try was one of the few chances Leeds had in the first 40 minutes and surprisingly they went to the sheds 8–6 ahead courtesy of an early penalty from the skipper Kevin Sinfield. This maintained his club record of scoring points in his last 51 games.

Not many Saints fans gave their side much chance as Leeds took advantage of the gale force wind in the final stanza. When the video ref was called on to decide a Scott Donald effort in the corner where it appeared he had snatched the ball from winger Ade Gardner, the Saints looked doomed, yet after three minutes of deliberation the try was ruled out. The decision lifted the Saints and soon after a neat combination of Sean Long and Leon Pryce sent fullback Paul Wellens over to take the lead at 10–8, but Leeds were not to be outdone. Again referee Klein awarded penalties to confuse players and fans alike but he missed a blatant knock-on from Ali Lauitiiti at the play the ball. This allowed big young prop Luke Burgess to come out of the shadow of his younger brother Sam to gain some glory himself with a strong barge over the line to seal the game.

The home fans were furious at the missed infringement but nothing could detract from Burgess' huge effort. He has settled into the Leeds squad well and looks another top prospect. With Sinfield and Peacock in delightful form the chance for St Helens to stage a late snatch and grab again was never on the cards as they drove on their side to bigger and better things in defence and attack. All in all it was an amazing performance from all the Rhinos.

Friday 28 March 2008

Kick off: 20.00, Venue: JJB Stadium, Att: 12,933, Match official: I Smith

Wigan (6) 8
T: S O'Loughlin 1 **G:** P Richards 2

Wakefield (4) 4
G: T Martin 2

Wigan squad
Richards, Calderwood, Goulding, Carmont, Colbon, Mathers, Leuluai, Fielden, McIlorum, Coley, Bailey, Hansen, O'Loughlin

Replacements: Higham, Palea'aesina, J Tomkins, O'Carroll

Wakefield squad
Blaymire, Gleeson, Demetriou, Atkins, Martin, Grix, Rooney, Watene, Henderson, Sculthorpe, Moore, MacGillivray, Ferguson
Replacements: Bibey, Wilkes, Golden, Pitts

Wigan were happy to snare a hard fought 8–4 win at the expense of visitors Wakefield who provided some stiff opposition in a game that was interrupted with a record 32 penalties by referee Ian Smith. Brian Noble was fuming, 'That was crap, we'll drive our fans away if this continues.' His point was backed up by new Wigan owner Ian Lenagan who was, 'Appalled at the number of stoppages.' Mr Lenagan added, 'Richard Lewis was at the game on Friday and to see 32 penalties in a game is far from ideal.'

Penalties and stoppages have been becoming a major problem for our game especially those penalties given after players have made several passes to obtain advantage as is the case in Union. Some fans have begun to chant, 'Swing low sweet chariot' at games. I hoped the message would get through to the ref boss Stuart Cummins that some flexibility was needed otherwise the fans would talk with their feet.

Either way Wigan held on with some tough defence to keep Wakefield scoreless in the second half where even they only added a Pat Richards penalty to the half time score of 6–4. The only try of the game came towards the end when Sean O'Loughlin crashed over from Mickey Higham's pass, a rare piece of skill in blustery conditions. Undeniably it was a forwards' day where Wigan's Andy

Sean O'Loughlin scores the only try in tough conditions.

Coley and Wildcats' Danny Sculthorpe were the stars, both enjoying the struggle and arm-wrestle throughout.

Trent Barrett was missing from the Warriors starting line up and Danny Brough was absent for the visitors but in those conditions it was never going to be a disadvantage to have creative players like those two missing. Wildcats coach John Kear still thought his side did enough to win it, 'I can't fault the effort, we could have levelled or even won it and when we get some of our pivotal players back we will be a good team.' Sadly the game was no classic with windy conditions and the stoppages for penalties but again we found the fans winding their way home discussing the referee and not the players' bravery and fortitude.

Saturday 29 March 2008

Kick off: 18.00, Venue: Halliwell Jones Stadium, Att: 7,444,
Match official: R Silverwood

Warrington (0) 6
T: P Johnson 1 **G:** C Hicks 1

Harlequins (8) 8
T: G Haggerty 1 **G:** H Paul 2

Warrington squad
Hicks, Riley, Martin Gleeson, King, Penny, V Anderson, Monaghan, Morley, Clarke, Rauhihi, Johnson, Westwood, Bracek
Replacements: Mark Gleeson, Parker, Pickersgill, Mitchell

Harlequins squad
Wells, Sharp, Clubb, Howell, Sheriffe, Paul, Rinaldi, Temata, Randall, Mbu, Barker, Worrincy, Purdham
Replacements: Grayshon, Haggerty, Walsh, Melling

By this time Bill Arthur had announced live on air that Dwain Chambers, the GB sprinter, was signing for the Tigers! The press boys were left working overtime—preparing copy for both the game and the sprinter, and to be fair it was the latter that grabbed the headlines the following morning. It was amazing to think these two teams battered it out in sludge, gave their all and left the field exhausted only to be usurped by a bloke who had never played rugby, nor could catch a ball! Publicity stunt or not, it grabbed the world press and became back page news. It also left most fans wondering what our game had come to in giving the athlete who was banned for taking drugs a chance to earn a crust. The fact we have allowed some of our league drug takers to resurrect their career was probably the reason why the RFL claimed they had no problem if Castleford wanted to register the flying 100 metres star. We all waited with baited breath as to when or where Mr Chambers would play his first game. Most fans claimed it was a farce with one fan suggesting someone from the local Council Chambers had more chance of playing a Super League game than him! Either way the bloke wanted to have a go so we sat back to see what he would do. A couple of tackles would sort him out one way or the other.

One bloke who was sorting a few things out was Warrington boss Paul Cullen. He slammed his players after a dismal performance against the Harlequins who showed more guile and strength to out muscle the Wolves 8–6. With water on the playing surface it didn't take Einstein to work out what game plan was needed and the London side missing top players like Hill, Orr and McLinden slugged it out in the mud, played simple basic rugby and kept the defence tight throughout. Outstanding performances from Rinaldi, Paul and Purdham was the platform for success as the youngsters around them took the ball up all day and made good metres forward by following hooker Randall for most of the match. With 12 players from Britain in the squad it shows what advances the London

outfit have made in throwing off the tag of fielding nearly all overseas players, which was so often the case in the past. Wolves boss Cullen admitted his side looked tired after the Easter games but wouldn't use it as an excuse for their first home defeat claiming that his side were, 'Absolutely awful...We were simply very poor, handling was poor, our completion rate was bad and we paid the price,' he added.

Prop Gareth Haggerty scored his first try for the Harlequins after intercepting an inside pass from Michael Monaghan and racing away from near the half way line to dive over near the sticks sending the visitors into the sheds with an 8–0 lead. Losing centre Martin Gleeson with a pulled calf muscle three minutes into the second half didn't help Wolves' cause, as they tried desperately to get back into the game. They managed this after some strong running from captain Adrian Morley who set up the position for Paul Johnson to crash over and give them hope but the London side hung on for a well deserved victory.

Coach Brian McDermott was more than pleased with his patched up side especially Michael Worrincy, Will Sharp and Tony Clubb, 'They all dug deep, we just rolled our sleeves up and were prepared to get mucky.' The patched up half back combination of Henry Paul and Julien Rinaldi worked well and they both showed spirit, direction and understanding to outplay their opposites.

Player of Round 9

Henry Paul, Harlequins
Still life left in the old dog yet. Paul gave a superb all round showing and directed the action like a traffic cop.

Gareth Raynor scored the final try which enabled Hull FC to draw with Catalans.

Saturday 29 March 2008

Kick off: 18.30, Venue: Stade Gilbert Brutus, Att: 8,450,
Match official: S Ganson

Catalans (24) 28
T: V Duport 1, D Pelo 1, T Bosc 1, G Mounis 1 **G:** T Bosc 6

Hull FC (16) 28
T: G Raynor 1, D Tickle 1, D Washbrook 1, S Wheeldon 1
G: D Tickle 6

Catalans Dragons squad
Greenshields, Stacul, Khattabi, Duport, Pelo, Wilson, Bosc, Chan, Gorrell, Guisset, Raguin, Croker, Carlaw
Replacements: Mounis, Fakir, Casty, Touxagas

Hull FC squad
Tony, Byrne, Yeaman, Hall, Raynor, R Horne, Lee, King, Berrigan, Fellous, Radford, Tickle, Washbrook
Replacements: Wheeldon, Manu, Houghton, Thackray

Like buses, draws also seem to come in two's and that was the case both in France and at Hull Kingston Rovers on Saturday and Sunday respectively. Super League had yet to witness a draw in

2008 and the way the Catalans had been playing, it was long odds they would be the first to break the duck. They were lucky to not lose the game with the last play of the match when a video referee turned down a Hull FC try after the TV replays hardly proved conclusive one way or the other that centre Craig Hall had touched the ball down.

A 28 all draw at Stade Gilbert Brutus was probably a fair result for the efforts of both sides who tried to play open rugby throughout despite both squads being without several injured star players. Hull's injuries have been well documented and it was no surprise that they signed Jamie Thackray from Leeds to start his second stint at the club. To say he was thrown in at the deep end was an understatement because the former Hull hero struggled to survive early on, giving away three penalties and dropping the ball a few times. Despite such misgivings he helped shore up the middle, a problem all season for coach Peter Sharp.

The game see-sawed throughout after Danny Tickle crossed for the first try after just seven minutes, only for Thomas Bosc to cross and make it 6–6 on the quarter mark. Wheeldon scored, so did Duport, then Mounis put the home side ahead 18–16. And when winger Pelo scrambled in near to the corner flag just before the break it put the Dragons in control at 24–16.

Both sides battled it out at the same score line in the second half until Danny Washbrook started the fight-back to score from a Berrigan pass and give them hope. When Khattabi was sin-binned it looked likely Hull would take control but it was Catalans who added extra points from Bosc's boot with two silly penalties given away by indiscipline from the visitors. At 28–22, with about five minutes remaining, winger Gareth Raynor took a superb cut out pass from Tommy Lee and dived into the corner leaving Danny Tickle a difficult conversion from the touchline. He duly slotted over the ball with nerves of steel to tie the game up.

Peter Sharp said it was the turning point for the season, 'Once our personnel are back onto the training field we will have a good side.' Catalans boss Mick Potter felt they had thrown the win away yet again, 'We worked away to get a good position for a field goal and didn't take it, I feel we dropped a point today.' It was surprising to see them spurn a golden chance to slot over the one pointer but elected to kick for the corner. This gave Hull the ball to work up field and get the equalizer.

Sunday 30 March 2008

Kick off: 15.00, Venue: Grattan Stadium, Att: 10,119, Match official: B Thaler

Bradford (22) 50
T: J Evans 1, P Sykes 1, S Hape 1, S Tadulala 3, B Jeffries 1, W Godwin 1, C Nero 1 **G:** P Deacon 6, I Harris 1

Castleford (4) 4
T: A Fletcher 1

Bradford squad
Halley, Evans, Sykes, Hape, Tadulala, Jeffries, Deacon, Lynch, Godwin, Burgess, Solomona, Nero, Langley
Replacements: Kopczak, Finnigan, Feather, Harris

Castleford squad
McGoldrick, Owen, Lupton, Dixon, Wainwright, Dorn, Sherwin, Huby, Henderson, Korkidas, Leafa, Clayton, Westerman
Replacements: R Fletcher, Higgins, Boyle, Massey

The Bulls exit the tunnel to cheers from their fans.

It could have been the Dwain factor that made Castleford put in one of the worst shows of the season by getting thumped to the tune of 50–4 by the Bradford Bulls at Odsal's Grattan Stadium. It was more a case of 'Horror Chambers' than Dwain Chambers as the injured Tigers lacked ideas and offered a creaky defence that allowed the Bulls to run at will and score nine tries in an easy win that saw winger Semi Tadulala race in for a hat trick.

Castleford's defence was woeful and coach Terry Matterson hoped that days like this could have been avoided but they struggled to get 17 fit players ready for this match. 'We haven't got a squad big enough to handle Super League never mind the Easter period.' Things

were made worse by Marc Leafa's injury —he looked to have broken his arm. This brought about the suggestion that the former disgraced sprinter could find himself playing next week against Saints. Matterson claimed he knew nothing about what was going on 'I don't want to talk about that,' he said.

It will take more than speed on the wings to lift the Tigers spirits, for their tackling was far from good enough at this level, as Paul Deacon and his half back Ben Jeffries ripped them apart with deft passes and solid kicking, both long and short.

Jeffries has injected much more spark in the Bulls attack and it looks unlikely that Iestyn Harris will find the form to oust him from the starting line-ups in future especially after the former Wakefield star

Shontayne Hape adds to the score in Bradford's hammering of Castleford.

scored a tremendous solo try producing a sidestep and dummy on the way. Bulls boss Steve McNamara was pleased for his players, 'This game was really tough after the Easter weekend and we played well, although we did drop a few chances over the line too.'

What a nightmare situation Matterson had for the forthcoming week. He not only had to lift the spirits of his side and bolster the defensive pattern, but he also had the added bonus of trying to turn a sprinter who has never played any sort of rugby in his life into a specimen worthy of taking on the full blooded challenge of our physical sport.

Best of luck Terry!

Sunday 30 March 2008

Kick off: 15.00, Venue: New Craven Park, Att: 7,101
Match official: P Bentham

Hull KR (18) 24
T: C Walker 1, Jake Webster 1, D Fitzhenry 2 **G:** P Cooke 4

Huddersfield (12) 24
T: C Thorman 1, P Whatuira 1, R Jensen 1, G Gatis 1 **G:** C Thorman 4

Hull KR squad
Briscoe, Fox, Walker, Jake Webster, Fitzhenry, Cooke, James Webster, Vella, Fisher, Crossman, Newton, Galea, Murrell
Replacements: Mills, Cockayne, K Netherton, Lovegrove

Huddersfield squad

Thorman, Lawrence, Whatuira, Lolesi, Jensen, Brown, Robinson, Mason, Gatis, Skandalis, Snitch, Crabtree, Jones Replacements: Raleigh, Jackson, Griffin, Hudson

Hull KR boss Justin Morgan was another to admit his side had blown a point as they had to fight back and snatch a 24–24 draw against a much improved Huddersfield. Unlike last term the Rovers have only lost one game at home this year and obviously Giants coach Jon Sharp was pleased to get a draw, 'Coming to Craven Park and getting a

Chris Thorman was in good form with a try and four goals in Huddersfield's draw with Hull KR.

point is really pleasing, we had a good feeling about today.' Jake Webster again hit top form and opened the scoring early when Paul Cooke brought him inside to score near the posts. After Daniel Fitzhenry took another superb pass from the Kiwi Webster to dive in at the corner one expected a runaway victory. Huddersfield are made of sterner stuff these days and had the added bonus of Sharp signing an extension to his contract. His players responded in kind with a try from George Gatis but Rovers still held the upper hand when a few minutes later Chev Walker crossed to keep a 12 point lead. It looked to stay that way to the break until Ryan Hudson strode through the defence to send Chris Thorman racing 30 metres to score under the posts and his conversion left them only six points adrift at half time.

The Giants couldn't believe their luck when Ben Cockayne spilled the ball. This allowed Paul Whatuira to go over near the corner flag, Thorman's deadly boot converted from the touchline to make it 18 all and set up a thriller. Midway through the half Rocket Rod Jensen showed his pace to outrace fullback Shaun Briscoe to a long downfield kick from Luke Robinson to go in at the corner. Yet again Thorman kicked a beauty from the touchline to take his tally to four from four and provide a lead of six points. Five minutes from time Fitzhenry scored his second of the day and when Paul Cooke converted to send the game into the final minutes at 24–24 it left the fans screaming for the one pointer. Thorman and Robinson for the Giants and James Webster and Cooke for Rovers obliged with attempts but none hit the mark. Justin Morgan wasn't happy, 'We were our own worst enemies, we made many breaks but failed to capitalise on them.'

engage
Mutual Assurance

Kick off: 19.30, Venue: The Galpharm Stadium, Att: 4,071,
Match official: R Silverwood

Huddersfield (6) 16
T: J Lolesi 1, D Griffin 1, R Hudson 1
G: C Thorman 2

Catalans (4) 20
T: T Bosc 1, J Fakir 1, D Ferriol 1
G: T Bosc 4

Huddersfield squad
Thorman, Lawrence, Whatuira, Lolesi, Cudjoe, Brown, Robinson, Mason, Gatis, Skandalis, Snitch, Crabtree, Jones
Replacements: Raleigh, Jackson, Griffin, Hudson

Catalans squad
Greenshields, Murphy, Raguin, Khattabi, Pelo, Mogg, Bosc, Chan, Gorrell, Guisset, Fakir, Croker, Carlaw
Replacements: Ferriol, Mounis, Casty, Touxagas

A record run of five games without defeat left Catalans coach Mick Potter a happy man after his side held on to a late flourish from Huddersfield to grab a hard fought 16–20 win in a match that had its share of controversy. In a hectic finish to the game the Giants nearly pulled off a victory that they didn't deserve. It was tingling stuff none the less as Darrell Griffin crashed over under the posts with just three minutes remaining with the conversion to come. Sadly for Huddersfield their skipper Chris Thorman ignored the kicking tee and went to drop goal the ball instead and even though the touch judge's flags went up the referee Richard Silverwood

rightly disallowed the goal. Thorman, aware of saving time didn't know the rules; Silverwood did though and the score line stayed as it was. This proved to be vital as Huddersfield should have been awarded a penalty in the dying seconds.

With time running out Thorman nearly came to the rescue with a darting run that eventually saw scrum-half Luke Robinson being tackled a few metres from the Catalans line by Aaron Gorrell. Robinson tried to get up quickly to play the ball, but despite interferance by the tackler, failed to gain the penalty and then dropped the ball. It was a dramatic end to a tough encounter where the French side showed up best in the first stanza and looked to be cruising at 12–20 in the final quarter with Thomas Bosc and Jason Croker playing their hearts out until those heart-stopping moments at the end.

One guy who didn't deserve to be on the losing side was Ryan Hudson who was amazing both in attack and defence. He could have won the game for his club on his own and it was a smart move from coach Sharp to throw him into the fray midway in the first half. He became the only player to create problems for the Catalans defence. Giants coach Jon Sharp admitted his side were second best and didn't deserve to be near to snatching a win although he was confused over the drop-goal conversion attempt. 'He [Thorman] did the same thing last year and was awarded a goal. Can anyone recall Thorman's drop goal conversion?'

he asked. To be fair a Giants win would have been an injustice to Catalans who played with more flourish and enthusiasm. The late surge from the Giants didn't exactly help to settle the nerves of coach Mick Potter who has seen his side lose two games in the dying seconds already this year. 'Early on in the year we would have dropped those two points, I was worried at the end.' Understandably, Potter is being pressurised by the Catalans club to make up his mind about next season as the media have him set to return to Australia or take up the St Helens job. It would be a bitter blow to the French club if he left as they have progressed quickly in three years to become a major force in Super League.

Friday 4 April 2008

Kick off: 20.00, Venue: The KC Stadium, Att: 13,617, Match official: B Thaler

Hull FC (6) 8
T: S Berrigan 1, **G:** D Tickle 2

Bradford (6) 24
T: S Tadulala 1, S Burgess 1, C Nero 1, M Cook 1 **G:** P Deacon 4

Hull FC squad
Tony, Byrne, G Horne, Yeaman, Raynor, R Horne, Lee, Dowes, Berrigan, Cusack, Radford, Manu, Tickle
Replacements: Thackray, Houghton, Washbrook, Wheeldon

Bradford squad
Halley, Evans, Sykes, Hape, Tadulala, Jeffries, Deacon, Burgess, Godwin, Lynch, Nero, Finnigan, Langley
Replacements: Kopczak, Cook, Feather, Harris

The return of Ewan Dowes to take on the Bulls was huge lift to Hull FC who have been hit with a horrific run of injuries. It was understandable that they struggled to contain the Bradford side late in the match. A fine effort from the home side in the first 60 minutes gave them hope of snatching a rare win this term and lifting the spirits of a club desperate to get back into the swing of things. The hope of coming home with a late run like last season appears to be slipping away as their star half back Richard Horne suffered a bad shoulder/spine injury in the first half that could threaten his career.

The effort of containing Bradford told in the final quarter as the Bulls started to find the gaps and run away with the game. The colour clash of strips didn't help either and players passed to the wrong team a few times. Despite this both sides started the second half all square at 6–6 and for the next 20 minutes the game was still in the balance! Two penalties, one from either side, left the match tied at 8–8 and all seemed set for a drop goal finish but Bradford's power told and Hull just ran out of steam. Cook, Tadulala, and Sam Burgess all scored in the final quarter to give Bradford a flattering score line and even more problems for Hull coach Peter Sharp who is under immense pressure from the fans. It will be interesting to see if the club officials support him.

Three wins out of 10 are hardly the stuff the boys from the KC are used to and it will be nervous times for the club. Peter Sharp at least saw some good signs from the display, 'It's encouraging but we just can't sustain for long enough.' Ben Jeffries again proved he was a smart buy from Wakefield, and Bulls coach Steve McNamara was elated just to grab a win, much of it down to the half back's promptings. 'We're all trying to scramble a team together, the injury problems run deep at all clubs and we're glad to get the two points at the moment.'

Kick off: 15.00, Venue: Twickenham Stoop, Att: 4,560, Match official: I Smith

Harlequins (18) 35
T: J Wells 1, M Gafa 2, R Sheriffe 2, R Purdham 1 **G:** H Paul 5 **DG:** H Paul 1

Hull KR (0) 16
T: B Cockayne 2, K Netherton 1
G: P Cooke 2

Harlequins squad
Wells, Clubb, Gafa, Howell, Sheriffe, Paul, Orr, Temata, Randall, Ward, Mbu, Worrincy, Purdham
Replacements: Rinaldi, Melling, Haggerty, Grayshon

Hull KR squad
Briscoe, Fox, Cockayne, Walker, Fitzhenry, Cooke, James Webster, Mills, Fisher, Vella, Newton, Lovegrove, Galea
Replacements: Crossman, Gene, I'Anson, K Netherton

Harlequins coach Brian McDermott was still not getting excited over his side's high position in the table despite a solid win against Hull KR 35–16. 'We had to run hard and strong but I knew they would have their crack at us.' Sadly for Rovers that came far too late as the London side took control early with tries from Jon Wells, Rob Purdham and Matt Gafa within the first 30 minutes to overrun completely the men from the east coast.

With Henry Paul and Danny Orr pulling the strings it was little wonder the Rovers coach was wondering where it was all going wrong and the exciting form of winger Rikki Sheriffe didn't help matters either as he broke the line with ease. A little more steadiness and the Quins

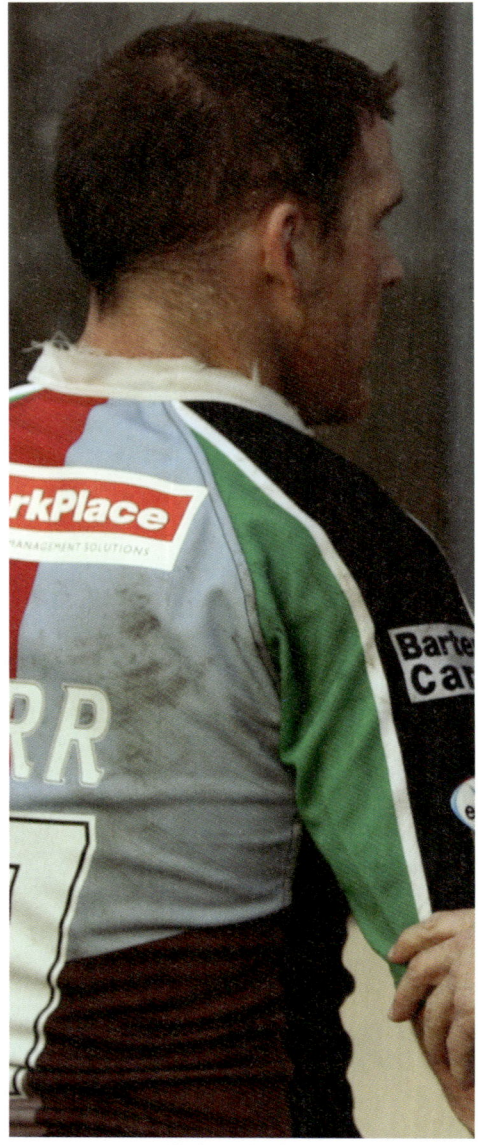

Danny Orr controlled much of the game in Harlequins' defeat of Hull KR.

could have seen at least 30 points posted on the scoreboard by half time but they were happy to turn ends ahead by 18–0. Rovers finally clicked after the break when Cockayne scored but a Paul field goal plus a Gafa try was making things look easy at 25–6. Some concern was etched on the face of coach McDermott (who has seen his side collapse a few times this term) when Hull KR went over for two tries in as many minutes, Cockayne grabbing his second try and Netherton diving over under the sticks to bring it back to 25–16. A last 10-minute push by Rovers could have snatched a win but Harlequins winger Sheriffe caught them out and snapped up two late tries to end any hope of a fight-back from the visitors. 'We made some silly plays, we are playing with little confidence but it will return,' said a disappointed Robins coach Morgan.

Saturday 5 April 2008

Kick off: 18.00, Venue: Headingley, Att: 18,769, Match official: S Ganson

Leeds (10) 10
T: S Donald 1, K Leuluai 1 **G:** K Sinfield 1

Wigan (14) 14
T: P Richards 1, T Leuluai 1
G: P Richards 3

Leeds squad
Webb, Smith, Ellis, Senior, Donald, Sinfield, Burrow, Scruton, Diskin, Leuluai, Peacock, Lauitiiti, Worrall
Replacements: Burgess, Tansey, Ablett, Bailey

Wigan squad
Mathers, Colbon, Goulding, Carmont, Richards, Coyle, Leuluai, Fielden, McIlorum, Coley, Hansen, Bailey, O'Loughlin
Replacements: Higham, Palea'aesina, Tomkins, O'Carroll

No way through for Luke Burgess in Wigan's surprise defeat of Leeds.

With 50 percent of all registered Super League players out injured it was little relief for both Leeds and Wigan who went into the Saturday clash depleted. Not that it stopped both sides producing some bone-crunching tackles nor did it prevent Warriors coach Brian Noble from once again pulling off a shock win at Headingley, something he enjoyed so often whilst boss at the Bradford Bulls in the past. Noble's tactics were to struggle with the man in the tackle and slow the Leeds outfit from getting the quick play the ball, which had reaped great reward over this season, and it worked a treat.

For once the referee Steve Ganson allowed the play to flow more often than of late and kept the whistle more in his pocket than in his mouth. Not that the Leeds fans were impressed when a few decisions went against the home side at crucial moments. In tight games players need a bit of luck and it came Wigan's way when talented Ali Lauitiiti limped off after just eight minutes. This was on top of the shoulder injury to Simon Worrall two minutes earlier, hardly helping the rotation system for Leeds coach Brian McClennan later in the game when both players were unable to return to the fray. The rub of the green continued for Wigan when just before the break Thomas Leuluai scored under the posts from what looked like a forward pass from big prop Iafeta Palea'aesina. This proved to be the winning try.

Nobody would have forecast that the second half would fail to yield a single point but with both sides desperately defending for their lives it soon became obvious that chances were few and far between in the second stanza. Leeds started out well with an unconverted Scott Donald try after 10 minutes when Wigan allowed a high bomb to bounce giving hooker Matt Diskin a chance to pass out wide for the winger to squeeze in at the corner with just inches to spare. Seven minutes later Pat Richards finished off one of the rare three quarter passing movements thanks to skilful play from centre George Carmont. The winger converted his own try and then kicked a vital penalty soon after to give the visitors a 4–8 lead. Leeds were soon back into the match when Sinfield worked a nice inside pass to send Kylie Leuluai crashing under the sticks, leaving the Leeds skipper an easy extra two points to take the lead again at 10–8. But, with seconds remaining, the controversial pass from Palea'aesina sickened the home fans into silence and sent Brian Noble's men into the dressing rooms 10–14 ahead. Another injury this time to centre Darrell Goulding soon after the restart failed to stop Wigan's defensive effort as they tackled everything in sight and when they did get breached out wide Mr Ganson pulled Lee Smith back for a forward pass and the try was turned down.

It was a tough old fashioned type of match with the kicking of Thomas Leuluai instrumental in repeatedly turning the Rhinos back deep into their own half. The ploy soon reduced the energy levels and secured a stranglehold on events. Wigan's fighting spirit showed that Leeds can be stopped, a point that most fans thought was out of reach of other clubs this season. Noble was pleased with his tactics, 'We were intense, we restricted territory for them, it's something you must do to have a chance here.' Brian McClennan realised the kicking tactics tired his side late in the game. 'They played well and we ran out of juice and lost a lot of shape and options on attack.' The return to

Headingley proved successful for Richie Mathers who shone at fullback and handled all the heavy stuff thrown at him. Thomas Leuluai's kicking in the second period proved vital and it showed Wigan could play without the skills of Trent Barrett, linked with a return to St George in Australia next season. Not that Wigan needed to worry after the neat showing from youngster Thomas Coyle, a kid who looks the goods.

Sunday 6 April 2008

Kick off: 15.30, Venue Belle Vue, Att: 5,436, Match official: A Klein

Wakefield (10) 16
T: S Grix 1, S Obst 1 **G:** D Brough 4

Warrington (2) 2
G: C Hicks 1

Wakefield squad
Blaymire, Gleeson, Martin, Atkins, Grix, Rooney, Brough, Watene, Obst, Moore, MacGillivray, Golden, Sculthorpe
Replacements: Bibey, Henderson, Wilkes, Leo-Latu

Warrington squad
Hicks, Riley, Johnson, King, Penny, Clarke, Monaghan, Morley, Mark Gleeson, Rauhihi, L Anderson, Westwood, V Anderson
Replacements: Parker, Pickersgill, Bracek, Harrison

Sorry to repeat myself, but yet another injury hit side struggled in great style to grab a 16–2 victory that many thought out of their reach. Warrington were playing well and not many (other than the home fans) expected Wakefield to upset the Wolves despite playing at Belle Vue. In what can be described as a scrappy game the Wildcats slugged it out to overcome a side that started out well, scored the opening points thanks to a

A good try from Sam Obst helped Wakefield in their win over Warrington.

Peter Lupton hauls down Paul Wellens in Castleford's defeat of St Helens.

penalty from Hicks and then lacked ideas from then on. By the time Ben Westwood received his marching orders for a high shot on Adam Watene 20 minutes into the second half the game was already lost for Paul Cullen's men. 'We made far too many errors and failed to control the ball, we got what we deserved,' said a sad coach after the match. His opposite John Kear was over the moon. 'To restrict Warrington to no tries is a magnificent effort, it was a win built on team spirit.'

That may be so but the likes of Danny Brough, and Danny Sculthorpe showed the way whilst prop Richard Moore has grown in stature each week. These three helped overcome a massive loss of no less than eight first teamer's from the starting line-up, a credit to players and coach alike. Brough's kicking added to good tries from Scott Grix and Sam Obst highlighting the team ethics of the Wildcats.

Sunday 6 April 2008

Kick off: 15.30, Venue: The Jungle, Att: 7,529, Match official: P Bentham

Castleford (10) 30
T: R Owen 1, K Dixon 2, L Dorn 1, J Westerman 2
G: C Huby 1, J Westerman 2

St Helens (16) 24
T: A Gardner 1, S Tyrer 1, P Clough 1, M Fa'asavalu 1   **G:** S Long 4

Castleford squad
McGoldrick, Owen, Clayton, Dixon, Wainwright, Dorn, Sherwin, Higgins, Henderson, Huby, Guttenbeil, Lupton, Westerman
Replacements: Thackeray, Korkidas, Boyle, Fletcher

St Helens squad
Wellens, Gardner, Gidley, Tyrer, Meli, Pryce, Long, Frodsham, Roby, Cayless, Clough, Wilkin, Flannery
Replacements: Bennett, Fa'asavalu, Eastmond, Dean

Bottom club they may well be but Castleford have done it again! The Tigers' win over St Helens was another slap in the face of those fans that thought Castleford couldn't handle the big time. Try telling that to coach Terry Matterson who, like at many clubs, has struggled with injuries. But he kept faith in his side and it proved a huge bonus to a club that was being ridiculed for giving former drug cheat sprinter Dwain Chambers a month's trial.

Chambers may have taken all the headlines over the past week but young Joe Westerman stole the show against a desperate Saints outfit trying to keep pace with the leaders Leeds and Wigan. Westerman and Dixon crossed for two tries midway through the first half to give the home side a 10–0 lead only for Clough to reply and keep Saints in it two minutes later. When the Challenge Cup holders scored tries through Fa'asavalu and Gardner near to the break even the most ardent Castleford fan expected the visitors to run riot after Saints went to the sheds 16–10 in front. All the publicity the Tigers had received in the past seven days was going to either lift them or provide a negative effect. Many of the public rated the Chambers trial as a stunt yet it appears it lifted the Tigers' players to grab a bit of the glory themselves.

Richard Owen scored a speedy try after latching onto Westerman's break early on after the restart to give them hope at 14–16. He looked to score again only to spill the ball and allow St Helens a chance to hit back with a 40 metre run from Steve Tyrer who flew into the corner to make it 14–20. Sean Long's conversion gave them an eight point gap but the outstanding Westerman once again found skill and speed to break down the Saints defence and narrow the gap to just four points. Even after the try scorer failed to convert, one got the feeling the home side were gaining the momentum despite the fact Long kicked a penalty goal to stretch the lead to 18–24. Castleford were buzzing, and so was the crowd as they battered Saints' goal line with successive sets of six. This brought about the second try for Kirk Dixon, Craig Huby converted and the game was tied with 16 minutes remaining. Silly play by Maurie Fa'asavalu in getting involved in a punch-up earned him the red card leaving St Helens one man down with six minutes to go. When the normally safe Paul Wellens fluffed a high bomb to allow Luke Dorn to score it sealed a good win by a side who wanted the spoils more than the visitors did.

Tigers' players Westerman, Luke Dorn and Ryan McGoldrick were superb, but it was a great team effort and Saints coach Daniel Anderson gave them credit for their enthusiasm. 'They performed and we didn't, it could have been much worse, we have to wake up.' Matterson was a proud Tigers coach and put it down to all the media that's been at the club all week, 'It was good to be in the spotlight for a change.' Two wins now, against top clubs Leeds and St Helens have lifted the spirits of the club and they, like many others, hope the momentum continues and their winning ways can help obtain that RFL Super League license for the next three years.

Player of Round 10

Luke Dorn, Castleford

Dorn's quick actions and being the man on the spot secured a great victory over St Helens together with a fantastic try that put the icing on the cake.

Dwain Chambers wonders what he's let himself in for.

engage
Mutual Assurance

Friday 11 April 2008

Kick off: 19.30, Venue: The Jungle,
Att: 8,136, Match official: S Ganson

Castleford (2) 12
T: P Lupton 1, M Cook 1 **G:** C Huby 2

Hull FC (18) 32
T: M Tony 1, C Hall 2, S Wheeldon 1,
J Thackray 1 **G:** D Tickle 6

Castleford squad
Owen, Donlan, Shenton, Dixon,
Wainwright, Dorn, Sherwin, Higgins,
Henderson, Huby, Lupton, Guttenbeil,
Westerman
Replacements: Clayton, Cook, Boyle,
Moore

Hull FC squad
Tony, Byrne, Hall, Yeaman, Raynor,
Washbrook, Berrigan, Dowes, Lee,
Cusack, Manu, Tickle, Radford
Replacements: Houghton, Wheeldon,
Burnett, Thackray

Troubled Hull FC coach Peter Sharp had
reasons to smile as his outfit proved too
strong for a Tigers side that failed to rise to
the occasion in a battle that could have
seen them come off the bottom of the
league table. Hull knew only too well a
loss would have seen them in the 'wooden
spoon' position, a factor that lifted the
side. However the Tigers did have the
chance to snatch the first points but
referee Steve Ganson ruled out Richard
Owen's effort on four minutes and after
that the black and whites earned the
spoils. The Tigers' effort couldn't be
faulted but they lacked the skills that were
on show when they shocked St Helens a
week before, a factor that irritated coach
Matterson. 'We were not clinical enough,

we had the chances and needed to be
more patient.'

The star of the show was Shaun Berrigan,
a man of many talents this term as he has
played in no less than four different
positions since he arrived from Australia
such have been the injury problems at the
club. With both sides showing plenty of
effort it needed that touch of class to tip
the scales and Berrigan provided it in
spoonfuls. Playing at scrum-half he
directed the play and was involved in three
of Hull's touchdowns on the night. Coach
Sharp has been calling for the fans to
judge him on his coaching ability when his
side is at full strength, not before, and this
win was a welcome relief to a man under
the cosh out Humberside way. Hull again
were without Carvell but the return of
Jamie Thackray from Leeds helped their
cause and produced some barn-storming
runs. He could well regain his form of a
few years back that earned him
international honours.

Late tries from Scott Wheeldon and Motu
Tony in the first half were added to Craig
Hall's score on 20 minutes and pushed Hull
to the break with a 2–18 lead. Again the
officials turned down a Tigers try that
could have sparked a revival midway
through the second half, Dixon not getting
the nod from the video referee. But it was
not long after that when Thackray dived
over to snuff out any chance of a fight-
back. A 32–12 victory looked unfair to the
home side and did little to portray the
Tigers hard work especially from the
talented Brent Sherwin, but it was a huge
effort from Hull who look likely to improve
from here on in.

A first half try by Motu Tony helped Hull FC claim the spoils at Castleford.

Kick off: 19.30, Venue: Knowsley Road, Att: 8,533, Match official: B Thaler

St Helens (28) 58
T: P Wellens 1, A Gardner 2, M Gidley 1, F Meli 1, L Pryce 3, S Long 1, J Roby 1
G: S Long 9

Harlequins (12) 12
T: M Gafa 1, G Haggerty 1
G: R Purdham 2

St Helens squad
Wellens, Gardner, Gidley, Talau, Meli, Pryce, Long, Hargreaves, Roby, Cayless, Wilkin, Sculthorpe, Flannery
Replacements: Bennett, Clough, Fa'asavalu, Frodsham

Harlequins squad
Wells, Clubb, Gafa, Howell, Sheriffe, Paul, Orr, Temata, Randall, Ward, Worrincy, Mbu, Purdham
Replacements: Melling, Haggerty, Grayshon, Sharp

It had been a long time since a St Helens side went into a match looking down the barrel of a four match losing streak and visitors Harlequins krew only too well the Saints would explode sometime. Boy didn't they blow the London side out of the water! Paul Sculthorpe's return added extra bite to the home side as he trotted out for his 250th appearance for the club, a great achievement after his injury problems and coming one week after Paul Wellens' 300th showing for the side. Still smarting from the defeat at Castleford the Saints started out with great vigour and when Long romped in for the first try after five minutes the result was never in doubt, Saints were running hot and the Quins had no answer. Despite being without Scott Hill, McCarthy-Scarsbrook and Daniel Heckenburg, their coach Brian McDermott refused to blame their absence for the team's 58–12 loss. 'It's pointless whinging about that, I thought we were poor throughout with the ball.'

One had to feel for the coach as his outfit came up against a side running red hot especially Leon Pryce and Jon Wilkin. Pryce scored a hat trick and put himself about in defence whilst Wilkin shrugged off any injury problems he had earlier in the year. As usual Danny Orr, Rob Purdham and Henry Paul tried all they could to stem the tide and help create two late first half tries for Haggerty and Gafa. But a 28–12 score line at the break was never going to see a change of fortune for the visitors and so it proved as Saints crossed for 10 tries while Long kicked nine goals from 10 attempts. St Helens boss Daniel Anderson admitted Pryce played well as did the rest of the lads, 'The challenge now is to do it consistently.' It was a welcome return to form by Saints and helped remove some of the fear that Leeds would run away at the top of the table. Don't write off the boys from Knowsley Road yet!

Kick off: 20.00, Venue: Headingley, Att: 16,327, Match official: I Smith

Leeds (8) 32
T: C Ablett 1, S Donald 2, R Burrow 1, L Burgess 1 **G:** K Sinfield 6

Warrington (6) 12
T: C Hicks 1, L Anderson 1 **G:** C Hicks 2

Leeds squad
Webb, Smith, Ablett, Senior, Donald, Sinfield, Burrow, Leuluai, Diskin, Bailey, Peacock, Ellis, Tansey
Replacements: Scruton, Burgess, Kaye, Williams

Warrington squad
Reardon, Hicks, Martin Gleeson, King, Penny, V Anderson, Monaghan, Morley, Clarke, Rauhihi, L Anderson, Johnson, Bracek
Replacements: Mark Gleeson, Parker, Riley, Harrison

'Leeds, Leeds, Leeds!' That was the cry from the South Stand as they urged on the league leaders to overcome a spirited Warrington performance that looked likely to snatch a rare victory at Headingley. The Rhinos, like many clubs, rejigged their side due to injuries using Tansey at centre, wing and half back and adding Danny Williams to the bench. Warrington withdrew Paul Johnson from the game after he pulled a hamstring in the warm-up. Not that it prevented the Wolves from taking an early lead after some fierce forward play from Rauhihi and Morley. This put Warrington into a good field position for half back Monaghan to send Louis Anderson in for the first try which Hicks converted to give Leeds a scare. Things got worse for the Rhinos after Gareth Ellis limped off with an ankle injury and an upset looked on the cards. Leeds showed their determination and skills to combat the early onslaught, tightened their defence and slowly got back into the game.

Some tremendous big hits from Bailey set the scene and when he smashed Morley to the ground in brutal fashion Leeds replied with a long range effort from winger Donald who raced away 40 metres after good work from Webb and Burrow. Sinfield converted and added

Gareth Ellis is intercepted by Matt King.

another two pointer just on half time to send the home side into the sheds with a two point lead.

Warrington soon suffered after the break by giving away silly penalties that allowed Leeds to gain the momentum and it came as no surprise when Donald dived over for his second of the match just six minutes after the restart. The penalty count brought criticism from Wolves coach Paul Cullen over referee Ian Smith's performance. 'We did well for the first 40 but the penalty count went against us and we had little possession.' Leeds took full advantage of Warrington's lack of discipline and surged forward for more points. When Jon Clarke was sent to the sin-bin for persistent interference the flood gates looked likely to open. Carl Ablett then scored out wide and when Sinfield added the conversion to make it 22–6 the game was virtually over. But to Warrington's credit they didn't throw in the towel and created a neat move that witnessed Hicks charging in at the corner. When the try scorer added the extras it looked as though it was going to be a thrilling finish as the visitors found new impetus and strength. Ten points adrift with just 13 minutes remaining, the Wolves went into top gear with King and Vinnie Anderson making good ground while the Leeds defence went into scramble mode. Nerves were eased when Rob Burrow produced a few touches of magic to take them away from danger with a smart unconverted try nine minutes from the end.

Burrow and Bailey were in great form with the latter back to his best both in defence and attack, whilst Burrow's field positional kicking proved vital. Another

young Leeds star Luke Burgess showed a vast improvement and was rewarded with the final touchdown from Sinfield's neat inside pass to make the scoreboard look exciting at 32–12. Full credit went to Warrington for putting up a brave fight but yet again the power and depth of Leeds made them hot favourites to retain their title and the question cropped up again as to who would be able to catch and match them. Rhinos coach McClennan knew only too well they had to dig deep to overcome a spirited showing from the Wolves, 'I'm proud of the boys it was a tough game.'

Friday 11 April 2008

Kick off: 20.00, Venue: JJB Stadium, Att: 13,044, Match official: A Klein

Wigan (8) 24
T: G Carmont 1, P Richards 2, E O'Carroll 1 G: P Richards 4

Catalans (10) 26
T: C Greenshields 1, J Murphy 1, J Guisset 1, D Carlaw 1 G: T Bosc 5

Wigan squad
Mathers, Calderwood, Colbon, Carmont, Richards, Coyle, Leuluai, Fielden, McIlorum, Coley, Bailey, Hansen, O'Loughlin
Replacements: Higham, Palea'aesina, O'Carroll, J Tomkins

Catalans squad
Greenshields, Murphy, Stacul, Raguin, Pelo, Mogg, Bosc, Guisset, Gorrell, Chan, Croker, Fakir, Carlaw
Replacements: McGuire, Ferriol, Mounis, Casty

Referee Ashley Klein again stumbled into controversy at the JJB Stadium following a last gasp win by the Catalans Dragons. Wigan were looking comfortable at 24–

16 with just 14 minutes remaining and when Jerome Guisset crossed three minutes from the hooter most fans thought it was just a consolation for the visiting French team. That was until Klein refused to penalise the onrushing Catalans for a tackle in the air on Calderwood that saw the winger drop the ball and give the Dragons a last flourish at scoring. It also looked like Clint Greenshields had knocked on in the build up to that final Bosc high kick but the official refused to stop play. Dane Carlaw must have thought it was Christmas as he picked up the Calderwood fumble to score in the dying seconds and rob what looked a sure and deserved win for the home side. To his credit, Wigan coach Brian Noble failed to criticise Klein after the game. 'We snatched a defeat from the jaws of victory,' he said.

Wigan's fine win at Headingley the week before obviously had taken some sting out of their play and they struggled early in the game when the French side took control allowing Greenshields to score the first try. Two goals from Bosc saw Catalans go to a 8–0 lead and Wigan could thank the boot and a try from Pat Richards to keep them in the hunt—they were just two points down at the break with a score of 12–10.

It was a better looking team that started the second half as Wigan scored two great tries in the space of 10 minutes to dump Catalans into the doldrums. Thomas Leuluai jinked his way through and served Eamon O'Carroll who scored his first of the season, followed shortly after by another piece of magic from the Warriors scrum-half who put in a neat grubber kick to send Richards in for the try and for him to go over the 500 points barrier for Wigan. At 24–16 it looked all over and even Catalans coach Mick Potter thought it was too. 'I thought the game had slipped away from us, we looked down and out and to find something late on was fantastic,' said the visitors' boss after an incredible 26–24 win.

Stevo watching the game at The Galpharm Stadium with Eddie Hemmings.

Jay Pitts stops the progress of Eorl Crabtree in Wakefield's victory over Huddersfield.

Saturday 12 April 2008

Kick off: 18.00, Venue: The Galpharm Stadium, Att: 5,693,
Match official: P Bentham

Huddersfield (12) 16
T: R Jensen 1, L Robinson 1
G: C Thorman 4

Wakefield (8) 18
T: A Murphy 1, T Martin 1, O Wilkes 1
G: T Martin 2, D Brough 1

Huddersfield squad
Thorman, Lawrence, Elford, Whatuira, Jensen, Brown, Robinson, Mason, Gatis, Raleigh, Snitch, Crabtree, Lolesi
Replacements: Jackson, Griffin, Hudson, Kirmond

Wakefield squad
Grix, Murphy, Martin, Atkins, Gleeson, Rooney, Brough, Bibey, Obst, Moore, Golden, MacGillivray, Sculthorpe
Replacements: Wilkes, Leo-Latu, Bibb, Pitts

Nobody could doubt the claim that the best player so far this season has been Wakefield's Danny Brough and it was the crafty half back's skills that put Huddersfield away 18–16. Wakefield, with 10 first teamers missing, looked ready for the kill by a Giants side that have had the wood on John Kear's men over the past few years. That nine game hoodoo would be hard to break as Adam Watene sadly had to return to New Zealand following the death of his father. It was heartening to hear John Kear dedicate the win to the Watene family. The Wildcats showed early promise scoring out wide through Aaron Murphy to take a 4–0 lead but a brace of touchdowns in the space of four minutes helped the Giants take control at 12–4. Luke Robinson scampered away from dummy-half to score, then Rod Jensen crossed from Thorman's kick three minutes later. Tony Martin helped keep the Wildcats in the match by scoring from a Sam Obst kick, again Brough missed the conversion and although his open play was outstanding it was of some concern to Kear that the golden boy was off form with the goal kicking boot. One couldn't say that about his kicking in general play for after the restart he sent a neat low kick into the goal area for Oliver Wilkes to level the scores and when Martin took the successful conversion Wakefield had the lead yet again at 14–12.

Chris Thorman was Huddersfield's best player by a mile and his two penalty kicks pushed the Giants in front again. Ironically Huddersfield gave away two penalties that were to prove their downfall in the end. First Martin slotted one over to level it again at 14–14 and when the second chance came a surprised crowd witnessed the introduction of the goalless Danny Brough to attempt what would prove to be the winner. Brough's form with ball in hand is second to none this term and his confidence is high but after his misses in the first half one wondered if he had taken on more than he could chew. He obliged by slotting the ball over from 45 metres out, much to the delight of the away fans. It left a desperate 20 minutes where both sides tackled like demons but failed to add any score.

John Kear was proud of his men, 'We lost four times to them last year which cost us a play-off spot place in the top six, I'm delighted, we dug deep.' Giants' boss Jon Sharp was upbeat about the loss, 'Our boys did well, I thought the best side lost.' These were no doubt encouraging words from Sharp but they will do little to lift the spirits of a side struggling to close out games, three wins from 11 will hardly inspire the

higher crowds they have been enticing to The Galpharm Stadium this season.

Sunday 13 April 2008

Kick off: 15.00, Venue: New Craven Park, Att: 8,377,
Match official: R Silverwood

Hull KR (14) 20
T: P Fox 1, B Cockayne 1, C Newton 1
G: P Cooke 4

Bradford (6) 18
T: P Sykes 1, S Tadulala 1, D Solomona 1
G: I Harris 3

Hull KR squad
Briscoe, Fox, Jake Webster, Cockayne, Fitzhenry, Cooke, James Webster, Vella, Fisher, Mills, Gene, Newton, Galea
Replacements: Crossman, Lovegrove, Murrell, K Netherton

Bradford squad
Halley, Evans, Sykes, Hape, Tadulala, Harris, Jeffries, Lynch, Godwin, Burgess, Nero, Morrison, Langley
Replacements: Newton, Solomona, Finnigan, Feather

The in-form Bradford Bulls arrived at Craven Park looking to snare a top three position in the table and continue their strong progress of five wins in the past six games. With the return of Newton, Solomona and Morrison into the fray it looked a tough task for the home side. Rovers also had reason to smile as Jake Webster and Scott Murrell returned to first team duty and stunned the Bulls with a try within two minutes, winger Peter Fox taking advantage of Tadulala's failure to defuse Paul Cooke's high kick, and crossing for an easy four pointer. Cooke added the extras to send the home crowd into raptures but their excitement soon disappeared when the Bulls struck back from the restart.

Hero Fox became the villain when he knocked on from the kick off which allowed Bradford the chance to erase Rovers' early bonus as Jeffries raced away from the scrum base to stretch the defence and throw a huge pass out wide for Tadulala to squeeze in at the corner. Iestyn Harris levelled the scores with a tremendous touchline conversion. Sadly for Bradford the absence of Paul Deacon was soon evident as their kicking game fell apart and the Bulls often lacked direction around the ruck area. A string of five penalties helped Rovers to take control and when Cockayne crossed from a neat Cooke kick the visitors looked to be struggling to get into the game but were given a lifeline when the referee, Silverwood, disallowed the try claiming the ball wasn't grounded correctly. Two minutes later Cooke added a penalty after Bradford's discipline failed yet again and on 22 minutes the stand off created a super off load for man of the match Clint Newton to dive in near the posts. Cooke added the conversion with ease to give his side an eight point lead, and that's how it stood at the break after Bradford finally found some defensive toughness.

With Cooke pulling the strings and Newton creating all sorts of problems for the Bulls, it was no surprise when Hull KR went further ahead through Cockayne's try midway through the second stanza. Again Cooke added the extra two to take his goal tally to four from four. Soon after, Clint Newton was yellow carded for a late challenge which offered the

green light to the Bulls who soon took advantage of the extra man as Paul Sykes crossed with just 13 minutes remaining. Harris converted to leave the home side a touch nervous. Bradford threw everything at the Rovers' defence who somehow scrambled back time and time again only to be breached by the big frame of Solomona. It came too late as the seconds ticked away during Harris's successful conversion attempt allowing Rovers to sneak home by two points. Bulls coach McNamara was disappointed. 'We lacked a bit of direction, Paul Deacon not being there didn't help but we should have done better.' Rovers boss Justin Morgan offered a simple equation for the win, 'There was no secret to our success, it was the willingness to compete, we had more desire.'

Man of the match Clint Newton gave a big performance in Hull KR's win over Bradford.

engage
Mutual Assurance

Kick off: 19.30, Venue: Halliwell Jones Stadium, Att: 13,024,
Match official: A Klein

Warrington (10) 22
T: K Penny 3, J Clarke 1 **G:** C Hicks 3

St Helens (14) 30
T: A Gardner 2, F Meli 1, P Clough 3
G: S Long 3

Warrington squad
Hicks, Riley, Martin Gleeson, King, Penny, Briers, Monaghan, Morley, Clarke, Rauhihi, L Anderson, Westwood, V Anderson
Replacements: Mark Gleeson, Parker, Bracek, Harrison

St Helens squad
Gidley, Gardner, Flannery, Talau, Meli, Roby, Long, Graham, Cunningham, Cayless, Gilmour, Sculthorpe, Wilkin
Replacements: Hargreaves, Clough, Fa'asavalu, Eastmond

Warrington once again found their bogey team St Helens far too strong despite getting away with a flyer and scoring after just six minutes. Young speedster Kevin Penny got the scoreboard clicking and it looked like the Wolves were in the mood especially after Saints had a late withdrawal of Leon Pryce and Fa'asavalu and Sculthorpe were taken off through injury during the first quarter. Penny showed blistering speed to go on and bag a hat trick but even that wasn't enough to down the visitors. Paul Clough came off the bench when Scully received a bad chest injury and proved to be the match winner in emulating the Warrington winger with a three try haul that changed the game.

Clough crossed for his first to bring the Saints back into the match after King dropped the ball and when Ade Gardner crossed on 27 minutes it looked likely the hoodoo of only beating St Helens once in 31 encounters was going to strike again. To Warrington's credit, they fought back strongly, also without key players Johnson and Reardon and it was again the combination of centre King sending Penny in at the corner and getting the nod from the video referee. Hicks failed with the conversion but the Wolves held a slender two point lead coming up to the break. Wolves continued to batter the Saints line and looked set to score until Monaghan threw out a stray pass which was gleefully intercepted by Francis Meli who raced away nearly 80 metres to score under the posts, Long added the extras and Daniel Anderson's men went in at the break 10–14 to the good.

Shortly after the restart Penny once again became the hero by avoiding Gardner to grab his third with some neat footwork. When Hicks converted, Saints looked down and out and when Hicks again added the two to a Jon Clarke try on 50 minutes they should have been. But even though they were 22–14 down the Saints outfit started to dig deep and start the fight-back. Good work from Roby sent in Clough for his second touchdown and the nerves kicked in for the home side and they started to look shaky. Paul Cullen's men did rally and had two good chances but both Penny and Riley spurned opportunities. This gave Saints a lifeline and they didn't fail to grab it either. Sean Long sending out a trademark long pass out wide to allow Gardner to squeeze in at the corner and when the crafty scrum-half kicked a beauty from the sidelines they took a 22–24 lead. Sadly for Warrington and centre Matt King, who had created three tries for his winger Penny, it was his mistake that allowed Saints possession 20 metres out to allow Bryn Hargreaves a chance to send hero Clough in for his hat trick and seal the match.

Wolves boss Paul Cullen was devastated at the loss, 'We made too many errors, though we tried to outplay them, we're never going to scrape a win against Saints and our attitude was good. We deserved a bit more from it,' he added. Saints showed great character in fighting back for only their second away win of the season and gave Cullen a headache over Warrington's fourth straight loss. Coach Anderson called it a gritty display, 'We've been a bit iffy this year, it was a great showing across the board.'

Friday 25 April 2008

Kick off: 20.00, Venue: New Craven Park, Att: 9,391,
Match official: R Silverwood

Hull KR (10) 22
T: P Fox 1, D Mills 1, S Murrell 1
G: P Cooke 5

Leeds (12) 36
T: B Webb 1, K Senior 1, S Donald 1, R Burrow 1, K Leuluai 1, M Diskin 1
G: K Sinfield 6

Hull KR squad
Briscoe, Fox, Cockayne, Jake Webster, Fitzhenry, Cooke, James Webster, Vella, Fisher, Mills, Newton, Gene, Galea
Replacements: Lovegrove, K Netherton, Crossman, Murrell

Leeds squad
Webb, Smith, Ablett, Senior, Donald, McGuire, Burrow, Leuluai, Kaye, Scruton, Sinfield, Worrall, Diskin
Replacements: Watkins, Burgess, Peacock, Tansey

Travelling to Craven Park these days is never going to be a picnic and with league leaders Leeds without six of their top stars the Robins were hungry to pick off the Rhinos. Yet the Headingley outfit produced enough skills to overcome an eager Rovers outfit 22–36. As expected with so many changes, Rhinos boss Brian McClennan was pleased, 'We played some good football for 65 minutes and there was more intensity than we have shown in the last few weeks.' The big factor in the win was the combination of half back Burrow and stand off McGuire who at times were too hot to handle and had the Rovers' defence stretched on many occasions.

Burrow was instrumental in kick starting the Rhino's charge after David Mills had given the home side the lead early on, Cooke's conversion giving them a 6–0 lead. The Leeds number 7 twinkle-toed through to give fullback Brent Webb an easy chance to level the scores. Two Paul Cooke penalties stretched Rovers to the front again only for Burrow to produce a sensational solo effort, side stepping through a bewildered defence to score near the posts for a converted try against the run of play. This took them to the break 10–12 in front. Rovers coach Justin Morgan would have been stunned as his

Player of Round 12

Rob Burrow, Leeds
His speed off the mark and sensational side stepping runs confused the Rovers. Burrow looked back at his best.

Ben Kaye and Kevin Sinfield grapple with Hull KR prop David Mills.

outfit had controlled the game for much of that first half. Losing James Webster to a bad dislocated shoulder didn't help matters on 16 minutes, an injury that could have seen him make his last appearance for the club. The player had not signed for next season and could retire to allow the club to get a replacement. It was a sad sight and it upset the Rovers' pattern of play for he was having a great game. Not that Leeds lost any sleep over it and extended their lead shortly into the second half when Kylie Leuluai barged over leaving Sinfield an easy conversion. Seven minutes later Burrow picked up a dropped ball from Ben Galea, racing away 40 metres for another speedy four pointer. Sinfield

again slotted over the extras and at 10–24 it was going to take something special for Rovers to get back into the fight. The Robins didn't take long to respond, Scott Murrell crossed from a Cooke pass and Murrell again featured with a neat kick to the winger Fox who obliged with glee, Cooke added extras to both tries including the Fox score from the sidelines to send the home side into raptures. Just two points separated the sides at 22–24 and the game was up for grabs but the veteran Keith Senior displayed some of his old magic with a barn-storming run to the line that allowed Sinfield yet again to convert from out wide, a kick that sent the home side's heads down. Diskin's try with less than four minutes left finished off any response by the Robins. Defeated coach Morgan was proud of his team's effort especially after losing the key player Webster, 'That's the fastest game we've played in and shows what progress we have made, we'd have been blown off the park if we had played 12 months ago, we did well to come back after being 14 points down.'

Saturday 26 April 2008

Kick off: 18.00, Venue: Belle Vue, Att: 5,016, Match official: S Ganson

Wakefield (6) 24
T: T Martin 1, J Rooney 2, S Obst 1
G: D Brough 4

Harlequins (20) 20
T: M Gafa 1, R Sheriffe 1, D Orr 1, M Worrincy 1 **G:** R Purdham 2

Wakefield squad
Blaymire, Gleeson, Martin, Atkins, Grix, Rooney, Brough, Bibey, Obst, Moore, MacGillivray, Golden, Pitts
Replacements: Blanch, Leo-Latu, Wilkes, Bibb

Harlequins squad

Wells, Clubb, Gafa, Howell, Sheriffe, Hill, Orr, Temata, Randall, Ward, Worrincy, Purdham, Paul
Replacements: Rinaldi, Melling, Haggerty, Mbu

The Danny Brough show continued and the cheeky scrum-half had prodded the Man of Steel selectors pretty hard with some outstanding displays. But not many Wildcats fans were singing their side's praises as the visiting Harlequins took them apart in the first half. Like I said the Brough story continued with a wonderful 40–20 kick after just five minutes that allowed Jamie Rooney to sneak over after good work from Ryan Atkins. When Brough converted from the touchline the hero of the hour basked in glory. It was short lived as the London side fired into action. It wasn't just about Wakefield putting the cue on the rack either as first off Rikki Sheriffe broke free to put Harlequins close to the Wakefield line allowing them the position for Chad Randall to put Danny Orr over. It was scintillating stuff with more to come as Matt Gafa accepted Scott Hill's sweet pass for the touchdown, 6–10 to the visitors which soon clicked on to 6–14 with the try of the match. Big prop Karl

Damien Blanch and Rikki Sheriffe challenge for the ball in the air.

Jamie Rooney scored twice as Harlequins were defeated by the Wildcats.

the second stanza got underway the Quins suffered a blow when Scott Hill had to leave the field with concussion. This gave Wakefield the green light, although it was only into the final quarter they decided to click. Enter Mr Brough, who had no option but to stand about in amazement as Quins weaved their magic in the first half. Danny Boy doesn't take to being out of the limelight and his probing kick gave Jamie Rooney a clear run and pick up under the posts. Another Brough chip over produced a try for Tony Martin soon after, and when Sam Obst spotted a gap near the line on 68 minutes the home side again took the lead when that man Brough added the extras. Harlequins tried desperately to snatch back the lead and it took a great tackle by Leo-Latu to prevent them from going home with a valuable two league points but an extra penalty success from Brough thwarted the visitors yet again.

John Kear was amazed with the transformation and praised his side for showing determination in the second half, 'We went from amateur to international in a half time break.' Quins boss Brian McDermott was furious, 'We had opportunities to kill three games off, we didn't play in the second half.'

Temata surprised the defence with a strong break, Orr carried it on before he off loaded to Michael Worrincy to score a try that had the home fans stunned. Rikki Sheriffe added another to take the Quins to a commanding 6–18 lead. Four tries in 10 minutes had blitzed John Kear's men and it could have been worse as Harlequins had two tries turned down just before the break.

It's amazing what a half time pep talk can do to a side and no doubt Kear stripped the wallpaper off the walls but whatever it was it worked. Soon after

Saturday 26 April 2008

Kick off: 18.30, Venue: Stade Gilbert Brutus, Att: 8,745,
Match official: P Bentham

Catalans (30) 38
T: C Greenshields 1, J Murphy 1, S Raguin 1, D Pelo 1, A Gorrell 1, J Guisset 1, G Mounis 1 **G:** T Bosc 5

Castleford (18) 30
T: A Fletcher 1, M Shenton 1, R McGoldrick 1, M Korkidas 1, J Westerman 1 **G:** K Dixon 5

Catalans squad

Greenshields, Murphy, Raguin, Mogg, Pelo, Bosc, McGuire, Chan, Gorrell, Guisset, Croker, Mounis, Carlaw
Replacements: Duport, A Bentley, Casty, Touxagas

Castleford squad

Donlan, Fletcher, Shenton, Dixon, Owen, McGoldrick, Sherwin, Higgins, Henderson, Korkidas, Cook, Lupton, Westerman
Replacements: Boyle, Moore, Thackeray, Hlad

The news that Catalans coach Mick Potter had accepted to coach St Helens next season did little to dampen the enthusiasm of the French outfit who had to dig deep to turn over the Tigers at the Stade Gilbert Brutus. The publicity surrounding sprinter Dwain Chambers' first game against a York reserve grade side days before may have fired up Castleford for a great effort that gave the Dragons a huge scare. With worldwide publicity over Chambers, the

Jerome Guisset added to Catalans' total as they overcame Castleford.

name of the Tigers went high profile. Coach Terry Matterson wanted to prove his side were not just part of a 'media show' and they produce some wonderful tactics that have brought them the scalps of Leeds and Saints in the past.

It was a high tempo game from start to finish, Dimitri Pelo scored after two minutes and with both sides keeping the ball alive it was obvious to all that the scoreboard attendant would earn his corn. Six minutes later Michael Shenton continued his good form to push the Tigers into the lead with a fine try. Dixon's conversion took the visitors into a 4–6 lead, and so it continued, Jerome Guisset's converted try swung the score back to 10–6. Then Joe Westerman crossed six minutes later from Sherwin's grubber to tie it up, Dixon converted to grab back the lead 10–12. Sebastien Raguin, Aaron Gorrell, Justin Murphy and Clint Greenshields scored tries in a hectic 18 minutes that should have blasted Castleford away. But a Michael Korkidas effort left Castleford with some hope and kept them in touch at 30–18 at half time.

The pace continued after the break and when Raguin took a spell in the sin-bin Castleford fought back. Ryan McGoldrick charged over under the sticks a quarter of an hour into the second half for a converted try. At 32–24 the Dragons looked wobbly and couldn't prevent Adam Fletcher picking up a Sherwin chip to score. This made it a two point ball game 32–30 after Dixon tagged on the conversion from the touchline with about 10 minutes remaining. Thomas Bosc became the hero yet again when his cross kick allowed Mogg to knock the ball back into the waiting arms of Gregory Mounis to race away for the clincher.

The win took Catalans into second place behind Leeds and extended their unbeaten run to seven matches. Consequently their coach, Potter, was full of praise. The Tigers gave their all but couldn't stop the formidable class of fullbacks such as Greenshields, Bosc and Mogg who are attracting much interest from other clubs. For Catalans' sake it would be a shame to lose the likes of Mogg who has helped the French outfit become a major threat in Super League.

Sunday 27 April 2008

Kick off: 15.00, Venue: Grattan Stadium, Att: 11,894, Match official: B Thaler

Bradford (16) 26
T: J Evans 1, S Hape 1, S Tadulala 1, B Jeffries 1 **G:** P Deacon 6

Wigan (2) 12
T: P Richards 1, P Bailey 1
G: P Richards 2

Bradford squad
Halley, Evans, Sykes, Hape, Tadulala, Jeffries, Deacon, Lynch, Newton, Burgess, Solomona, Langley, Morrison
Replacements: Nero, Finnigan, Kopczak, Harris

Wigan squad
Mathers, Colbon, Goulding, Carmont, Richards, O'Loughlin, Leuluai, Fielden, Higham, Coley, Hansen, Bailey, J Tomkins
Replacements: Hock, Palea'esina, O'Carroll, Barrett

A rain sodden Odsal pitch did little to lift the spirits of players wanting to display open style rugby league but Bradford didn't mind too much as they produced solid basic play, no frills but effective. So much so that they controlled the first half through great work from the forwards and a tough defence that allowed Wigan few chances to wake up the scoreboard attendant in the first 40. In fact Pat Richard's penalty goal just before half time registered Wigan's first points. By then Bradford had scored three tries and were sitting comfortably at lemons with Tadulala, Hape and Jeffries crossing. They could have extended that lead if Paul Deacon's boot had added the conversion for the first two tries.

Wise words from Warriors coach Brian Noble seemed to lift them out of the doldrums after the restart. With a glut of penalties they got back into the match and Pat Richards was rewarded with a try on 60 minutes after both sides battled against the conditions and tough defences. It was hardly pretty stuff and Deacon took advantage to stretch the lead to 18–6 with a penalty goal, leaving Wigan a huge mountain to climb with just 10 minutes remaining. Nerves started to jangle after Wigan scored a controversial try two minutes later. Bradford stopped and expected referee Ben Thaler to blow for a knock-on but to their amazement he allowed play to continue. Mickey Higham scooped up the loose ball and raced downfield to give Phil Bailey the four pointer amid jeering from the home crowd. Deacon added another penalty to give Bradford an eight point buffer with five minutes remaining. This relieved many of the fans aware of Wigan's sensational fight-back last year in the play-offs where they grabbed a win after being down 30–6. Both sides felt the tension and fighting broke out several times in the final minutes as Wigan tried desperately to snatch a victory. That faded away when James Evans took advantage of a neat break from Paul Sykes to wrap things up, Deacon's goal giving Steve McNamara's men a well fought win.

James Evans intercepts a bomb.

'I thought we were good from start to finish and defended well. It's all about field position and possession in these conditions,' McNamara claimed after the match. Brian Noble, the Wigan coach commended his former club's effort and work ethic and rightly claimed the conditions were hardly helpful in chasing the game. In wet conditions the Bradford fullback Dave Halley produced an amazing performance, ran with vigour and defused everything that Wigan threw at him. Old stager Terry Newton showed his experience and settled the side when things got tough.

Kick off: 15.15, Venue: The KC Stadium, Att: 12,420, Match official: R Laughton

Hull FC (18) 28
T: T Byrne 2, C Hall 1, D Washbrook 1, D Tickle 1 **G:** D Tickle 4

Huddersfield (8) 20
T: P Whatuira 1, L Robinson 1, S Snitch 1 **G:** L Cudjoe 1, T Hemingway 3

Hull FC squad
Tony, Byrne, Yeaman, Hall, Raynor, Washbrook, Dykes, Dowes, Berrigan, Cusack, Radford, Manu, Tickle
Replacements: Thackray, Houghton, Burnett, Lee

Huddersfield squad
Cudjoe, Aspinwall, Lawrence, Whatuira, Jensen, Brown, Robinson, Mason, Hudson, Skandalis, Snitch, Crabtree, Lolesi
Replacements: Raleigh, Jackson, Griffin, Hemingway

Hull FC at long last gave their suffering fans plenty to shout about after overturning visitors Huddersfield 28–20, although they had their moments of fear when the Giants staged a fight-back in the second stanza. Until this game Hull had only scored 187 points in 11 rounds, a stat that hardly encourages the critical black and white supporters and when the home side raced away to a convincing 18–0 lead in just 28 minutes they expected the flood gates to open. Full credit went to the Giants for never throwing in the towel. They could thank scrum-half Luke Robinson's converted try just before the half time hooter for giving them some sort of hope. But Todd Byrne, Craig Hall and Danny Washbrook had scored early and it was all smiles, sweet light and happiness at the KC stadium. For once coach Peter Sharp could feel some of the weight off his shoulder. With Todd Byrne and Adam Dykes hitting top form it was little wonder that Huddersfield struggled early on as the KC boys' defence ripped into the Giants.

An 18–8 score line indicated the Giants needed to score first after the break and they nearly did but Jensen's effort was ruled out by referee Laughton for a forward pass. Hull celebrated their luck with a try from hard working Danny Tickle who failed with his own conversion attempt but at 22–8 they were sitting pretty. Ugly work from Hull gave away two penalties to allow Huddersfield back into the match. Steve Snitch powered over under the posts leaving Cudjoe an easy conversion making the score 22–14 with 25 minutes remaining. This gave Jon Sharp's men a sniff of success but Hull's defence held for the next onslaught and some fine work from the forwards gave Willie Manu a chance to go close allowing Todd Byrne to cross from Dykes' dummy-half pass. Again some outstanding defence kept Huddersfield out until the Giants scored a consolation converted try with six minutes to go. The eight point buffer was always going to be enough to ensure Hull picked up a vital win.

Once again Jon Sharp was convinced that the Giants had turned the corner, 'We won the second half 12–10, but things just don't seem to be going for us, yet we finished the game strongly.' It still doesn't take away the fact the Giants have slipped to 11th on the table, a worrying time for the club. The other Sharp, Peter, was more than happy, 'We are taking some small steps in the right direction, we've got people back in training and we are building in confidence.'

ROUND 13

engage
Mutual Assurance

Saturday 3 May 2008

Kick off: 15.00, Venue: Millennium
Stadium, Att: 12,000,
Match official: B Thaler

Huddersfield (22) 34
T: R Jensen 1, M Lawrence 1,
L Robinson 1, J Skandalis 1, A Raleigh 2
G: L Robinson 3, T Hemingway 2

Warrington (6) 36
T: S Reardon 1, L Briers 2,
M Monaghan 1, A Bracek 2
G: C Hicks 6

Huddersfield squad
Jensen, Aspinwall, Lawrence, Whatuira,
Elford, Brown, Robinson, Griffin,
Hudson, Skandalis, Snitch, Raleigh,
Lolesi
Replacements: Crabtree, Jackson,
Mason, Hemingway

Warrington squad
Reardon, Hicks, Martin Gleeson, King,
Penny, Briers, Monaghan, Morley,
Mark Gleeson, Rauhihi, L Anderson,
Westwood, Harrison
Replacements: Parker, Johnson, Riley,
Bracek

All roads led to Cardiff for another
League bonanza for the Millennium
Magic weekend. The trains were full, so
were the busses and car parking was at
a premium. One was lucky to get served
quickly at the many pubs in the city
centre. After last year's huge success the
RFL were hoping for a bigger
attendance—they beat it by just under
5,000—the increase indicated again
what a bonus the weekend has become
for league fans.

Few players were as happy as the
boisterous crowds, as the roof was
closed and the ground sweated like a
sticky peach in the midday sun leaving
some of our superstars looking like
converts to *Dancing on Ice*. It was the
same for all sides and the beer flowed as
quickly as the feet slipped.

First up was the Warrington vs
Huddersfield clash and when Michael
Monaghan threw the dummy to stroll
under the posts it looked like the
bookies' favourites were going to take
the Giants apart. Hicks converted the

The fans make their way in to the Millennium Stadium.

Aussie's touchdown and things looked bleak for Huddersfield given the ease with which the scrum-half split the defence.

The Giants had other ideas and staged a stunning spell of blistering skill and speed that left the Wolves fans baying for coach Cullen's head. It was without doubt the best display from the Giants this term as first Michael Lawrence crossed to level the scores after good work from Luke Robinson. He was having the time of his life teasing the Warrington defence who for some unknown reason failed to move up and waited for what was on offer resulting in them conceding four tries in the first half. Robinson himself scored from quick thinking by Ryan Hudson who stabbed a kick into the danger zone, Robinson failed to convert yet he was at it again forcing Warrington to drop out from under the posts twice in as many minutes. The pressure told with big Andy Raleigh backing up another Robinson break to put the Giants in a commanding 16–6 lead. The Wolves supporters at this point were jeering and calling for Cullen's head, and probably wanted it presented on a platter when Rod Jensen touched down after a long break from Shane Elford. This left Warrington in tatters and a moody look on Paul Cullen's face going to the sheds for what would turn out to be an amazing pep-talk.

Huddersfield continued where they left off after the restart when Jensen made another break and arced around for the return pass only to knock on with the line at his mercy. This proved to be the turning point for it should have extended the lead to 28–6. Warrington took advantage of their luck by storming back up field for a controversial try from Reardon who appeared to be tackled, and when the referee Ben Thaler allowed play on even after shouting the number of the tackle, Reardon stretched over. The video ref Ashley Klein stunned all and sundry by awarding the try! Jon Sharp was beside himself over the incident, 'I have a different opinion than the fella who made the decision in the end.'

The decision was a bitter blow that ignited Warrington into action. They scored an amazing four tries in nine

The Gleeson brothers square up to Rod Jensen in Warrington's narrow defeat of Huddersfield.

minutes with Briers quickly following up Reardon's effort. Two tries from Andy Bracek amazingly put the Wolves back in front at 30–22. John Skandalis offered some respite with a close range four pointer which Robinson converted to leave them just two points adrift. Yet the man who had steered the comeback, Lee Briers, took it into his own hands to seal the win. Briers was hardly seen in the first stanza but it was the opposite in the second as the magic flowed from the talented half back and it was fitting when his solo run saw him go under the posts to score. Andy Raleigh surged over with two minutes remaining to make it a nervous finish but Warrington's defence held to hang onto an amazing victory. Paul Cullen was a relieved coach bearing in mind he had the look of a man awaiting the gallows at half time and looked just as stunned as the Warrington fans over this amazing turn about. Full credit to Cullen for sticking by his tactics in the second half, 'We didn't have much ball first half and when we did in the second we knew we could fight back.'

Saturday 3 May 2008

Kick off: 17.00, Venue: Millennium Stadium, Att: 15,000,
Match official: I Smith

Castleford (6) 16
T: M Shenton 1, R Owen 1,
J Westerman 1 **G:** K Dixon 2

Wakefield (24) 54
T: R Atkins 1, S Grix 3, A Watene 1,
S Obst 1, R Moore 1, D Blanch 2
G: D Brough 9

Castleford squad
McGoldrick, Donlan, Dixon, Shenton, Owen, Dorn, Sherwin, Higgins, Moore, Huby, Guttenbeil, Cook, Westerman

Replacements: Henderson, Korkidas, Clayton, Catic

Wakefield squad
Blaymire, Gleeson, Martin, Atkins, Grix, Rooney, Brough, Watene, Obst, Moore, MacGillivray, Golden, Dale
Replacements: Wilkes, Leo-Latu, Bibb, Blanch

The stadium was still buzzing over the exciting finish to the previous game when Wakefield and Castleford trotted out. The crowd expected much of the same and to say they were disappointed was an understatement. The Tigers didn't tackle, looked shell-shocked and had no answer to Danny Brough who was returning to the same stadium where his magic boot helped win the Challenge Cup for Hull three years previously. Brough was in no mood to lower his standards on this occasion, in fact he improved them. He simply ran the show with elegant kicking, shrewd passing and dynamic pace off the mark to blitz a Tigers outfit that left their coach Terry Matterson apologising not only to his fans but to all league fans who witnessed a pathetic performance. If the game had been a boxing match the referee would have stopped it in the first round! Woeful is the only word that does justice to Castleford's effort but it would be insulting not to give credit to the Wildcats showing.

With the likes of Richard Moore charging about the field with a hit and destroy mentality it was little wonder Brough enjoyed the stage yet again. The highlight came midway through the first half when Brough sidestepped past defender after defender before handing off the last line of defence and off loading, looking back with a smile as he witnessed the big prop Moore charging

Ryan Atkins gets the ball down in Wakefield's big defeat of Castleford.

25 metres into the corner for an amazing touchdown.

Not that Castleford were smiling and after watching this capitulation one felt even Dwain Chambers, the sprinter, would be having second thoughts about staying at the club. It would be hard to pick out a top performer in black and gold and the final words from coach Matterson summed it all up, 'It's hard for me to say it, but we gave up.' Richard Owen did at least score just before the break but it was mere consolation as Trinity held a 24–6 lead at half time.

I won't bore you with the try scorers but one has to mention the last try of the match. It came from Brough again sending out a long, looping pass to Damien Blanch who squeezed in at the corner with just seconds left. Who else could add the finishing touch? None other than Mr Brough who booted over a beauty from the touchline. The simple

fact is that if you were picking the Man of Steel now then Brough would get the nod and it's going to take a bad loss of form or injury from preventing him being a front runner come the season's end.

Saturday 3 May 2008

Kick off: 19.00, Venue: Millennium Stadium, Att: 18,000,
Match official: R Silverwood

Bradford (10) 26
T: S Hape 1, S Tadulala 2, S Burgess 1
G: P Deacon 5

Leeds (6) 40
T: B Webb 1, R Hall 1, K Watkins 1, K Senior 1, S Donald 1, K Leuluai 1, E Anselme 1 **G:** K Sinfield 6

Bradford squad
Halley, Evans, Sykes, Hape, Tadulala, Harris, Deacon, Lynch, Newton, Burgess, Solomona, Langley, Morrison
Replacements: Tupou, Finnigan, Godwin, Nero

Leeds squad
Webb, Hall, Watkins, Senior, Donald, McGuire, Burrow, Leuluai, Diskin, Scruton, Ablett, Peacock, Sinfield
Replacements: Tansey, Burgess, Worrall, Anselme

What should have been a classic finish to Saturday's games turned out to be a damp squib. This was hard to take when the Rhinos were pitted against the Bulls. Thankfully the first half was close as both outfits tried to steam roller the opposition after Bradford's Semi Tadulala's early try and a response from talented Leeds' youngster Kallum Watkins. It was no surprise to see the teams finish the first 40 minutes with a 10–6 advantage to Bradford courtesy of Deacon's kicking.

With both previous games of the day producing 70 points the fans were more than happy to see a crunch clash from some of the best players in the land. Peacock and Morrison took it upon themselves to tackle like demons and crash into the defence with no respect for their own bodies. It was a surprise to see after the break a sluggish effort from Bradford who looked to have run out of steam in the hot atmosphere of the enclosed Millennium Stadium. The Rhinos sensed as much and started to give the ball much more air leaving a big chance to Kallum Watkins to shine again by splitting through before off loading to man of the match Brent Webb who in turn gave Frenchman Eric Anselme the chance to race under the sticks. Sinfield's goal put the Rhinos in front again. This was soon followed by a smart pass from McGuire which found Simon Worrall who raced away before giving Keith Senior the chance to finish off with a breathtaking 70 metre effort.

Webb and Donald added more pain to the Bulls' side to leave them chasing a 28–10 deficit, although Bradford did show some sort of revival when Tadulala

Kylie Leuluai off loads to Danny McGuire as Deacon and Langley tackle.

crossed for his second of the match and when Shontayne Hape brushed aside Senior there was a glimmer of hope at 28–20. The eight point buffer was to prove too much for Steve McNamara's side and whilst forcing the pace to cut the lead Hall intercepted to close the game down at 34–20. Four minutes later Kylie Leuluai stretched it even further, Sinfield kicking his sixth from seven attempts to crush Bradford into the ground. The hard working Sam Burgess snatched one with only seconds remaining but the Rhinos knew a long time ago they had the spoils. Steve McNamara claimed that losing James Evans didn't help matters but accepted Leeds were the better side in the second half. 'We only held the ball five times in the second half and it needs fixing.' Leeds boss McClennan admitted it wasn't a great game, 'It was an error ridden match, but we're happy to get away with it.'

Sunday 4 May 2008

Kick off: 14.30, Venue: Millennium Stadium, Att: 15,000,
Match official: A Klein

Catalans (6) 18
T: J Murphy 1, J Croker 1, J Touxagas 1
G: T Bosc 3

Harlequins (10) 16
T: S Hill 1, M Worrincy 1, C Melling 1
G: R Purdham 2

Catalans squad
Greenshields, Murphy, Mogg, Raguin, Pelo, Bosc, McGuire, Chan, Gorrell, Guisset, Carlaw, Croker, Mounis
Replacements: Ferriol, A Bentley, Fakir, Touxagas

Harlequins squad
Wells, Clubb, Gafa, Howell, Sheriffe, Hill, Orr, Temata, Randall, Ward,

Worrincy, Purdham, Paul
Replacements: Rinaldi, Melling,
Haggerty, Mbu

With 206 points scored on the first day
the supporters were getting value for
money and looked forward with
anticipation to even more drama
unfolding. The pubs in Cardiff were
doing big business as the gala feeling
was becoming better by the minute.
Thousands of followers were eager to
book again for next year, only to be hit
with a rumour the RFL were thinking of
taking the Magic weekend away from
Wales and going to Murryfield or even
Dublin instead.

Spokespersons from the RFL had made it
quite clear they were far from impressed
by the support given by those who ran
the stadium even though there had been
an increase in attendance from last year.
This must have come as a huge shock to
the Celtic Crusaders who felt the Magic
weekend was a huge spin off for their
attempt to gain a licence for Super
League, so whilst the rumours swept
through the stadium Catalans and
Harlequins stood toe to toe in what
wasn't a classic to say the least.

The atmosphere appeared to get to both
sides who decided to play a waiting
game despite Jason Croker stretching
out for a Dragons try after just six
minutes. This was wiped out by Michael
Worrincy's effort soon after. Defences
were on top with chances few and far
between until Harlequin's Scott Hill took
advantage of a slick off load from Chad
Randall to cross out wide on 22 minutes
but any hopes of a score fest again died
down and the sides went to lemons with
the London outfit 10–6 in front.

Mick Potter's side came out inspired for
the second stanza and looked the faster

outfit even though they had a scare
when Scott Hill had a try turned down
through a clearly seen obstruction. This
was the key to lifting the Quins' pace,
Scott Hill was having one of his best
games and created a try for Melling after
good work by Jon Wells. The try took
them further away from the Frenchmen
at 16–6 and they held on until nine
minutes from the end before Danny Orr
fumbled a pass to allow Catalans' Julien
Touxagas to snap up and race away 85
metres to score leaving a desperate Ward
and Sheriffe grasping air. Why Harlequins
were trying to force the pass with a
commanding lead is anyone's guess and
it was no surprise when Thomas Bosc
chipped over for Justin Murphy to score
and tie the match. Bosc had no problems
adding the extras to snatch the win 18–
16 leaving Harlequins wondering where

Jamal Fakir barges through the Quins defence in Catalans victory.

it all went wrong.

Quins' coach Brian McDermott was furious and in the press meeting he questioned his side's commitment to the cause of keeping league in London alive. 'I'm asking some questions whether the whole bit of being in London works.' The media latched onto what they perceived to be a point where McDermott could quit the Quins after watching his team throw away a winning lead yet again in the past two games. Thankfully for the London outfit he was quick to downplay any such action and later made it clear he was fully committed to the cause. Mick Potter was amazed they had won the game with just a few minutes remaining. 'I'm happy with the comeback, I thought they looked better than us for most of the game and probably deserved victory.'

Sunday 4 May 2008

Kick off: 16.30, Venue: Millennium Stadium, Att: 22,000,
Match official: S Ganson

Hull FC (10) 17
T: G Raynor 2, D Washbrook 1
G: D Tickle 2 **DG:** A Dykes 1

Hull KR (10) 22
T: P Fox 1, C Walker 1, Jake Webster 1, D Fitzhenry 1 **G:** P Cooke 3

Hull FC squad
Byrne, Sing, Yeaman, Hall, Raynor, Washbrook, Dykes, Dowes, Berrigan, Cusack, Manu, Tickle, Radford
Replacements: Lee, Whiting, Thackray, Wheeldon

Hull KR squad
Briscoe, Fox, Walker, Jake Webster, Fitzhenry, Cooke, Murrell, Vella, K Netherton, Mills, Newton, Gene, Galea
Replacements: Crossman, Fisher, Cockayne, Chester

Probably the best game of the weekend proved to be the humdinger between the two Hull clubs where the score line switched no less than five times. Six weeks earlier Rovers had snatched a winner thanks to James Webster's drop goal and Hull FC must have felt it was their turn to drop one over their close rivals when Adam Dykes put over the one pointer to take them to what looked like a 17–16 win on 73 minutes. Sadly for Hull FC the chance to hang on to the lead was wiped away when Shaun Berrigan was adjudged to have knocked on when Cooke kicked off after the Dykes drop goal. The resulting scrum allowed the Robins to camp down in Hull's quarter and after some hectic defending for a tense period it looked likely that Paul Cooke would be setting up for the drop goal to at least grab a draw.

It wasn't possible to keep the Rovers side down for long and it was to be another Webster, this time Jake, that gave them the spoils yet again when Cooke ignored the chance to set himself up for a shot. Instead he sent the ball wide to find Ben Galea who provided centre Webster with the ball sending him storming over. It was cruel blow to Hull coach Peter Sharp who had witnessed a spirited display from the likes of Dykes, Berrigan and Byrne but the major factor was the introduction of Ben Fisher off the bench for the Rovers. Kirk Netherton looked sluggish at dummy-half and coach Morgan knew the introduction of Fisher would spark them up a bit. He did more than that and produced some effective control of the ruck which gained the Rovers good ground to launch their attack.

Gareth Raynor got Hull FC away to a fine start, showing speed and finesse going in at the corner after only two minutes but

Daniel Fitzhenry launches an incisive tackle on Todd Byrne in Hull KR's victory over Hull FC.

with Cooke taking control and producing some neat kicks and passes they were rewarded with a try out wide from Peter Fox, Cooke again being the creator. Not to be outdone the other Rovers' winger Fitzhenry touched down after good handling from Galea and Gene to stretch the score to 10–4 Rovers' way. Just before the break Hull forced an error from winger Fox who fumbled a Whiting kick to allow Raynor to pounce for his second try of the match. The video ref took a while to adjudge if Raynor had got downward pressure and when they got the nod the score was tied 10–10 at the half time hooter.

Washbrook's try soon after the restart gave Hull the lead again, Tickle adding the extras but five minutes later Chev Walker took yet another Cooke pass to charge over and when Cooke kicked the conversion it was all square again 16–16. Rugged defence from either side left little chance to get the scoreboard working again until Dykes' one pointer and a power score from Jake Webster. Rovers' coach Morgan was happy, 'A great win and we dedicate this victory to

Webbo [James] and his contribution to this club.' Black and Whites' boss Peter Sharp was critical of the officials. 'It could have gone either way and we can build momentum from here.' But the thing that probably hurt the Hull fans most was the fact that former Hull FC star Paul Cooke ran the show and with good support from Ben Fisher and Ben Galea deserved to grab the win.

Sunday 4 May 2008

Kick off: 18.30, Venue: Millennium Stadium, Att: 28,500,
Match official: P Bentham

St Helens (35) 57
T: A Gardner 2, W Talau 2, F Meli 1, S Long 3, L Gilmour 1, J Wilkin 1
G: M Gidley 1, S Long 7 **DG:** S Long 1

Wigan (0) 16
T: T Leuluai 1, M Higham 1, H Hansen 1
G: P Richards 2

St Helens squad
Wellens, Gardner, Gidley, Talau, Meli, Pryce, Long, Cayless, Cunningham, Graham, Gilmour, Flannery, Wilkin
Replacements: Roby, Bennett, Hargreaves, Clough

Wigan squad

Mathers, Colbon, Goulding, Carmont, Richards, Barrett, Leuluai, Fielden, Higham, Prescott, Hansen, Coley, O'Loughlin Replacements: Coyle, Palea'aesina, J Tomkins, O'Carroll

Mick Potter sat in the stands eager to see how the club that he will take charge of next season would fare against old rivals Wigan and it didn't take 'long' for him to realise he's got so much talent to work with next year. 'Long' was the word, Long was the difference, Long was the star, Long simply blew the Warriors apart in a performance that left opposition coach Brian Noble embarrassed.

For the record the final score was 57–16 but it could have been worse with the Saints lifting the foot off the gas pedal midway through the second half. It was no coincidence that Wigan's only smell of success came when Mr Long left for the bench after scoring a hat trick and a record 27 points in a match against Wigan. I say 'match' with tongue in cheek because put simply this wasn't a match at all. When the cheeky scrum-half crossed for his first try on six minutes the floodgates opened. The former GB scrum-half enjoyed every minute of it before taking a rest midway through the second 40. It was only then that Wigan sparked into life and scored two consolation tries through Harrison Hansen and Mickey Higham Saints still in first gear decided to have the last laugh and produced tremendous support play yet again, a feature throughout the game, to send in Lee Gilmour to add the gloss to a polished showing from Daniel Anderson's charges.

Up until this game the likes of Lee Briers and Danny Brough had snatched the limelight and one wonders if that old fox of a brain inside Mr Long just wanted to prove a point, not to Wigan but to the rest of Super League. Either way he was outstanding, and so were the players around him who enjoyed the freedom Wigan's defence offered them.

Anderson was over the moon at the fact his team had the ball for 21 sets and completed them all, 'Scoring 21 from 21 is unheard of, that was the best team we have been able to put out this year and having such talent out on the field makes us much stronger.' 'The first 20 to 25 minutes was embarrassing, we just didn't compete and Saints capitalised,' was the sad summing up from Wigan coach Brian Noble after the game. 'We talked about having a good start all week but the only thing we did well really was kick off,' he added. It wasn't the best start for a man who had just signed a new contract to stay at the JJB and it was no shock to learn that new Wigan chairman Ian Lenagan was flying out to Australia the day after to sign up a few players to help get the Warriors out of the doldrums.

The Saints fans danced in the Cardiff streets and sang their hearts out, whilst the real faithful cherry and white supporters looked stunned, taking it all on board as the ribbing and sledging got louder as the night got longer. The fact that such coming together of so many supporters from all the clubs who linked arm in arm and enjoyed the banter without a hint of trouble was a tribute to all who were at the Millennium Stadium. Putting it simply, it was magic, but tell that to the Wigan fans.

Player of Round 13

Sean Long, St Helens

Long's best showing for ages, amazing game, a hat trick and outstanding direction with passing and kicking. Sensational.

engage
Mutual Assurance

Friday 16 May 2008

Kick off: 19.30, Venue: JJB Stadium, Att: 15,537, Match official: A Klein

Wigan (8) 38
T: G Carmont 1, L Colbon 1, T Barrett 2, G Hock 1, J Tomkins 1 **G:** P Richards 7

Warrington (14) 14
T: V Anderson 1, M King 1, A Bracek 1
G: C Hicks 1

Wigan squad
Richards, Calderwood, Bailey, Carmont, Colbon, Barrett, Leuluai, Coley, Higham, Prescott, Hansen, Hock, O'Loughlin
Replacements: Mathers, Fielden, Palea'aesina, J Tomkins

Warrington squad
Hicks, Penny, Martin Gleeson, V Anderson, King, Briers, Monaghan, Morley, Clarke, Rauhihi, L Anderson, Westwood, Grix
Replacements: Parker, Harrison, Mark Gleeson, Bracek

The pressure on Warrington coach Paul Cullen continued at the JJB stadium with Wigan staging a strong second half to instil more doom on the Wolves boss. With both Johnson and Reardon out for the season it was a reshuffled outfit and Cullen knew they had to take control early on if they had any chance to pick up vital league points and keep in the race for the play-offs.

But Wigan took the lead with a neat try from centre George Carmont and it proved a spur to get the Wolves working. Switching Matt King to wing worked a treat with the big Aussie diving over on 14 minutes to level the scores. Five minutes later Chris Hicks had

Iafeta Palea'aesina hit the high spots in Wigan's game against Warrington.

a try turned down by the video referee when it was deemed Trent Barrett had been obstructed in the build up, but it was clear to everyone bar the video official Phil Bentham that Barrett had been standing in an off side position and the try should have stood. Despite this setback they soon took the lead after a mistake from Pat Richards gave them possession for Vinnie Anderson to score from Monaghan's wonderful grubber kick. More was to come following a Mark Gleeson break that enabled his brother to provide a slick pass to send in Andy Bracek out wide. Sadly for Warrington, Chris Hicks failed to tag on the conversions of both tries but it still left them playing well with a commanding lead at 6–14 and only three minutes to half time. The sin-binning of Vinnie Anderson just before the break did little to help their cause and when Pat Richards slotted over a penalty just before the break Wigan had plenty to play for with a half time score of 8–14.

Warrington's defence was under immense pressure after the restart and the 12 men handled it well, yet it seemed the struggle before Anderson's return had taken its toll. So it proved with Wigan scoring 32 unanswered points and smashing the visitors to pieces. The writing was on the wall when Leuluai had a try turned down by the video referee but three minutes later Trent Barrett crossed to start the procession as Warrington just caved in under the pressure. Warrington's discipline hardly helped as they struggled to stop the flow and hung on at the ruck area far too often for referee Ashley Klein to ignore and with so much ball and field position a high score was on the cards.

Paul Cullen looked a doomed man afterwards and admitted the defensive effort took it out of the side but it was clear he didn't want to blame the officials. 'We caved in for the last 30 minutes, we won't make any excuses about injuries or the officials' decisions.' Wigan boss Brian Noble was convinced they could turn the tide after going behind early in the match, 'Stop giving penalties away, improve the skills and given an even share of possession, and I think you'll win this game,' he said. That they did with gusto and with some great performances from Barrett and Hock who teased the Warrington side throughout the second stanza.

Poor Warrington looked a sad outfit as they trudged off the playing area at full time. The travelling fans made it quite clear they were not getting value for money and were left wondering when the likes of King and Monaghan would hit top form again to ensure they stay in the top six. On this showing I didn't bet on them making the play-offs.

Player of Round 14

Trent Barrett, Wigan

At last the real deal. Barrett was back to his top form, two tries and a great kicking game.

Friday 16 May 2008

Kick off: 20.00, Venue: Headingley, Att: 17,647, Match official: R Silverwood

Leeds (36) 58
T: K Senior 2, D McGuire 3, R Burrow 1, M Diskin 1, C Ablett 1, E Anselme 1, S Worrall 1 G: R Burrow 2, K Sinfield 7

Wakefield (6) 12
T: D Brough 1, S Obst 1 G: D Brough 2

Leeds squad
Webb, Hall, Ellis, Senior, Donald, McGuire, Burrow, Leuluai, Diskin, Peacock, Ablett, Anselme, Sinfield Replacements: Tansey, Scruton, Worrall, Bailey

Wakefield squad
Blaymire, Blanch, Martin, Atkins, Grix, Rooney, Brough, Moore, Obst, Wilkes, MacGillivray, Golden, Sculthorpe Replacements: Dale, Bibey, Leo-Latu, Drew

Leeds were at it again with an easy win over Wakefield who tried hard but just couldn't get anywhere near the speed of the Rhinos. Four converted tries in just 13 minutes would be enough to blitz any team in the world and Leeds looked just that, world beaters. Rhinos' boss Brian McClennan was somewhat nervous about his side before kick off as they had tip-toed through the defence with sheer class.

Barely seconds had gone by before McGuire started the procession by sending Ablett away down the touchline before receiving the inside ball to score. It took some tremendous rearguard action from Wakefield to hang on as Leeds unfolded move after move. It came as a surprise to see the Wildcats score on 19 minutes through Obst who backed up the fine run from Rooney to level the scores but it just poked the home side in the eye as they started the whirlwind of attacks that blew Wakefield away. On loan Eric Anselme charged over on his home debut and then Rob Burrow bagged a four pointer after great work from Ellis and McGuire who also bagged his second soon after. Wakefield were stunned and couldn't stop the flow of sensational support play. For each break Leeds made, there were numbers of players around to finish off the efforts. Four minutes before the break Simon Worrall went over and the old man of the party Keith Senior, who was playing like a youngster, sealed it all off with a crunching effort seconds before the hooter sounded.

At 36–6 at half time it was a question of how many. Trinity tried hard but when McGuire bagged his hat trick on 61 minutes there was a sense that Leeds would reach the magic 50 mark. Matt Diskin scampered over soon after a consolation try from Danny Brough that left an easy conversion for Sinfield who on the night equalled Andy Farrell's Super League record of scoring in 48 consecutive matches. But this was no individual success, this was all about team work and exhilarating power play for the full 80 minutes. It left the fans wondering who could stop the Rhinos.

Brian McClennan was somewhat nervous before the kick off.

struggled to overcome Harlequins in the Challenge Cup the previous week and even he was stunned by the way his side gelled together, 'We played really well, that spell before half time was hard to defend against.' It sure was as the Leeds outfit produced sublime rugby skills, Sinfield steered the ship, Leuluai charged like a—well a rhino, and Danny McGuire

Saturday 17 May 2008

Kick off: 18.00, Venue: GPW Recruitment Stadium, Att: 8,550, Match official: P Bentham

St Helens (16) 28
T: A Gardner 2, L Pryce 1, K Cunningham 1, J Graham 1, C Flannery 1 **G:** S Long 2

Catalans (0) 10
T: C Greenshields 1, A Mogg 1 **G:** T Bosc 1

St Helens squad
Wellens, Gardner, Gidley, Talau, Meli, Pryce, Long, Cayless, Cunningham, Graham, Gilmour, Flannery, Wilkin Replacements: Roby, Bennett, Hargreaves, Clough

Catalans squad
Greenshields, Khattabi, Mogg, Wilson, Pelo, Bosc, McGuire, Chan, Gorrell, Ferriol, Raguin, Croker, Mounis Replacements: Guisset, Carlaw, Fakir, Casty

St Helens was one side that thought they could overcome the Rhinos. Over the season they slowly but surely regained their confidence and open style of play that made them famous for years. I know it hurt them deep down as Leeds had all the accolades yet after seeing them coast against Catalans for a 28–10 victory they needed to improve.

It could have been a case of the Saints coming down to the French side's level for they irritated the fans by holding down and slowing the pace of the game. The 14–3 penalty count against Catalans indicates the referee wasn't too fond of their tactics either and it came as no surprise when Clint Greenshields took a spell in the sin-bin. It was a poor game with little chance of open play but the home side just did enough to get the win.

Chris Flannery opened the scoring on three minutes and with most of the

James Graham added his name to the score sheet in Saints' win over the Dragons.

possession Saints should have hammered them early but the succession of penalties seemed to frustrate them as much as it should have the visitors. Midway through the first half Cunningham bagged the second touchdown with Long adding another 10 minutes before the break to send them in 16–0 up. This seemed to leave the result confirmed and I hoped for the fans' sake the game could become a contest at least in the second stanza. As it turned out the French side came out with a different attitude than the one they had shown earlier.

An otherwise quiet Casey McGuire suddenly burst into life with a weaving run to flip a fine inside pass to allow Mogg to score under the posts which Bosc converted to make it 16–6. Suddenly the crowd woke up and found their voices only to witness yet another interference at the play the ball that earned Greenshields a yellow card. It wasn't much later before Saints sealed the win. Matt Gidley's super quick off load sent Gardner into the corner for a fine try, a feat that Gidley repeated soon after to send in Gardner yet again to give them a 24–6 lead. Leon Pryce capped off a fine game by running on the arc from 12 metres out to stretch the lead even further. Even though Greenshields picked up a consolation try the fact was that the Catalans failed to hit the high spots throughout leaving a few St Helens fans wondering what type of tactics their new coach would bring to the club.

Michael Potter's attempt to show off his coaching prowess fell short leaving more than the odd Saints fan walking away wondering if the club had got the right man to take over from Daniel Anderson. Anderson summed the game up nicely, 'We were poor and they were terrible.'

Kick off: 15.00, Venue: Twickenham Stoop, Att: 3,793, Match official: B Thaler

Harlequins (6) 34
T: C Melling 2, T Clubb 2, J Rinaldi 1, M Worrincy 1 **G:** H Paul 5

Hull FC (16) 26
T: M Sing 1, K Yeaman 1, D Washbrook 1, R Whiting 1, T Lee 1 **G:** C Hall 3

Harlequins squad
Wells, Melling, Gafa, Howell, Sheriffe, Hill, Orr, Temata, Randall, Ward, Clubb, Mbu, Paul
Replacements: Rinaldi, Haggerty, Worrincy, Grayshon

Hull FC squad
Byrne, Sing, Yeaman, Hall, Raynor, Washbrook, Dykes, Dowes, Berrigan, Cusack, Manu, Radford, Whiting
Replacements: Burnett, Lee, Wheeldon, Thackray

Another club in crisis was the Hull FC outfit, who threw away a 6–16 lead at half time to go down 34–26 in the end to a spirited Harlequins' fight-back. Black and whites' coach Peter Sharp still felt they could make the play-offs but the loss left them next to bottom. Time was running out for the club and the coach and so it proved when Sharp was sacked two days later. Sharp would have sensed the mood in the camp as they frittered away a 10 point lead and allowed the Quins back into the match after they dominated things for the first 39 minutes.

Melling dropped a high bomb and gave Whiting an easy try after two minutes and with most of the possession Hull looked strong yet too many errors allowed the London side to stay in contention until another Dykes kick undid them, this time Sheriffe spilled the bomb and Tommy Lee dived over to make it 0–12. It should have been worse for the Harlequins but Todd Byrne somehow lost the ball in the act of scoring. The reprieve was short lived after a Raynor break split the defence which allowed Danny Washbrook to score from the next set of six. At 0–16 up Hull were looking pretty to go in at the break with a commanding lead only for Quins to bounce back with the last play of the first half. Tony Clubb bustled his way over after strong pressure on the Hull line and gave the home side some hope.

Hull were by far the better outfit and should have scored more points in the first 40 and they soon realised their mistakes when the home side crossed only seconds after the restart. Substitute Julien Rinaldi stole the ball 30 metres out and trotted over for an easy try whilst the black and whites' players stood looking at the referee for what they thought was a two on one tackle. Referee Ben Thaler ignored their protests and pointed for the try. Henry Paul's conversion took Harlequins to just four points adrift and Hull looked stunned.

Brian McDermott's half time speech did the trick as the Londoners started to breach the defence with ease. Clubb and Worrincy produced strong breaks for the Quins that should have seen the scoreboard click over but against the run of play Hull stretched the lead with a long range effort from Raynor who just squeezed in at the corner. Hall failed to convert and at 12–20 it looked like the visitors had weathered Quins' storm. Then came a purple patch for the home side as Scott Hill produced some of that old Australian magic to create two tries in as many minutes. First Hill's inside pass to

Howell off loaded to Worrincy made for an easy score, then Hill again made some good ground before sucking in fullback Byrne to ensure Melling scored. Henry Paul gladly converted both tries to put them in the lead for the first time in the match at 24–20.

Worse was to come for Hull after about 25 minutes of the second half when Tony Clubb snatched his second try of the day to make it 28–20 and the home side were well in control. Eight minutes before full time Hull did fight back with a try to Matt Sing after tremendous work from Richard Whiting who kicked through twice to enable the winger to score. Sadly his collision whilst putting in the second kick saw him carried from the field of play with a broken leg. It was a heavy price to pay and rocked the visitors enough to allow Chris Melling to seal the game four minutes from time. This was one game the Quins were determined not to throw away.

Sunday 18 May 2008

Kick off: 15.00, Venue: The Galpharm Stadium, Att: 7,248,
Match official: I Smith

Huddersfield (20) 50
T: L Cudjoe 1, M Aspinwall 1,
M Lawrence 2, P Whatuira 1, S Elford 1,
L Robinson 1, J Skandalis 1, A Raleigh 1
G: C Thorman 7

Hull KR (6) 16
T: P Fox 1, S Murrell 1, R Lovegrove 1
G: P Cooke 2

Huddersfield squad
Cudjoe, Aspinwall, Lawrence, Whatuira, Elford, Brown, Robinson, Jackson, Hudson, Skandalis, Jones, Raleigh, Snitch
Replacements: Thorman, Crabtree, Griffin, Kirmond

Hull KR squad

Briscoe, Fox, Walker, Jake Webster, Fitzhenry, Cooke, Murrell, Vella, Fisher, Mills, Newton, Lovegrove, Chester
Replacements: Crossman, Cockayne, Aizue, K Netherton

When Hull KR took an early lead at the Galpharm Stadium even the most ardent Huddersfield fans suggested the Rovers would take them to the cleaners, especially as they had knocked the Giants out of the challenge cup the previous week. Scott Murrell continued his top form with the opening try after a neat pass from Paul Cooke sent him in between the sticks and when Cooke added the extras they looked a confident side. Six minutes later the game switched around as the Giants produced some outstanding play not seen at the stadium for quite some time. Tries from Martin Aspinwall and Shane Elford in the space of four minutes shocked the Robins, and it was the Giants who were 'bobbing along'. Luke Robinson crossed soon after and when man of the match Michael Lawrence dived over the home side held a 20–6 lead at the break and the buzz around the ground was electric, thanks mainly to the skills of the youngster Lawrence who showed great skills to undo Rovers' defence. Coach Jon Sharp as ever was reluctant to heap praise on the young kid but did admit his talent is of the highest order, 'We've known since

The Huddersfield team take the field at The Galpharm Stadium.

Luke Robinson scores in Huddersfield's defeat of Hull KR.

he was 15 that he was going to be a fantastic prospect,' and so it proved even more in the second half where he continued to grow in stature and tease the defence.

Giants' fans must have been pinching themselves at the break, such was the dominance the home side had and it wasn't much longer after the restart for them to realise a good thrashing was on the cards. Skandalis's try three minutes in made it 24–6, Cudjoe, another young talent picked up a four pointer soon followed by Whatuira who stretched the lead to an incredible 36–6 with just over 20 minutes remaining!

Rhys Lovegrove did offer some hope for the visitors but Huddersfield were running hot, Andy Raleigh got his name on the score sheet before the young kid Lawrence again stole the limelight in the dying seconds leaving Thorman an easy conversion to take them to 50.

Rovers' coach Justin Morgan summed up his side's performance as, 'Disappointing, effortless,' harsh words indeed but they looked nothing like the outfit that played the previous week in the cup. Take nothing away from Jon Sharp's men who at long last fired on all cylinders and showed with the likes of youngsters Lawrence and Cudjoe in the squad the future looks bright.

Sunday 18 May 2008

Kick off: 15.30, Venue: The Jungle, Att: 7,855, Match official: R Laughton

Castleford (14) 24
T: M Shenton 1, M Wainwright 1, R McGoldrick 1, L Dorn 1, J Westerman 1 **G:** L Dorn 1, J Westerman 1

Bradford (28) 46
T: M Platt 1, P Sykes 1, B Jeffries 1, T Newton 1, S Burgess 1, J Langley 1, G Morrison 1, S Finnigan 1 **G:** P Deacon 7

Castleford squad

Donlan, Fletcher, Shenton, Dixon, Wainwright, McGoldrick, Dorn, Higgins, Moore, Huby, Guttenbeil, Catic, Westerman
Replacements: Korkidas, Henderson, Hlad, Owen

Bradford squad

Platt, Evans, Sykes, Nero, Tadulala, Jeffries, Deacon, Lynch, Newton, Burgess, Solomona, Langley, Morrison
Replacements: Finnigan, Tupou, Harris, Kopczak

Wooden spoon favourites Castleford shocked the visiting Bradford Bulls with an opening salvo that saw the home side leading 10–0 after just 16 minutes and it took some outstanding defence to ensure they didn't go further behind. In-form centre Michael Shenton got the scoreboard clicking after receiving from Westerman's break down the right. He could have been away over the horizon if referee Ronnie Laughton had given two disallowed tries. Yet the team were rewarded eventually when Luke Dorn produced a neat kick to allow McGoldrick to score. Dixon's conversion gave them a handy lead but Bradford worked hard to get back in the game through some good work in the forwards, especially Sam Burgess, and it came as no surprise when Deacon and Jeffries combined to give Paul Sykes his chance but Deacon couldn't add the extras.

The Tigers' defence was a problem and whilst they could score good tries they suffered when it came to tackling the man with the ball. Poor defence was on the cards again when sloppy play allowed the Bulls to even the scores at 10–10, even then the Tigers would not lie down and the young star Joe Westerman put them in front again 14–10, Dixon missing the conversion.

Not even the travelling Bulls fans would have expected a burst of skill that bagged three tries within four minutes just before the half time hooter was blown. Burgess, Morrison and Langley crossed to blow the Tigers away after Castleford looked likely to go to the sheds in front. They trudged in 14–28 down instead for another uplifting speech from coach Terry Matterson. Castleford never recovered from that quick three try blitz despite a try from Wainwright and a touchline conversion from Westerman after Bulls' centre Evans was sent to the sin-bin. Soon after Westerman's effort Bradford kicked back with a superb solo try from Platt who jinked his way in and out and showed pace to score leaving an easy conversion for Deacon right in front of the posts that left it 20–34 to the Bulls.

Further tries from Jeffries and Finnigan kept the scoreboard lads busy and the Bulls fans happy but coach Steve McNamara had little to smile about despite the win, 'Our performance was erratic and, although we have some players in form, we have to improve.' Terry Matterson was a dejected figure. 'I thought we were the better side for 20 minutes but we made three mistakes and they scored off them.' Matterson realised the fans were frustrated and he expected the team to get better, 'We are in a tough competition.' Sadly, the Tigers conceded 182 points in their last four games and defence was the key. One thing was for sure, Castleford would not throw in the towel, they had two big scalps in Leeds and St Helens and anyone who took them lightly would be punished for they were able to score some good tries. Add more venom in defence and they could provide a few more bad moments for the top sides fighting for a play-off spot.

engage
Mutual Assurance

Friday 23 May 2008

Kick off: 19.30, Venue: Grattan Stadium, Att: 14,013, Match official: P Bentham

Bradford (8) 14
T: D Halley 1, D Solomona 1, T Tupou 1

Leeds (12) 30
T: B Webb 1, K Senior 1, D McGuire 1, R Burrow 1, A Lauitiiti 1 **G:** K Sinfield 5

Bradford squad
Platt, Halley, Sykes, Hape, Tadulala, Morrison, Jeffries, Vagana, Newton, Lynch, Solomona, Langley, Burgess Replacements: Kopczak, Finnigan, Karlile, Tupou

Leeds squad
Webb, Hall, Ellis, Senior, Donald, McGuire, Burrow, Leuluai, Diskin, Scruton, Ablett, Peacock, Sinfield. Replacements: Burgess, Bailey, Lauitiiti, Tansey

The big derby at the Grattan Stadium, Odsal, would prove that Bradford could compete with their near neighbours in a race for Old Trafford. During the first 25 minutes it looked like they were going to boss the game. Within the first five minutes Terry Newton had a try disallowed whilst the Rhinos looked shaky despite the Bulls having two late withdrawals in Deacon and Harris. Both pulled muscles at their last training session.

It wasn't the first time the video ref would go against them as a further three tries were handed upstairs only to come back with the same decision, 'No Try'. It was an unlucky day for the Bulls in the end when Leeds' two offerings to the video ref got the green light. They

Danny McGuire tries to evade the clutches of Ben Jeffries.

also had bad luck in losing winger Semi Tadulala with a dislocated shoulder and Glenn Morrison who was playing at stand off limped throughout with a foot injury. David Solomona and Newton were bossing the first quarter and not surprisingly they took the lead when the former crossed on 14 minutes. Halley had a try wiped by video two minutes later but nothing was going to stop Halley scoring the second time and take the lead at 8–0. Leeds just couldn't get going and it took some exciting play that enabled McGuire to squeeze in at the corner to lift the visitors especially when Sinfield kicked a beauty from the sideline that pushed him past Andy Farrell's record of scoring in consecutive matches. This took the skipper to 49 games and he went on to kick five from five during a commanding showing. The Rhinos were on a roll and a skilful pass from Sinfield sent Senior racing downfield who passed inside to the supporting Burrow to score under the sticks with just three minutes left in the half. The Bulls couldn't believe the score at lemons as they trailed 8–12 after having all the position and possession.

The break helped slow the Leeds momentum and when substitute Tame Tupou charged over from Newton's pass to take the lead again with a converted try, it looked likely the Bulls would stretch the lead even further. Again the video ref turned down Tupou's effort on 59 minutes, and this lifted the Leeds side to respond. They did so with a neat try from Ali Lauitiiti, Sinfield was on target yet again and the lead went back to the

Sam Burgess feels the force of the Rhinos defence.

visitors. It became a thrilling encounter—tempers flared and big hits were the order of the day but it was all skill when Kylie Leuluai burst through the middle and off loaded to Jordon Tansey who in turn traded passes with McGuire before sending fullback Webb over for a remarkable 80 metre raid downfield. Bradford were battling to get back into the game at 14–24 and had even more bad luck when Tupou was again turned down by the video referee with a score that would have made life interesting to say the least. Yet Leeds hung on and sent in Senior for a late try to seal it up at 14–30. The score line failed to explain the tightness of the two sides for both played well and it was a joy to watch a good old fashioned style of game.

The Bulls coach, Steve McNamara was full of praise, 'I thought the effort was superb, we tried really, really hard.' Rhinos boss McClennan again was hard to please and he made it clear he thought it was a scrappy game. 'It was slow in the ruck and it wasn't enjoyable to watch.'

Saturday 24 May 2008

Kick off: 18.30, Venue: Stade Gilbert Brutus, Att: 7,785, Match official: A Klein

Catalans (20) 48
T: C Greenshields 2, J Murphy 1, J Wilson 1, D Pelo 1, G Mounis 1, J Fakir 1, R Casty 1 **G:** T Bosc 8

Huddersfield (0) 0

Catalans squad
Greenshields, Murphy, Wilson, Raguin, Pelo, Mogg, Bosc, Guisset, McGuire, Chan, Croker, Mounis, Carlaw Replacements: Elima, Duport, Fakir, Casty

Huddersfield squad
Cudjoe, Aspinwall, Lawrence, Whatuira, Elford, Brown, Robinson, Jackson, Hudson, Mason, Jones, Raleigh, Lolesi Replacements: Thorman, Snitch, Griffin, Crabtree

Huddersfield Giants flew down to the South of France in a buoyant mood after last week's thumping win over Hull KR and coach Jon Sharp must have been thinking the tide had turned for his side. The Dragons are usually a hard side to beat at home and it proved to be the case for the Giants when they failed to score a point, a result that must have left the Giants and their coach on thin ice. At least they prevented the Catalans from topping the 50 point mark but that was poor consolation for the Giants who looked like dead men in the water. Sharp was scathing, 'I'm devastated with what I've seen tonight, we were outmuscled and bullied and that disappoints me.'

Nothing went right for the visitors as the French side ripped them apart with speed skill and tough tactics that put the Giants on the back foot throughout the game. It took only four minutes for Catalans to open the scoring with a penalty goal and then man of the match Clint Greenshields tip-toed through a poor defence to sneak in next to the posts. Gregory Mounis soon followed with another easy try and when Dimitri Pelo crossed with ease out wide after Mogg's 40/20 kick it was curtains for Huddersfield at 20–0 at half time.

The much needed half time speech from coach Sharp hardly brought about much change, in fact Huddersfield got worse as they failed to gain any ground position to launch any attack. With so much defending, it was clear Huddersfield's energy level would plummet and Catalans put them to the sword. Jamal Fakir crossed on 49 minutes and then a procession of tries, Wilson, Murphy and Casty all joining in the fun and games. It was fitting that Greenshields finished the try scoring spree the same way he started it, scoring a great try after good work from Sebastien Raguin who also shone throughout the match. Huddersfield never really got into the game until the final quarter but even then they lacked ideas and were pleased when the final whistle went. It was a poor showing for the Giants and the chance of making the play-offs were slim on this form.

Sunday 25 May 2008

Kick off: 15.00, Venue: New Craven Park, Att: 8,084,
Match official: S Ganson

Hull KR (4) 22
T: M Dobson 2, S Gene 1, C Chester 1
G: P Cooke 3

Harlequins (8) 8
T: M Worrincy 1, J Grayshon 1

Hull KR squad
Briscoe, Fox, Walker, Jake Webster, Fitzhenry, Cooke, Dobson, Vella, Fisher, Crossman, Newton, Gene, Murrell
Replacements: Mills, Chester, Cockayne, Watts

Harlequins squad
Melling, Wells, Clubb, Howell, Sheriffe, Hill, Orr, Temata, Randall, Ward, Worrincy, Paul, Mbu
Replacements: Rinaldi, Haggerty, Grayshon, Barker

The new recruit, Australian Michael Dobson, was making his debut for Hull KR as they took on the Harlequins at Craven Park. The home fans were hoping the crafty scrum-half could help the Robins shake off last week's sad loss to Huddersfield and they didn't have to wait long to realise what a talented player he is. Dobson played with confidence, scored two tries and showed his kicking game was up there with the best and teased the Quins with some clever open play. Not that it was easy as Harlequins had the better of play in the opening stages and were rewarded with a good try from Michael Worrincy who continued to impress each week. Sadly Henry Paul couldn't convert but there was little doubt who was bossing the game especially when Scott Murrell left the field with a dislocated shoulder. It wasn't long before Dobson popped up for his first try to level the scores. A big hit by Chev Walker stunned Gareth Haggerty and lifted Rovers no end. It put the Quins under immense pressure but Jake Webster was sent to the sin-bin and Harlequins took full advantage soon after when Scott Hill provided the pass for Jon Grayshon to barge over. Again Paul missed an easy kick but Quins went to the break 4–8 up.

Barely seconds after the restart Hull KR took the lead after a sensational pass off the floor from Paul Cooke sent in Chris Chester and the provider tagged on the extras to take the lead. Things got worse for the struggling Quins when Chad Randall got his yellow card which allowed Rovers to take control of the match with a Stanley Gene try that pushed the advantage even further at 16–8. Harlequins, to their credit, produced some gutsy defence to stop the rampant Rovers running away with it but they could do nothing to stop the man of the moment Michael Dobson from sealing the win with a nice kick through to score, earning him the man of the match award. Rovers' coach Justin Morgan heaped praise on his new signing, 'I thought the chemistry between Cookey and Dobbo was very good considering they have had only 80 minutes training together.' Stanley Gene also impressed his coach. 'He's just like a nice bottle of Bordeaux, you've just got to lay him down for a couple of weeks here and there.'

Sunday 25 May 2008

Kick off: 15.30, Venue: Belle Vue,
Att: 6,370, Match official: B Thaler

Wakefield (12) 30
T: M Blaymire 1, T Martin 1, D Blanch 2, J Pitts 1 **G:** D Brough 5

Wigan (14) 38
T: L Colbon 1, P Richards 1, T Leuluai 1, A Coley 1, H Hansen 1, G Hock 1
G: P Richards 7

Wakefield squad
Blaymire, Gleeson, Martin, Atkins, Blanch, Grix, Brough, Bibb, Obst, Wilkes, MacGillivray, Golden, Sculthorpe
Replacements: Murphy, Drew, Moore, Pitts

Wigan squad
Mathers, Colbon, Bailey, Carmont, Richards, Barrett, Leuluai, Coley, Higham, Fielden, Hansen, J Tomkins, Hock
Replacements: Goulding, Palea'aesina, McIlorum, O'Carroll

Wigan went to Belle Vue knowing that their coach Brian Noble had never won there with the Warriors in Super League. It looked like it would stay that way when Damien Blanch scored after just five minutes. Wakefield, despite missing several top players including Jamie Rooney, made it quite clear who was going to be boss as they blitzed Wigan with some rugged defence in the opening quarter. The tactics made it clear

Despite five goals from Danny Brough Wakefield were unable to overcome Wigan.

that they were going to crunch the opposition. With so much momentum, it wasn't surprising to see Danny Brough take control. His neat kick claimed the try for Blanch and they should have scored again when Brough charged down a Barrett kick and raced over. The referee stated he was offside, yet again the maestro scrum-half created a chance for Sam Obst but he lost the ball over the line.

Amazingly after so much pressure Wigan's first real attack resulted in Thomas Leuluai going over near the posts to level the scores. That man Brough came back with a great response putting in a grubber kick into the in goal area where Grix amazingly flicked the ball back for Jay Pitts to score, Brough's conversion took the Wildcats 12–6 clear. Three minutes later Wigan bounced back with a strong lunge for the line from Andy Coley, Pat Richards added the extras to tie things up and added a penalty after Sculthorpe's high shot on Hock just before the break to bring a surprising lead. Wakefield must have been gutted at being behind as they had most of the play throughout the first half

but credit went to the Warriors for taking their few chances.

With the wind behind them most expected Wakefield to take control through the kicking game of Brough and like the first half they dominated the early period thanks to a 40/20 from the scrum-half who was having a field day teasing the Wigan defence. It came as no surprise when Brough combined with Brad Drew to send in Tony Martin. Once again Wigan took their chance three minutes later when Barrett threw out a wonderful long ball to winger Liam Colbon to make it 18–18, and game on. The tall figure of Pat Richards helped Wigan's cause by plucking the ball out of the air to put the visitors in front then five minutes later Richards added a penalty to make it 18–26. Man of the match Gareth Hock appeared to have won the game when he waltzed over after Brough put the restart into touch on the full. At 18–32 it looked all over for the home side but they scored two quick tries from Blaymire and Blanch to bring it back to 30–32 only for Harrison Hansen to finish off a Carmont break to seal it. The Wildcats coach John Kear was not happy, 'We should have had more points on the board early on and I'm disappointed in some of our defensive work.' Brian Noble knew they had been in a battle, 'It's a very difficult place to come here because they are always in your face.'

Sunday 25 May 2008

Kick off: 18.00, Venue: The KC Stadium, Att: 14,653, Match official: R Silverwood

Hull FC (4) 8
T: K Yeaman 1, G Raynor 1

St Helens (10) 16
T: S Tyrer 1, L Pryce 1, J Wilkin 1
G: S Long 2

Stuart Fielden battles his way through in Wigan's defeat of Wakefield.

Hull FC squad

Byrne, Sing, Hall, Yeaman, Raynor, Washbrook, Berrigan, Dowes, Houghton, Cusack, Manu, Tickle, Radford

Replacements: Thackeray, Lee, Carvell, G Horne

St Helens squad

Wellens, Tyrer, Gidley, Talau, Meli, Pryce, Long, Cayless, Roby, Graham, Gilmour, Flannery, Wilkin

Replacements: Cunningham, Hargreaves, Bennett, Fa'asavalu

It was going to be a tough baptism for Hull's new young coach Richard Agar who, following the departure of Peter Sharp, was handed the reins on a two and a half year contract. St Helens were the visitors and would be a tough test for Agar whose side had to stand up to the skill and toughness of the Challenge Cup holders. They didn't get the result they wanted but Agar's players displayed a different attitude which added fuel to the rumours that Sharp had lost the dressing room.

This was a battling performance by the black and whites. They fought tooth and nail against a Saints outfit that started like a house on fire scoring within five minutes when Wilkin raced 40 metres to score out wide evading the diving tackle from fullback Byrne. Hull had further problems soon after when Shaun Berrigan left the field with a bad shoulder injury leaving the black and whites with few attacking options. But they stuck at it as Saints made six clean breaks that should have produced tries yet Hull's crumbling defence got there time and time again, never more so when Manu chased back to grab Gilmour who looked set to score. It was one of many defensive cameos that prevented the visitors running away with

the game, a fact backed up by Saints' boss Daniel Anderson, 'They showed great attitude, we made loads of breaks but they stopped us on the last tackle or near the line. That showed their commitment.'

Agar was disappointed about not winning but admitted it was an improved showing, 'We've got effort in bucket loads but we ran out of gas.' With no real ball player available it was down to hard work to have any chance of pulling off an upset. Hull knew it as their forwards clashed with the opposition pack with some rugged tackles that had Saints going backwards at times and it took touches of skill to break the home side down. The KC stadium hasn't been kind to Saints over the years and they had to dig deep to get any reward. Quick hands from Pryce and Gidley sent Tyrer in at the corner after 20 minutes, Long's conversion was successful and put them 10–0 up. Saints suddenly went to sleep when Raynor patted back a huge kick from Byrne to the corner. This left the visitors standing, still claiming to the official that it was a knock on. Whilst Long was slow to snap up the ball, Yeaman kicked through and pounced to put them back in the game, Tickle missed the extras but it gave Hull a huge boost when they went to the sheds three minutes later.

At 4–10 St Helens couldn't relax and Hull threw everything into the fray. Both defences held despite some huge hits that rocked the ground. Thackray and Carvell especially worked overtime, so did Cayless and Graham who were staging their own little war in a torrid period over 20 minutes only for Leon Pryce to provide the breakdown play. The classy stand off had had little chance to shine amongst the forwards' battle but his speed and swerve produced a try of the highest quality as he ran on the arc close to the line and forced his way over. Surprisingly Long missed the conversion and at 4–14 Hull still had a sniff at getting back into the game. With little invention to add to their determined hard work Hull never looked like breaking through and when it did it was too late. Raynor's score in the corner showed the home side at least had shown much spirit but the fact is they still occupy second bottom of the league table and the chance of making the play-off's seem remote. Agar certainly lifted the side and added more spark and any improvement from this showing will make a trip to Hull a far from happy experience.

Monday 26 May 2008

Kick off: 19.30, Venue: Halliwell Jones Stadium, Att: 7,788, Match official: I Smith

Warrington (10) 28
T: C Hicks 1, C Riley 2, K Penny 1, V Anderson 1 **G:** C Hicks 4

Castleford (14) 36
T: S Donlan 1, M Wainwright 1, R Owen 1, M Shenton 1, A Fletcher 1, L Dorn 2 **G:** C Huby 1, J Westerman 3

Warrington squad
Hicks, Riley, Martin Gleeson, King, Penny, Briers, Monaghan, Morley, Clarke, Rauhihi, L Anderson, Westwood, V Anderson
Replacements: Mark Gleeson, Grix, Bracek, Harrison

Castleford squad
Donlan, Wainwright, Owen, Shenton, Fletcher, McGoldrick, Dorn, Huby, Moore, Guttenbeil, Catic, Lupton, Westerman
Replacements: Henderson, Korkidas, Higgins, Boyle

As there was to be no relegation in rugby league in 2008 we accepted that the usual sacking of coaches would not happen! Hull coach Peter Sharp was sacked and on his way back to Australia and suddenly some coaches were looking over their backs including one Paul Cullen. He hosted the arrival of bottom club Castleford to the home of the Wolves and had been getting plenty of stick from sections of the crowd. He must have realised a loss to the favourites for the wooden spoon could spell trouble in the Warrington camp. A loss at home would see Warrington drop out of the top six position and the fans knew it too. Many refused to leave the ground after the game whilst chanting for Cullen's head. One hour later the Wolves coach obliged, said farewell inside the dressing room and walked away from the club.

The string of Warrington injuries didn't help Cullen's cause but he insisted throughout the campaign that he would not blame injury for the poor performances of some of the players. Despite paying big money for the likes of Matt King and Michael Monaghan, Warrington failed to gel into a winning outfit. The team started out badly and suffered from poor defence allowing Castleford to glide through gaps out on the fringe and it was no surprise they took the lead through good tries from Richard Owen and Michael Shenton, a reported target for Bradford. Warrington looked lethargic and were in all sorts of trouble with a defence that failed to meet up face to face with the rampaging Tigers and it took some time before they found the spark. It came through Vinnie Anderson and Chris Riley and allowed Warrington to sneak back into the match but Castleford fully deserved to go in at half time 10–14 up when Adam Fletcher crossed.

Cullen's words of wisdom certainly had the right effect for they appeared a much tighter bunch for the second stanza and when Catic earned a 10 minute sin-bin stint it gave the green light to the home side. Both wingers, Riley and Penny, picked up a try apiece and when Chris Hicks scored, the home side had a 28–14 advantage with just over 10 minutes remaining. It could have been more but the referee pulled them back for a controversial knock-on. TV evidence appeared to suggest the try should have been given, but even that aside nobody expected the capitulation that was about to unfold. Warrington not only put the cue on the rack, they dismantled the table and threw the balls away doing little to prevent Castleford staging the finest fight-back in years. Three tries in the space of five minutes was amazing and the home crowd looked on in horror as first Wainwright crossed, then Luke Dorn and Stuart Donlan but more tragedy was to come when Dorn picked off Monaghan's long pass and raced away 90 metres to seal the match for good. What was going through Cullen's mind as he watched the former Broncos and Salford half back speeding away towards the post would have done little for his health or his job. When the hooter went one knew it didn't just herald the end of the game it brought down the curtain on Cullen's reign with the club. Cullen was involved with Warrington over 25 years and it must have been a sad time in the dressing room afterwards. Full credit went to Castleford, they came with a game plan that fell apart when Catic got sin-binned and allowed the Wolves to race away but coach Terry Matterson was proud of the way they stuck at it. 'I don't know who needed the win more but if you look at the table, I think maybe we did. I think the hungriest side won.' So it was two coaches down, surely there wouldn't be any more sackings?

Luke Dorn scored two tries in the defeat of Warrington which ended the reign of Paul Cullen.

engage
Mutual Assurance

Friday 6 June 2008

Kick off: 19.30, Venue: GPW Recruitment Stadium, Att: 8,404, Match official: P Bentham

St Helens (30) 52
T: P Wellens 1, A Gardner 3, M Gidley 2, W Talau 1, L Pryce 1, M Fa'asavalu 1
G: P Wellens 1, S Long 7

Hull KR (0) 10
T: S Briscoe 1, M Vella 1 **G:** P Cooke 1

St Helens squad
Wellens, Gardner, Gidley, Talau, Meli, Pryce, Long, Cayless, Cunningham, Graham, Flannery, Wilkin, Sculthorpe
Replacements: Roby, Hargreaves, Clough, Fa'asavalu

Hull KR squad
Briscoe, Fox, Jake Webster, Fitzhenry, Steel, Cooke, Dobson, Crossman, Fisher, Vella, Newton, Gene, Walker
Replacements: Mills, Cockayne, J Netherton, Chester

St Helens welcomed a Hull KR side they had struggled to beat in the previous weekend's Challenge Cup 24–18. Many expected another tight contest at the GPW Recruitment Stadium on a bright Friday night but it was obvious that the sting had been taken out of the Rovers after just 15 minutes. The injury to Chev Walker after seven minutes didn't help matters, neither did it auger well for Saints when Chris Flannery hobbled off too but it was the home side who looked in the mood and, when Gardner accepted a neat pass from Matt Gidley to cross in the corner, one sensed a big score was on its way for Saints. St Helens didn't disappoint either with Matt Gidley

the star of the show, scoring twice himself and providing some outstanding flick passes to give Gardner a hat trick in a performance that had the crowd in raptures. Many St Helens fans were disappointed when they lost Jamie Lyon to Manly two years ago, but not even the skills of Lyon could have come near to Gidley's showing. His play was first class and he had wrapped up the man of the match award by half time and ensured Saints went to the break 30–0 up.

Poor Jon Steel, the Rovers winger had a nightmare although he wasn't helped by his team mates who failed to cover on many occasions leaving the winger stranded time and time again. Nothing could take away the class and power of the right centre combination of Gidley and Gardner who were magical at times. The only sour spot in that first half was the bad injury to Jason Cayless who, like Flannery, suffered a long term knee injury and could well miss the rest of the season. It was a bitter blow to Saints who looked threatening each time they had the ball and Rovers just couldn't match the effort, although they were rewarded with two tries back-to-back midway through the second stanza from Mick Vella and Shaun Briscoe. But the game was over soon after Gidley had started to weave his stuff. Leon Pryce was again in good form and crossed eight minutes after the restart. Pryce showed his skill factor enough to ensure his seat was booked on the plane to Australia and the World Cup. Surely Gardner would be seated next to him after this showing but what a boost it would have been if Gidley could have found a Grandparent from England that would make him eligible to play for the St George mob. The Gardner and Gidley combination has become a thing of legend down St Helens' way.

Robins' boss Justin Morgan was at a loss for their showing. 'We had the same issue after our last cup game. We put so much effort into beating Huddersfield and were on the end of a similar score line the week after. We had poor discipline and we need to fix it.' For Saints coach Daniel Anderson it was a mixed bag due to the two long term injuries to Flannery and Cayless, 'It's a bit of a downer but it was a scintillating performance in attack. There was lots of energy and I was pleased with the return of Paul Sculthorpe.' One hoped Sculthorpe could shrug off his injury jinx and settle back into the side. His performance was encouraging and he was involved in creating three tries. They were going to need him as Flannery looked set to be out for a few weeks.

Friday 6 June 2008

Kick off: 20.00, Venue: Headingley, Att: 16,886, Match official: B Thaler

Leeds (4) 38
T: K Senior 1, S Donald 2, R Burrow 2, G Ellis 2 **G:** K Sinfield 5

Hull FC (18) 22
T: G Horne 1, W Manu 1, D Tickle 1
G: D Tickle 5

Leeds squad
Webb, Hall, Ablett, Senior, Donald, McGuire, Burrow, Leuluai, Diskin, Bailey, Anselme, Ellis, Sinfield
Replacements: Scruton, Tansey, Burgess, Jones-Buchanan

Hull FC squad
Byrne, Sing, G Horne, Yeaman, Briscoe, Hall, Dykes, Dowes, Houghton, Carvell, Manu, Radford, Tickle
Replacements: Wheeldon, Burnett, Dale, Thackray

The Headingley South Standers are famous for noise but on this occasion for the first half hour they were stunned into silence. There's little doubt the introduction of new coach Richard Agar has brought a new belief to the Hull FC side. Even after their shock win in the Challenge Cup the previous week at Bradford not many black and white fans would have believed they would rip Leeds apart and lead 18–0 with just five minutes of the first half remaining.

Adam Dykes proved to be the key, all three tries coming from his expertise with the boot, his cross kick allowing Willie Manu to score, then his high bomb found Tickle who slipped a risky pass that Senior intercepted but fumbled

Gareth Ellis battles through the Hull defence.

Rob Burrow scores in Leeds' win over Hull.

to give Graeme Horne an easy score. When Tickle jumped highest to snatch a touchdown the Rhinos were looking down and out. With Dykes in control one wondered if Leeds had the determination to hit back. They were surely relieved to grab a try through Senior who, as the game wore on, became more of a danger to the visitors.

At 4–18 at the break, one wondered if the Hull side could continue with the same gusto but from the kick off they allowed the ball to go dead. From the drop out Rob Burrow produced a side stepping run and speed to the line that lifted the home side's spirits. Leeds were powering into action and the fans were shouting at long last but not even they could have envisaged the scintillating effort from winger Donald. Webb caught the kick off and sent a long pass out to Scott Donald who displayed amazing speed and agility to go inside Wheeldon and then outside Hall to score one of Headingley's greatest tries for years. It was the fillip they needed and soon after the scores were level when Senior, in great form, burst through to put Leeds in

a commanding position. This saw Adam Dykes, the hero for so long, sent to the sin-bin for a professional foul, leaving McGuire from the tap to send in Ellis in at the corner for Leeds, Sinfield converting from the touchline. Danny Tickle added a penalty on 58 minutes to stretch the lead to two but Leeds were in no mood to lie down and Burrow and Webb combined to send in Donald for his second of the night, Sinfield yet again converted to make it 26–22. The steam had gone out of the Hull side and not surprisingly the Rhinos extended their lead to 32–22 when Sinfield and Ellis interchanged for the second rower to touch down. Rob Burrow sealed the score for Leeds with a neat try with 10 minutes remaining making the score 38–22.

It was a remarkable fight-back from Leeds who showed they have the spirit and guts to dig deep, and they needed to against a Hull outfit with plenty of flair and effort. Hull's new boss Richard Agar was pleased with the effort but not happy with the way they changed the tactics, 'We went 18–0 up and started playing like we were 40 up. If we had stuck to what was working we might not have had to chase the game.'

Saturday 7 June 2008

Kick off: 18.00, Venue: The Jungle, Att: 8,236, Match official: I Smith

Castleford (10) 16
T: R McGoldrick 1, L Dorn 2
G: K Dixon 2

Wakefield (18) 32
T: M Blaymire 1, D Blanch 2, J Rooney 1, D Brough 1 **G:** D Brough 6

Castleford squad
Donlan, Dixon, Shenton, Owen, Wainwright, McGoldrick, Dorn, Higgins, Moore, Huby, Guttenbeil, Lupton, Westerman
Replacements: Henderson, Boyle, Clayton, Catic

Wakefield squad
Blaymire, Gleeson, Martin, Atkins, Blanch, Rooney, Brough, Moore, Obst, Wilkes, MacGillivray, Go den, Sculthorpe
Replacements: Grix, Bibey, Henderson, Bibb

Castleford and Wakefield games are not for the faint hearted and the battle down at the jungle on a warm Saturday evening was going to be no different. The Wildcats were buoyed by the fact they went into the match having won the last eight in succession but grabbing the ninth would take some effort against a Tigers team desperate to stop the rot. Things looked good when Luke Dorn accepted the neat short kick from Ryan McGoldrick early in the game to split the Trinity defence. When Kirk Dixon added the extras the home crowd were hoping for revenge of that 54–16 thrashing at the Millennium Stadium in Cardiff the month before.

The Tigers were in the mood for revenge although a touch of luck went against them when Danny Brough, returning to The Jungle for the first time since his Castleford days, stabbed a grubber towards the in goal area. The kick took a wicked diversion off Awen Guttenbeil's leg and offered the little half back a simple try which he converted easily to lock up the scores. Ryan McGoldrick was in great form and a thorn in Wakefield's defence throughout. It was pleasing to see him rewarded with a touchdown that restored the lead for the home side. He came on the angle from 25 metres out and arced his way over with a strong thrust that sent the home crowd into raptures, rightly so, as it was a classy piece of football. Sadly Dixon missed the conversion and Wakefield sighed in relief and were soon rewarded when McGoldrick went from hero to zero by throwing out a long pass that was intercepted by winger Damien Blanch who raced the length of the field for a runaway touchdown. Brough's conversion gave them the lead at 10–12. Once again Danny Brough was the architect of so many of Wakefield's moves and with the tireless Sam Obst they started to take control of the game. This gave them the position for Sean Gleeson to send in Matt Blaymire to extend the lead at the break to 10–18 after Brough added the extra two.

Wakefield were unlucky to have a video referee decision turned away when Tony Martin crossed soon after the kick off.

The home side struck first, McGoldrick yet again producing some fine play to send Luke Dorn in for a converted try to cut the lead to just two points. The fightback was well and truly on. Both sides threw everything at each other and it took a controversial decision to jolt the home team's momentum. Video referee Ashley Klein earned himself no favours with the home fans when he awarded a try to Jamie Rooney after winger Sean Gleeson appeared to have dropped the ball in the act of scoring. Klein suggested otherwise and awarded the touchdown saying the ball had been reefed out of the hands by Michael Wainwright. It was cruel blow and the Tigers never recovered especially when Brough added another penalty to take it to 16–26 with eight minutes left. To their credit, Castleford

launched a last gasp attempt only to see the ball spilled near the Wildcats line giving winger Blanch another long range effort to seal the match.

Tigers' boss Terry Matterson felt the result was cruel, 'If you break the game down we weren't as bad as the 32 points suggest and the video referee's call was a massive decision.' John Kear was happy with his charges saying, 'It's a tough place to come and I am delighted with the way we played.' Again the Tigers put in much effort but sadly looked destined for the wooden spoon. On this showing they could still hurt other clubs' chances of making a top six play-off. They might only have three wins but their CV is not bad: Leeds, St Helens and Warrington. Wakefield, on the other hand, were bouncing, a cup semi final and a good chance of making the play-offs was just reward for John Kear's coaching.

Ryan McGoldrick attempts to break through the Wakefield line.

Sunday 8 June 2008

Kick off: 15.00, Venue: Grattan Stadium, Att: 8,346, Match official: A Klein

Bradford (12) 16
T: P Sykes 1, B Jeffries 1, S Burgess 1
G: I Harris 3

Catalans (8) 24
T: J Murphy 1, J Wilson 1, S Raguin 1, C McGuire 1 **G:** T Bosc 4

Bradford squad
Bradford: Platt, Evans, Sykes, Hape, Halley, Harris, Jeffries, Vagana, Newton, Lynch, Solomona, Langley, Burgess
Replacements: Kopczak, Finnigan, Cook, Tupou

Catalans squad
Greenshields, Murphy, Wilson, Raguin, Pelo, Mogg, Bosc, Guisset, McGuire, Chan, Croker, Mounis, Carlaw
Replacements: Casty, Elima, Fakir, Duport

Another side hurting from a Challenge Cup defeat the week before were Bradford Bulls who started favourites to turn over visitors Catalans Dragons at a hot, sunny Grattan Stadium, Odsal. The French outfit had Casey McGuire at hooker and Bosc and Mogg forming the half back combination in a reshuffled side. But despite having all the play and possession, Catalans found themselves 12–2 down after 30 minutes.

Sam Burgess barged over from close range after a neat break from Jamie Langley on 22 minutes and six minutes later Ben Jeffries latched onto a superb chip over from Iestyn Harris to stun the visitors. They were playing by far the best football of the two sides. Without Tadulala, Godwin, Morrison, Nero and Deacon, Bradford were hardly a full strength side but they were happy to ride their luck and take the advantage. The French team had different ideas and the prompting from new hooker McGuire soon had them on track to get back into the match. Things started to click when winger Dimitri Pelo raced 70 metres downfield only for an amazing tackle from Dave Halley to prevent a touchdown but it left them in a good position for McGuire to cross just before the break. Bosc's conversion added to his early penalty and left them just four adrift at the hooter 12–8. Only brave defence kept Catalans out after the restart, again Pelo being bundled into touch near the corner flag. They couldn't stop Sebastien Raguin accepting Adam Mogg's lovely little kick through that bounced into the centre's hands to score, Bosc added the extras to make it three from three and a 12–14 lead for Catalans. This was short lived when Sam Burgess sent a looping pass out wide to Sykes who took full advantage of Pelo going for the intercept to leave a clear

Jerome Guisset and Dane Carlaw put the brakes on big Joe Vagana in the defeat of Bradford.

run to the line. Sadly Harris couldn't tag on the extra two but it gave them a slender two point lead at 16–14.

A controversial penalty given against Iestyn Harris didn't help matters and Bosc levelled the scores yet again but it was all Catalans from here on in, although Bradford did have a great chance when David Solomona broke clear only for his pass to Harris being deemed forward. Clint Greenshields' pass put John Wilson in at the corner on 65 minutes for an unconverted effort that appeared to take the steam out of Bradford. With six minutes remaining the French side sealed the victory with some fine play from McGuire who kicked into the in goal area and watched with glee as Michael Platt hesitated enough for Justin Murphy to touch down.

Bulls' boss McNamara couldn't deny his side's effort. 'We still lacked a touch of quality in a couple of areas and lacked composure yet for some reason we are giving away far too many penalties and I have to find out why and fix it.' It was a great game from stand in hooker McGuire that left coach Mick Potter with a choice of selection for next week. 'I'm extremely happy with McGuire, he's played well and with Aaron Gorrell due back anytime it leaves me with a headache, but one I'm happy with.' This win left Catalans holding down the third spot on the league table and on track for a play-off spot. Not many fans expected this result but Potter had done a fine job and the team has gained in confidence each week. The big question on everyone's lips was whether they could challenge the front runners Leeds and St Helens. Only time would tell.

Sunday 8 June 2008

Kick off: 15.00, Venue: Twickenham Stoop, Att: 3,622,
Match official: R Silverwood

Harlequins (12) 24
T: T Clubb 1, R Sheriffe 1, M Worrincy 1, G Haggerty 1 **G:** R Purdham 4

Warrington (12) 40
T: C Riley 2, Martin Gleeson 1, M King 1, M Monaghan 1, J Clarke 1, L Anderson 1 **G:** C Hicks 6

Harlequins squad
Melling, Sharp, Clubb, Howell, Sheriffe, Purdham, Orr, Temata, Randall, Ward, Worrincy, Barker, Paul
Replacements: Haggerty, Grayshon, Hill, Mbu

Warrington squad
Hicks, Riley, Martin Gleeson, Grix, King, Briers, Monaghan, Morley, Clarke, Rauhihi, L Anderson, Westwood, V Anderson
Replacements: Mark Gleeson, Parker, Bracek, Harrison

Jimmy Lowes has made it quite clear he wants to take over Warrington on a full time basis after the resignation of Paul Cullen. There were a few pointers that must have made him think he was in with a good chance after watching Wolves spark back into life against a Harlequins side that looked lacklustre at times. The 24–40 score line read well but the truth was that the Quins gifted the game to the visitors during the first 20 minutes of the second half when they spilled the ball so often it looked likely the London outfit could be in for a record defeat.

Jon Clarke created the first try, using the blindside to full effect and sending in winger Chris Riley on 13 minutes soon followed by Louis Anderson who took full advantage after Michael Monaghan and Matt King combined in a scintillating move that took Warrington to a 0–12 lead. Lowes must have been smiling as Warrington looked the goods despite some poor defence by the home side but the grin was wiped from his face when Scott Hill provided some magic with a neat pass that sent Chris Melling charging through, who in turn sent Tony Clubb over. Rob Purdham's conversion spurred them on even further and just before the break the home team sneaked in out wide after great work from Melling again sent another young London star Michael Worrincy in at the corner. Purdham's superb kick from out wide sent them into the sheds on level terms.

What occurred after the break was not of the highest quality from the home side and coach Brian McDermott was furious at the way they kept dropping the ball. This allowed Warrington the position and possession to take control of the match. Martin Gleeson was the first to cross after poor defence, and even more pain was to come Harlequins' way when Sheriffe knocked on allowing Michael Monaghan to cross under the sticks from the resulting scrum. Matt King regained some self confidence of sorts when the winger crashed over out wide. When Chris Hicks sent in Jon Clarke the game was over bar the shouting. Hicks added all four conversions to take them to a commanding 12–36 score line. In boiling conditions the scene was set for a riot to unfold but the Quins dug deep to regain some pride with tries from Haggerty and Sheriffe to make the score respectable at 24–36 with just over 10 minutes to go. Again bad handling left them squandering good field positions and it was no surprise when Chris Riley picked up his second of the day just before the hooter. Quins coach McDermott was unhappy, 'I'm concerned that we're giving away too easy tries.' Lowes on the other was happy with the showing. 'It's been a tough couple of weeks. I asked players to do little things they might not have done in the past and they did, Vinnie Anderson, Jon Clarke, Adrian Morley were outstanding, I could go across the board.' It's hard to say if this win would help Lowes' attempt to snare the job on a full time basis, but there were some good passages of play from his side and a win is a win irrespective of how the opposition play.

Friday 25 July 2008
Delayed match played between Round 18 and 19.

Kick off: 20.00, Venue: JJB Stadium, Att: 12,216, Match official: Ian Smith

Wigan (0) 4
T: P Richards 1

Huddersfield (18) 34
T: P Whatuira 1, D Hodgson 2, R Hudson 1, J Lolesi 1, D Griffin 1
G: C Thorman 5

Wigan squad
Richards, Colbon, Goulding, Carmont, Phelps, Barrett, Leuluai, Fielden, Higham, Coley, Hock, Bailey, Tomkins
Replacements
Smith, Hansen, O'Carroll, Palea'aesina

Huddersfield squad
Cudjoe, Aspinwall, Brown, Whatuira, Hodgson, Robinson, Mason, Hudson, Raleigh, Kirmond, Lolesi, Wild
Replacements
Jones, Snitch, Jackson, Griffin

It's one thing getting your bottom kicked by St Helens to the tune of 46–12, but it's another when it comes to playing at home to low placed Huddersfield and getting another hiding. To put it mildly, the Warriors were shocking, poor defence, bad handling and a lack of enthusiasm that left their coach Brian Noble bewildered to say the least. 'It was very flat and we didn't tackle enough,' was his stark response to a performance that had the home crowd booing the team and even singing out that none of them were fit to wear the shirt.

It was embarrassing to watch as Huddersfield ran in three tries in the first half to give Wigan no hope of a comeback even after half time, where the cherry and white faithful crossed their fingers and hoped there would be some sort of response after a lecture from Noble at the break. The fact it didn't materialise proved too hard for many fans who trudged out of the JJB stadium well before the final whistle.

Take nothing away from Huddersfield for they showed real passion and an eagerness to keep the ball alive and send the Warriors defence into a mess of misunderstanding. It was the Giants first away win of the season and they were happy to get the monkey off their backs.

This was a factor that pleased stand in coach Kieron Purtill no end, 'A performance like that has been coming for some weeks, today we showed what a quality side we are and got just reward for all the hard work we've been doing.'

Chris Thorman opened the scoring with a penalty on 10 minutes and the Giants went further ahead when David Hodgson crossed for the first try midway through the first half thanks to a fine grubber kick into the corner from Luke Robinson. Thorman added the extras and one felt the writing was on the wall as Wigan kept dropping the ball in a similar way to the previous week against Saints. Gareth Hock was the worst culprit—he can be a world beater at times yet other times can be the team's own worst enemy. This was going to be a night where it became worse for the talented second rower who man handled the referee Ian Smith with just six minutes remaining of the match. Smith had no alternative but to send him off.

It made little difference to the outcome of the match as the Giants held a 4–30 lead at the time but they were eager for more points and a dejected Wigan side could only look on in horror as Hodgson went over for his second of the night just before the hooter sounded. Hock dropped the ball that allowed Paul Whatuira to scoot in for an easy try on 30 minutes and eight minutes later the Giants added another from Darrell Griffin. He finally scored after Aspinwall had snapped up another dropped ball, this time from George Carmont and raced away 60 metres to leave them in a good position for Stuart Jones to give Griffin his chance. It left a dejected home crowd furious as Wigan left the field for half time 0–18 down.

Coach Brian Noble has the knack of bringing out the best of his charges when in trouble at the break but on this occasion nothing was going to work. When Barrett dropped the ball from the Giants' kick off you suspected this was not going to be Wigan's night. Soon after Lolesi threw a dummy and strolled over for Huddersfield's fourth try of the evening. Number five followed soon after Hudson picked up yet another loose ball and crossed for yet another gift try that left the home side with their heads held low in shame and looking like an outfit willing the full time whistle to sound.

Midway through the second stanza Pat Richards did get Wigan on the board but even his goal kicking talent failed to convert but it was mere consolation for the home side. Then came the bizarre incident with the referee and Hock, who had been declared to have failed to ground the ball after Higham had set him up to dive over. It proved to be too much for the excited Great Britain star and he pursued the man with the whistle and pulled him back! Ian Smith quickly pulled out the red card and sent Hock to the dressing rooms. It was the final act of a player who showed the entire team's frustration at being outplayed and it was fitting that Noble stated afterwards that he could, 'Understand the fans' frustrations.'

Not that Huddersfield were worried over the incident for they played the Warriors off the park and it was a wonderful performance from Luke Robinson, one of five former Wigan players playing for the Giants who stole the show against a poor home side. Noble has plenty of work to do before Wigan can think of a play-off spot but he's done it in the past so don't write them off yet.

Friday 13 June 2008

Kick off: 19.30, Venue: GPW Recruitment Stadium, Att: 9,009, Match official: R Silverwood

St Helens (22) 58
T: S Tyrer 1, L Pryce 1, J Graham 1, B Hargreaves 3, J Wilkin 2, J Roby 1, M Fa'asavalu 1 **G:** S Long 9

Bradford (14) 20
T: D Halley 1, S Tadulala 1, P Sykes 1, I Harris 1 **G:** P Sykes 2

St Helens squad
Wellens, Gardner, Tyrer, Talau, Meli, Pryce, Long, Graham, Cunningham, Hargreaves, Gilmour, Wilkin, Sculthorpe
Replacements: Roby, Clough, Fa'asavalu, Thompson

Bradford squad
Platt, Halley, Evans, Hape, Tadulala, Sykes, Jeffries, Vagana, Harris, Kopczak, Solomona, Finnigan, Langley
Replacements: Feather, Cook, James, Carlile

The London result on Saturday was welcome news for the Saints who the night before had ripped a brave Bradford side apart late in the game, just like they had done the week before against Hull KR. It was magical stuff from the red and whites who slowly but surely dragged themselves back into the match after the Bulls had taken a 0–8 lead and were in charge in the opening 20 minutes or so. Bradford's coach Steve McNamara had been buoyed by the fact the club had made it clear his job was not under threat and he wouldn't become the fourth coach to leave Super League in the past four weeks. Their support was well founded as the visitors gave Saints a lesson in fine open play and with Solomona once again producing magical off loading skills it appeared an upset could be on the cards. Injury problems had forced the Bulls coach to stick Iestyn Harris into the hooking role and Paul Sykes into stand off. It worked a treat as both showed fine skills and it was no surprise when Tadulala picked up the first score via the video referee, who was to work overtime in the opening stanza. Paul Sykes' effort again had to be referred upstairs and he got the nod which took Bradford into a 0–8 lead leaving Saints bewildered. Maurie Fa'asavalu lifted the home side's spirits with another charging run to twist in the tackle and get the ball down, allowing Long an easy conversion to bring the deficit back to just two points. The Bulls were not overawed by the big forward's effort and when Iestyn Harris stole the ball from Sean Long near the Saints line to send Matt Cook close, the hooker silenced the home crowd with some neat play. Harris barged over from dummy-half and appeared to have been pulled up short of the line but the gods were smiling and again the video referee, after a long deliberation and many replays, awarded a try. At 6–14 the look on coach Daniel Anderson's face was like thunder and nobody needed a replay to realise he was far from happy with his side's defence. The response from the Saints outfit was superb, they scored three tries in nine minutes to turn the match. Jon Wilkin set off with a fine try, soon followed by Steve Tyrer who had been drafted in in the absence of Matt Gidley and when James Graham busted under the posts the home fans were in good voice. The sides went to the dressing sheds with a score line of 22–14. Graham's score just before the break left Bradford clutching at straws and looking a little tired. It was no surprise when Saints blitzed them late in the second half, not helped by Simon Finnigan's 10 minutes in the sin-bin.

Wilkin grabbed his second try soon after the restart and the result was never in any doubt. Leon Pryce was in outstanding form and produced a fantastic display of power and even worked hard as a make-shift forward, getting over the advantage line time and time again. His man of the match performance was run close by prop Bryn Hargreaves who after scoring his first try for the club on 59 minutes went on to complete his hat trick. 'They came along just like busses,' he quipped after the match obviously delighted. So was the home side's boss Anderson who witnessed yet another classic display of power and skill late in the game. Wilkin, Roby, Hargreaves (3) and Pryce completed the second half score sheet for the Saints. The only bright spark for Bradford was Dave Halley's neat try. To be fair to Bradford the score line didn't show the hard work and effort they brought to the match and only emphasised the quality of the home side these days. Again the Bulls were the villains of the match as they gave away too many penalties leaving their coach with a huge problem. 'Saints were good, and on the back of 19 penalties they were even better, we had our chance at 28–20 when we made that break from Hape on the left hand side, the game was still in the balance,' claimed McNamara. The result left no doubt the

clash in the next round with Leeds at Headingley would be a cracker and ensure the 'Full House' signs were put up.

Kick off: 17.00, Venue: Twickenham Stoop, Att: 3,769, Match official: A Klein

Harlequins (14) 28
T: W Sharp 2, S Hill 1, C Randall 1
G: H Paul 7

Leeds (12) 24
T: K Senior 1, S Donald 2, R Burrow 2, J Peacock 1 **G:** K Sinfield 2

Harlequins squad
Melling, Bryan, Clubb, Howell, Sharp, Hill, Orr, Temata, Randall, Ward, Worrincy, Paul, Mbu
Replacements: McCarthy-Scarsbrook, Rinaldi, Haggerty, Janowski

Leeds squad
Webb, Smith, Ablett, Senior, Donald, McGuire, Burrow, Leuluai, Diskin, Bailey, Ellis, Peacock, Sinfield
Replacements: Tansey, Worrall, Scruton, Jones-Buchanan

The big question was still doing the rounds as to who could stop Leeds from racing away with the League Leader's Shield? Many thought that not even hot shots St Helens could catch the Rhinos who had been magnificent all season. Not many gave Harlequins much hope when they took on the league leaders on a sunny Saturday evening. Naturally, a coach will always give his charges a chance, but not even Brian McDermott could have wished for a better performance that was to crush the Super League Champions and the best club in the world. With so many injuries, McDermott brought in two debutants in Lamont Bryan and Adam Janowski, the latter not even listed in the first team squad! To say it was one of the London club's finest hours was an understatement as the crowd went wild watching a see-saw match that was charged with energy and tension. With barely five minutes gone, Jamie Peacock strolled over some weak defence to score a try. At this point most people sat back and wondered, 'By how many?'

Maybe the Leeds players thought the result was a foregone conclusion too and eased off but it didn't faze Scott Hill who soon after Peacock's effort sent David Howell racing down the left wing to allow winger Will Sharp in for his first try for the club. Little did they know that late in the second half that Sharp's second try would seal the Rhinos' fate. Leeds tried hard to regain their confident mood but Quins' defence was in top form. Not surprisingly Scott Hill again took the London side into the lead. His grubber kick into the in goal enabled them to regain possession and from it the former Australian star ducked under defenders to touch down and take a 12–6 lead. The visitors hit back midway through the first half when Danny McGuire broke free and sent in Rob Burrow who showed amazing speed to go under the posts.
Unfortunately the video referee ruled there had been an obstruction by Sinfield and turned down the try much to the disgust of Rhinos' fans for it was a close call.

Henry Paul added another penalty to his two conversions and with the score line at 14–6, the chance of an upset suddenly sprang to mind. Yet in-form winger Scott Donald had other ideas when he crossed out wide from a superb Burrow pass that had debutant Lamont Bryan grasping at thin air. Sinfield's superb touchline conversion dragged the visitors back into the match 14–12 and left coach Brian McClennan a touch more happy when he spoke to his team at the break. The method of catching Harlequins out wide left the crowd wondering if off-form Leeds would find their straps for the second stanza and start playing their open, fast, wide flowing football that has seen them demolish so many sides.

The answer was soon to come only it was nothing for the travelling fans to cheer about. Despite a more up beat, defensive set by Leeds, a smart dummy and dive took hooker Chad Randall over the whitewash and stretched the lead to 20–12 sending the Rhinos into panic mode. With 20 minutes to go, Keith Senior continued his super form this year with a block-busting charge to reduce the deficit to 20–16 and even when Sinfield hit the post with his conversion attempt one wondered when the home side would fall in a heap, for Leeds were beginning to regain their touch. With the clock ticking towards the final quarter it appeared Harlequins had settled for hanging in and defending for their lives and when Ellis broke clear it looked as though the tide had turned but the big second rower dropped the ball and the chance had gone. Tempers were beginning to fray and, as anticipated, a good old fashioned bust up saw Senior and McCarthy-Scarsbrook sent to the sin-bin for fighting, a factor that seemed to upset Leeds more than the Quins. Henry Paul again extended the advantage to 22–16 with a solid long range penalty goal but it was just seconds later that the home side, steered magnificently by Scott Hill, grabbed what turned out to be the winning score. Hill's neat grubber kick into the corner allowed winger Will Sharp to touch down for his brace and left a dejected group of Champions looking at each other for guidance. Paul added even more pain with a magical touchline kick to see his side go 28–16 up. Full credit went to the Rhinos for trying their best to snatch the game. When Burrow crossed with eight minutes remaining, nerves started to jangle and one's mind went back to that last gasp win over the Quins a few weeks previously in the Challenge Cup. But it wasn't to be, even when Scott Donald grabbed his second three minutes from time, as Kevin Sinfield failed to add the extras to their two late tries. Harlequins deserved to hang on despite Leeds scoring five tries to four but the kicking of Henry Paul's six from six proved decisive.

Brian McDermott was lost for words and could only splutter some sort of thanks for his guys' effort although he later heaped praise on his experienced players like Paul, Hill and Randall who all had fine games. The other Brian, Leeds coach, McClennan had no excuses and even thought late on they could have snatched it just like they did in the challenge cup game. 'I thought our half backs were outplayed and that proved vital.'

Player of Round 17

Scott Hill, Harlequins

Hill put Leeds to the sword, creative with ball in hand he demonstrated fine passing skills and scored a neat try.

Saturday 14 June 2008

Kick off: 19.00, Venue: Stade Gilbert Brutus, Att: 9,125,
Match official: I Smith

Catalans (14) 45
T: C Greenshields 3, J Wilson 1, S Raguin 1, A Mogg 1, O Elima 1
G: T Bosc 8 **DG:** A Mogg 1

Wigan (18) 38
T: C Phelps 1, G Carmont 1, P Richards 1, A Coley 1, I Palea'aesina 1, J Tomkins 1 **G:** P Richards 7

Catalans squad
Greenshields, Stacul, Wilson, Raguin, Pelo, Mogg, Bosc, Chan, McGuire, Guisset, Croker, Mounis, Carlaw
Replacements: Elima, Duport, Fakir, Casty

Wigan squad
Mathers, Colbon, Phelps, Carmont, Richards, Barrett, Leuluai, Fielden, Higham, Coley, Hock, Bailey, Hansen
Replacements: McIlorum, Prescott, Palea'aesina, J Tomkins

When the third and fourth sides in the Engage Super League table clash, one expects plenty of points scored and at the Stade Gilbert Brutus in Perpignan the fans were not disappointed. A 45–38 score line is good value for money and the crowd of more than 9,000 enjoyed every minute of it. Not even the Wigan fans who had travelled to the South of France could complain about the standard on display. The home side fought back after Pat Richards set the scoreboard ticking 10 minutes into the game with a controversial try to put Wigan in front but the lead was short lived when John Wilson scored under the posts shortly after to make it all square at 6–6. A Bosc penalty put Catalans ahead 8–6 but the Warriors were rewarded from Trent Barrett's perfectly timed pass to Joel Tomkins which sent him over to regain the lead despite the home side dominating in the forwards both in defence and attack. Clint Greenshields' try off Thomas Bosc's pass made it 14–12 and one soon realised the chaps on the scoreboard would earn their money big time. But Wigan were not to be outdone and seven minutes from the break George Carmont latched onto a fine kick from Barrett which allowed Pat Richards to convert and go in at the break 14–18 in front.

Catalans fans must have been puzzled at the score line as they bossed most of the first half but Wigan found holes down the left side of the French defence. A late challenge on Fakir just before the hooter resulted in a punch-up which left the crowd buzzing as both sides took to the sheds. Four minutes into the second half Olivier Elima crossed to make the lead change yet again, Bosc's conversion taking them 20–18 ahead, only for Richards to tie it up again with a long range penalty. Neither side could break clear of each other but Catalans were looking dangerous and when Mogg and Greenshields touched down it looked likely that they would race away with the match. Bosc added both conversions to make it 32–20 going into the final quarter. The skills of Adam Mogg were teasing Wigan, he created three tries and scored one try to pick up the man of the match award but the Warriors were not done yet. Andy Coley's try for Wigan after a neat pass from Palea'aesina set the alarm bells ringing at 32–26 and 13 minutes remaining.

Again Catalans put together a brace of four pointers to put the brakes on Wigan's fight back. Raguin and Greenshields' converted touchdowns gave them what surely was a winning margin at 44–26 but the substitute Palea'aesina crossed to give Wigan some hope with just six minutes left. But the home side hero Adam Mogg topped off a fine match with a field goal soon after to seal the victory. A consolation try just before the hooter by Wigan debut sub Cameron Phelps finished off a fine display of open rugby league but it was Catalans' day. It was an amazing game where both goal kickers were on target throughout, Thomas Bosc kicking eight from eight whilst Richards slotted over seven from seven.

Sunday 15 June 2008

Kick off: 15.00, Venue: Halliwell Jones Stadium, Att: 9,095, Match official: B Thaler

Warrington (16) 38
T: C Riley 1, Martin Gleeson 1, L Briers 2, P Rauhihi 1, B Westwood 1, B Harrison 1
G: C Hicks 5

Hull KR (14) 20
T: S Briscoe 1, P Fox 1, B Fisher 1, C Chester 1 **G:** P Cooke 2

Warrington squad
Hicks, Riley, Martin Gleeson, Grix, King, Briers, Monaghan, Morley, Clarke, Rauhihi, L Anderson, Westwood, V Anderson
Replacements: Mark Gleeson, Parker, Bracek, Harrison

Hull KR squad
Briscoe, Fox, Cockayne, Jake Webster, Fitzhenry, Cooke, Dobson, Mills, Fisher, Vella, J Netherton, Lovegrove, Chester
Replacements: Crossman, K Netherton, Watts, Welham

Winning is everything! That's the difference between holding down a job and lifting some silverware or getting your marching orders. Not that Warrington's caretaker coach James Lowes was thinking of silverware but he certainly knew his two wins in charge following his side's victory over an out of form Hull KR wouldn't automatically give him the coach's mantle for the rest of the season. There's plenty of time remaining for him to push for an extension to next year and beyond but he realised his side still needed a big improvement. 'There's still work to be done but I'm just enjoying working with the boys. Nothing's been decided yet,' he added but the Warrington board were quite happy to hand him the job for the rest of the year a day later.

Like previous coach Paul Cullen, Lowes knew only too well that if Lee Briers was in form, so were the rest of the lads. So it proved with the half back showing flair and skills to create the chances for Warrington to score seven tries, two for himself in the second half against a makeshift outfit from the East coast whose coach Justin Morgan struggled to find 15 fit men. Rovers tried hard but lack of ball control and poor defence at times enabled the Wolves to take charge late in the match, but it could have been different if the visitors had built on their 6–10 lead halfway through the first stanza. Against the run of play Paul Cooke and Ben Fisher crossed to wipe out the early effort from Westwood but they couldn't hold onto the ball at crucial moments and it took some outstanding handling to give Warrington the lead again. Jon Clarke started the run, Monaghan, Briers and Anderson supported and centre Martin Gleeson sent the home fans wild with a great team try to level the scores. Briscoe swung the game Hull KR's way on 30 minutes to 10–14 and could have extended even more but referee Ben Thaler brought winger Fox back for a knock-on and disallowed the try. Warrington bounced back with a solid try from Ben Harrison who crossed out wide from Monaghan's pass. Hicks' conversion gave Warrington a shallow lead of 16–14 at the break. It was all Warrington in the second half as first Rauhihi, then Riley and Briers (2) wrapped up the match. Peter Fox scored on the bell for a consolation touchdown but it was all over soon after the restart as Wolves took advantage of some poor defence from Rovers. 'It was a poor display from us in the second half, we were confident at half time,' said Rovers' boss Justin Morgan. It must have been

Lee Briers added two tries in Warrington's defeat of Hull KR.

sweet dreams for coach Lowes who no doubt enjoyed the telephone call the following day telling him he had been given the chance to stake his long term future at the club.

Sunday 15 June 2008

Kick off: 15.15, Venue: The KC Stadium, Att: 12,681, Match official: P Bentham

Hull FC (18) 40
T: K Yeaman 2, T Briscoe 1, C Hall 3
G: D Tickle 8

Castleford (8) 14
T: C Huby 1, N Catic 1 **G:** K Dixon 3

Hull FC squad
Byrne, Sing, G Horne, Yeaman, Briscoe, Washbrook, Dykes, Dowes, Berrigan, Carvell, Manu, Tickle, Radford
Replacements: Thackray, Houghton, Wheeldon, Hall

Castleford squad
Donlan, Dixon, Shenton, McGoldrick, Wainwright, Dorn, Sherwin, Higgins, Moore, Huby, Catic, Lupton, Westerman
Replacements: Henderson, Clayton, Boyle, Owen

New Hull FC coach Richard Agar observed an improved performance from his team.

Another young British coach was enjoying his day in the sun—Hull FC's Richard Agar must have enjoyed their 40–14 mauling of the Tigers. Hull's effort over the previous two weeks must have impressed Agar, as the team had won a Challenge Cup victory over Bradford followed by a great battle against Leeds a week later. Agar's team must have felt confident playing a side that had let in over 500 points.

Again the home side took control in the second half after Castleford went toe to toe with the black and whites in the opening half hour. Castleford looked the more dangerous in the opening 10 but Hull set the scoreboard going when winger Tom Briscoe scored after Hull's first real attacking move. Tickle and Dixon shared penalties to make it 8–2 until Wainwright's take of Sherwin's neat chip over allowed him to off load to Craig Huby who crashed over. Dixon's

conversion tied it up at 8–8 yet Hull ended the first half in charge after Craig Hall and Kirk Yeaman scored in the last 10 minutes to leave them 18–8 in front.

Four minutes after the restart, Ned Catic gave the visitors much hope when he crossed from another great Sherwin pass. Sherwin's battle with Adam Dykes was a treat to watch. At 18–14 Hull looked worried but a penalty goal from Tickle settled the nerves and when Craig Hall got his second of the match the home side started to pull away. Even when Hull went to 12 men after Carvell was shown the yellow card for a late tackle on Sherwin, Hull extended the lead. Hall completed his hat trick and Yeaman finished it off.

The Hull coach was happy to get his first Super League win in charge, 'We have lacked a little ability to score this year but it's gradually starting to happen for us.' Terry Matterson was keeping a brave face, 'Our last plays didn't help, we were chasing the game towards the end.' Would the magic of Agar continue to send Hull towards the play-offs? On this showing the answer was yes, although at seven points behind Wakefield (in sixth place) it still left the black and whites with plenty to do.

A bad tempered Wakefield v Huddersfield game erupted into a brawl.

Sunday 15 June 2008

Kick off: 15.30, Venue: Belle Vue,
Att: 6,271, Match official: S Ganson

Wakefield (18) 28
T: S Grix 1, J Rooney 2, J Demetriou 1,
K Henderson 1
G: J Rooney 1, D Brough 3

Huddersfield (8) 26
T: D Griffin 1, J Skandalis 1, J Lolesi 1,
E Crabtree 1 **G:** C Thorman 5

Wakefield squad
Blaymire, Grix, Gleeson, Atkins, Blanch,
Rooney, Brough, Wilkes, Obst, Bibey,
Golden, MacGillivray, Sculthorpe
Replacements: Moore, Drew, Demetriou,
Henderson

Huddersfield squad
Cudjoe, Aspinwall, Brown, Whatuira,
Elford, Thorman, Robinson, Griffin,
Hudson, Skandalis, Wild, Lolesi, Raleigh
Replacements: Jackson, Crabtree,
Kirmond, Jensen

A rough and tough encounter unfolded at Belle Vue as the Wildcats entertained the Huddersfield Giants who came late with a three-try burst but failed by two points 28–26 to take the spoils. Huddersfield angered the home fans with their style of defence and Kevin Brown was put on report for a spear tackle on Danny Brough, which incensed coach John Kear, 'The tackle on Brough was a disgrace.'

Not surprisingly things flared up soon after when Danny Sculthorpe and Darrell Griffin clashed enough to offer referee Steve Ganson the chance to brandish the yellow card to both but it didn't prevent more trouble throughout the match. Half way through the first half Jamahl Lolesi scored a try to pull back Wakefield's early lead from Rooney's penalty goal. When Thorman converted things quietened down somewhat although the defences were eager to get to grips with each other and another penalty from Thorman extended Huddersfield's lead to 2–8. Two minutes later came the try of the match as Rooney, who was outstanding for the full game, sidestepped his way through and arced towards the line for a classic touchdown. He failed with the extras, although a Scott Grix try took them in front 12–8 after Thorman was sin-binned for dissent and that's how it should have stayed at half time, but referee Ganson failed to hear the half time hooter and a play the ball later Jamie Rooney crossed for his second controversial try. Brough who had returned from the early knock converted to the sound of loud booing from the Giants fans and left the field 18–8 up.

Giants' caretaker coach Kieron Purtill admitted he didn't hear the hooter either, 'I was on my way down from the gantry at the time and the lads didn't mention it at half time.' The amazing

Ryan Atkins tries to sprint clear of the Huddersfield defence.

recovery from Brough stunned the crowd, he had been stretchered off after the Brown tackle and expected not to return. He returned late in that first half to put in the kick that created Grix's try and added the extras from Rooney's post-hooter effort. Brough again stretched the lead when he was instrumental in sending Kevin Henderson over to make it 24–8 after he added the extra two. It looked all over for the visitors yet a late flourish made Wakefield nervous.

Eorl Crabtree got the ball rolling with his try on 50 minutes to bring the score to 24–14 when Thorman converted. Jason Demetriou's try soon after looked to have sealed an easy win for the Wildcats, especially when Luke Robinson offered unwise words to the referee that earned him a red card and left Huddersfield down to 12 men with 20 minutes remaining. The home side were expected to run riot but it was the other way around as Skandalis and Griffin crossed for converted tries to make it a

breathtaking final 10 minutes. Wakefield held on against some fierce attacks and were more than pleased at taking the two league points that put them back into the top six. Not that the Giants fans left with a smile on their face—they trudged out still complaining about the referee not hearing the half time hooter. It was a costly error for them.

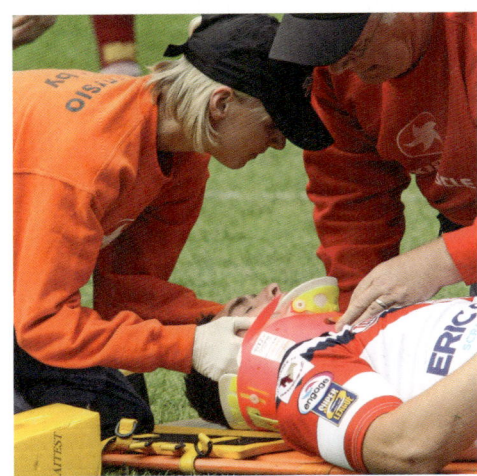

Danny Brough was on the receiving end of some rough tackling.

engage
Mutual Assurance

Friday 20 June 2008

Kick off: 19.30, Venue: Headingley, Att: 18,303, Match official: S Ganson

Leeds (6) 12
T: S Donald 1, K Sinfield 1
G: K Sinfield 2

St Helens (10) 26
T: F Meli 2, L Pryce 1, B Hargreaves 1, M Fa'asavalu 1 **G:** S Long 3

Leeds squad
Webb, Smith, Ellis, Senior, Donald, McGuire, Burrow, Leuluai, Diskin, Bailey, Peacock, Ablett, Sinfield
Replacements: Scruton, Tansey, Burgess, Jones-Buchanan

St Helens squad
Wellens, Gardner, Gidley, Talau, Meli, Pryce, Long, Graham, Cunningham, Hargreaves, Gilmour, Wilkin, Sculthorpe
Replacements: Roby, Clough, Fa'asavalu, Thompson

Just over 18,000 fans crammed into Headingley to see the battle of the big boys, Leeds versus St Helens, and boy what a game it turned out to be! Referee Steve Ganson was again the centre of controversy in the game but it was not his fault as his boss, Stuart Cummins, decided to let him take charge of a game involving his home town club St Helens. Not surprisingly the volatile South Standers were eager to disagree with all his rulings if it went against the home team but Ganson had no hesitation in sending off Nick Scruton for a spear tackle on Keiron Cunningham. Many tried to blame his dismissal on the Rhinos loss but to be fair when Ganson sent him packing 25 minutes into the second half the game was well and truly going Saints' way at 6–14. Francis Meli scored twice within 12 minutes to stretch the lead even

Jamie Peacock evades the tackles of James Graham and Paul Clough.

further and the chance of the Rhinos getting back into the match was minimal.

It was always going to be a tough encounter and several clashes looked ugly especially when Ryan Bailey was put on report for a high shot on Fa'asavalu who had stepped off the bench seconds earlier. The big Saints fellow brought the first try of the game, his power taking him over the top of Webb's tackle to crash over. Sinfield hit back four minutes later to level the scores and with McGuire in super form it looked likely the home side would find even more breaks. Saints' defence held strong and they took the lead again thanks to a bit of fortune when Long's kick hit the padding on the left post and bounced back to give Hargreaves an easy touchdown. Unexpectedly Long put wide an easy conversion attempt but it was enough to send his side in at the break with a 6–10 lead.

With McGuire stepping this way and that throughout the match it was

Leon Pryce is seized by Kevin Sinfield and Brent Webb.

inevitable that his opposite number, Leon Pryce, would lift his game and he sure did by supplying the telling passes for three tries and crossing for the clincher with 10 to go to take Saints to a comfortable 12–24 advantage. This followed a spirited fight-back from Leeds midway through the second stanza that rewarded them with a try for Scott Donald but Saints were in control, especially in the forwards where Graham and Wilkin yet again were a tower of strength. The home fans and players were confused over Mr Ganson awarding the visitors five straight penalties after the restart which certainly helped them secure good field positions. Yet nobody could deny the fact that Saints were playing with great gusto and never rushed or panicked. It was a master class in controlling a match which frustrated Leeds even more late in the game. With four minutes to go Sean Long personified the professional attitude within the team by slotting over a penalty to wrap things up at 12–26.

Daniel Anderson was licking his lips at the way his side performed, 'We are in a good vein of form and our intensity was great.' Leeds' loss left them only two points ahead of Saints in the league table and one wondered what effect it would have when the England squad was selected, both sides knowing that the bulk of their stars would be on international duty next Friday and could leave them light in depth for next weekend's Super League clashes. It was more of a worry for Rhinos' boss Brian McClennan who was surely going to be without Scruton who earned a red card. Also their clash with Castleford would be on Saturday, less than 24 hours after England's match. Saints players would have the extra day to recover before

they hosted an up and down Huddersfield Giants. A lot would depend on how many of the England players would double up for their clubs.

Kick off: 19.00, Venue: Stade Gilbert Brutus, Att: 9,040,
Match official: R Silverwood

Catalans (38) 52
T: J Murphy 2, J Wilson 1, S Raguin 1, Y Khattabi 1, A Mogg 1, T Bosc 1, C McGuire 1, O Elima 1 **G:** T Bosc 8

Warrington (0) 14
T: C Riley 1, P Rauhihi 1, B Westwood 1 **G:** C Hicks 1

Catalans squad
Greenshields, Murphy, Wilson, Raguin, Khattabi, Mogg, Bosc, Chan, McGuire, Fakir, Carlaw, Croker, Mounis
Replacements: Elima, Duport, A Bentley, Casty

Warrington squad
Hicks, Riley, Martin Gleeson, Grix, King, Briers, Monaghan, Morley, Clarke, Rauhihi, L Anderson, Westwood, V Anderson
Replacements: Parker, Bracek, Harrison, Blythe

Warrington's revival was always going to be tested with a trip down to the South of France against a Catalans outfit that has clocked up some huge scores at the Stade Gilbert Brutus this term. The game against Warrington proved to be no exception as Catalans ran out easy winners with a score of 52–14. Nine tries and eight goals from the reliable boot of Thomas Bosc did little to lift the spirits of new Wolves coach James Lowes and I suspect didn't help the players' mood either. To be frank, the home side smashed Warrington in all departments and at 38–0 at half time it would have been a good idea for any fan to have stayed clear of the half time talk in the Warrington dressing room. Dragons' coach Mick Potter had done a great job in expanding his side's ball skills and despite his penchant to playing safety first and slow down tactics when his side were on the road, one couldn't fault his eagerness for his side to play fast open football at home. Playing into a bright sun didn't help Warrington and proved a problem from the kick off. The home side capitalised on this time and time again and as the error count rose, so did the scoreboard. The score was 30–0 before the midway mark of the first half, giving an idea of the power and control Catalans had over their opponents. The numerous travelling Warrington supporters were left with little else to do but enjoy the hot sun, have a few beers and a *jambon* sandwich.

The Warrington supporters did have something to cheer about soon after the restart when Chris Riley made good use of a fine Martin Gleeson pass. Four minutes later Paul Rauhihi gave Warrington a glimmer of hope when he brushed off defenders to cross the line. Sadly Hicks couldn't convert either try so the score stayed at 38–8 until Justin Murphy started the scoreboard working again in the home side's favour. Westwood's try on 66 minutes was just a consolation but it did allow Hicks the chance to get on the score sheet with his only goal of the match. Catalans were not finished and Khattabi and Elima rounded off a fine day for the Dragons who for the third time in succession scored over 40 points on their home ground. They sent out a warning that this outfit would cause more pain to teams chasing a top six spot. They of course were looking for at least a third spot and a home tie in the play-offs.

Kick off: 19.30, Venue: New Craven Park, Att: 8,427, Match official: A Klein

Hull KR (6) 18
T: P Fox 1, M Vella 1, C Newton 1
G: P Cooke 3

Wakefield (4) 26
T: R Atkins 1, D Blanch 1, J Rooney 1, B Drew 2 **G:** D Brough 3

Hull KR squad
Briscoe, Fox, Jake Webster, Cockayre, Fitzhenry, Cooke, Dobson, Vella, Fisher, Mills, Newton, Gene, Chester
Replacements: Crossman, Lovegrove, J Netherton, I'Anson

Wakefield squad
Blaymire, Gleeson, Martin, Atkins, Blanch, Rooney, Brough, Wilkes, Obst, Sculthorpe, Golden, MacGillivray, Demetriou
Replacements: Watene, Drew, Henderson, Moore

The game of rugby league was stunned over the death of former Great Britain captain David Topliss who suffered a heart attack at the age of 58 and it was fitting that Wakefield played Hull KR wearing armbands in memory of one of its favourite sons. It was an amazing comeback by the visitors to Craven Park as they were 18–4 down with just 15 minutes of the match remaining. The Robins had controlled the match until that point. To say Brad Drew was the saviour would be an understatement, for when coach John Kear threw him back into the fray from the bench, the result was a foregone conclusion and two precious league points looked set to go to Hull KR—or did they?

Gene went close early on but lost the ball, and despite the home side having the better of things Wakefield struck first through winger Blanch in a rare excursion into Rovers' ranks but it was obvious that the run of silly penalties would allow Rovers back into the game. Rovers' try eventually came from Clint Newton and a conversion by Paul Cooke on 30 minutes made it 6–4. That's how it stayed at half time but the home side should have made more of the enormous possession they had.

Wakefield were happy to be just two points adrift after the 10–2 penalty count in the first half and were expected to utilise the strong wind after the restart. Yet Hull KR started to play the better football and scored two tries in as many minutes midway through the last half to take a commanding lead, Mick Vella and Peter Fox crossed whilst Cooke added both extras to hold what should have been a winning score line of 18–4. Then in an amazing turn of events, Drew pulled out all the skills in creating a chance close to the line, a quick tap penalty and the Australian crashed over to give Wakefield a slim hope. Brough added the extras to make it 18–10 but needed two more scores to grab an amazing win. With just six minutes to full time Danny Brough sent a long, speedy pass out wide to find Ryan Atkins who crossed in the corner and despite Brough's missed conversion the 18–14 score line looked anything but safe for the Robins. The Wildcats suddenly had the momentum and when Drew produced a fantastic chip over on the right side it found Sean Gleeson in full flight who off loaded to Sam Obst who ran towards the sticks and in a wonderful inside pass found Jamie Rooney who raised his fist in a triumphant manner whilst diving in near the posts. Danny Brough's conversion silenced the stunned home fans who couldn't believe what had happened. Drew wasn't done either, for he produced another burrowing lunge at

the line with seconds to go and picked up his second of the night leaving a smiling Brough to add the two points after the hooter had sounded to finish with an incredible score line of 18–26.

'It was a marvellous last quarter that typifies the group,' said a more than relieved and happy Wakefield coach after the match. Kear was also full of praise for Drew, 'He really had a fantastic last 15 minutes.' Rovers' boss Justin Morgan was stunned to say the least at witnessing such a winning margin clawed back.'At 18–4 we should have put that away, silly penalties and dumb play cost us in the end.' The first half was pretty even despite that lack of control from Wakefield who gave away too many penalties but at least both sides tried to keep the ball alive in poor, wet conditions with a wind that favoured the home side in the first half. It wasn't all gloom and doom in the Rovers camp when 24 hours later their winger Peter Fox was selected for England to take on France in Toulouse. It was a just reward for a player who has given his all over the season.

Kick off: 15.00, Venue: Grattan Stadium, Att: 9,511, Match official: I Smith

Bradford (20) 36
T: P Sykes 1, S Hape 1, S Tadulala 2, T Newton 1, A Lynch 1, M Cook 1
G: I Harris 4

Hull FC (12) 22
T: K Yeaman 2, D Houghton 1, W Manu 1 G: D Tickle 3

Bradford squad
Platt, Halley, Sykes, Hape, Tadulala, Harris, Jeffries, Vagana, Newton, Lynch, Solomona, Burgess, Langley
Replacements: Kopczak, Finnigan, Cook, Evans

Hull FC squad

Hall, Sing, Yeaman, Broughton, Briscoe, Washbrook, Berrigan, Dowes, Houghton, Carvell, Manu, Radford, Tickle
Replacements: Thackray, Dale, Burnett, Wheeldon

'We needed to win...' said Bulls coach Steve McNamara.

Bradford Bulls were back in winning ways with a convincing display over Hull FC to the tune of 36–22. After three losses on the trot these were desperate times for Steve McNamara the Bulls coach and he at least would have gained some confidence knowing that his side had turned the corner. Within the first 15 minutes the home side had clocked up three tries and it looked like plain sailing with the black and whites in all sorts of problems. Andy Lynch started it off by supporting Terry Newton after just three minutes, Harris's conversion proved easy and when Danny Tickle made a right porridge of the kick off, Bradford stormed downfield to score again from Paul Sykes who powered over after good work from David Halley. Harris again added the extras to make it look easy at 12–0. Less than 10 minutes later Newton and Solomona combined to send Tadulala in at the corner, Harris missed this time but at 16–0 the Bulls fans were thinking by how much?

Hull did get some momentum going when Willie Manu kicked forward to enable Danny Houghton to win the race to touch down, Tickle's goal made it 16–6 and any thoughts of a runaway looked doomed. All this happened in the opening 17 minutes, so fans were getting plenty of action for their money although things stayed even until 10 minutes from the break where Newton again supplied the pass for Hape to score an unconverted try to keep the Bulls in charge at 20–6. In swirling, windy conditions the players were offering a treat and Hull would not lie down, eventually rewarded after some great stuff from Berrigan who squeezed in near the corner flag just before half time. Tickle's superb touchline conversion lifted their chances and at 20–12 the visitors were still in with a chance. Man of the moment Semi Tadulala, in good form, grabbed his second eight minutes into the second half and to add to Hull's woes the busy Terry Newton backed up fullback Michael Platt's break to go under the posts. With Harris tagging on his third attempt out of six the Bulls were in a rampaging mood and in control at 30–12. Manu and Yeaman scored consolation four pointers but it was too late to make any difference. Matt Cook made it a day to remember with his try on 72 minutes, Harris added the extra two and left his boss with a smile. 'We needed to win, not for revenge for that Challenge Cup defeat but to find a way to win,' said McNamara. Hull boss Richard Agar still thought he could get some positives out of the game, 'Our senior players were outstanding but we did our best to make up for that 16–0 deficit, it ultimately cost us.'

Kick off: 15.00, Venue: The Galpharm Stadium, Att: 4,176,
Match official: P Bentham

Huddersfield (8) 26
T: M Lawrence 1, S Jones 1, J Lolesi 1
G: T Hemingway 7

Harlequins (10) 16
T: T Clubb 1, M Worrincy 1, K Temata 1
G: H Paul 2

Huddersfield squad
Cudjoe, Aspinwall, Lawrence, Wild, Elford, Whatuira, Hemingway, Skandalis, Jones, Mason, Lolesi, Snitch, Raleigh
Replacements: Crabtree, Jensen, Kirmond, M Brown

Harlequins squad
Melling, Bryan, Clubb, Howell, Sharp, Hill, Orr, McCarthy-Scarsbrook, Randall, Ward, Worrincy, Paul, Mbu
Replacements: Rinaldi, Temata, Haggerty, Heckenburg

With only four wins this season the Giants were eager to take apart the travelling Harlequins to ensure they kept clear of bottom club Castleford who were just three points adrift on the league table. It was a tight struggle in the first half and the Giants went into the break 8–10 down but realising they had played into a gale force wind in the first half, caretaker coach Paul Anderson was not too concerned and realised it would work for them for the last 40. 'Tom Hemingway played the conditions very well and got the team around the park.'

It was praise indeed for the youngster who slotted over seven from seven goals to ensure they took the spoils. He also had a hand in the Giants' first try and won the man of the match award by a country mile. With such a gusty wind swirling around the Galpharm Stadium it was always going to be difficult to play open football and Hemingway's decisions to continue kicking for goal proved to be right. Harlequins started well when Tony Clubb crossed just after five minutes but Henry Paul failed with the conversion but it was enough to overcome Hemingway's earlier penalty and lead 2–4. Michael Lawrence then crossed for an easy try after fullback Chris Melling dropped the ball. Hemingway added the extras and the Giants were in front again 8–4.

Handling became difficult for long periods and it was 23 minutes before the scoreboard ticked over again. Rinaldi's pass looked to have evaded prop Karl Temata but he leaped high to grab the ball and just dropped over the line near the post leaving Henry Paul the easiest of conversions to take the lead 8–10. That's how it stayed until the half time hooter. Another Hemingway penalty soon after the restart levelled the score at 10–10 after his 40/20 put them in a good position downfield and for the next 20 minutes the home side took a grip on the match. Lolesi and Jensen went close, however stubborn defence by the Quins somehow kept them out but on 55 minutes they couldn't stop Jamahl Lolesi crashing over to put Huddersfield in a winning position. Five minutes later the Giants wrapped it up with some fine play from Crabtree that allowed Stuart Jones to race away for the clinching try that was once again converted by the dead eye boot of Hemingway to make it 24–10. Michael Worrincy scored a consolation try before the end but Mr Hemingway finished off in big style by kicking another penalty goal to put the icing on the cake at 26–16.

Sunday 22 June 2008

Kick off: 15.30, Venue: The Jungle, Att: 7,048, Match official: B Thaler

Castleford (14) 22
T: R McGoldrick 1, A Henderson 1, P Lupton 1 **G:** C Huby 5

Wigan (6) 22
T: P Richards 1, T Barrett 1, T Leuluai 1, M Higham 1 **G:** P Richards 3

Castleford squad
McGoldrick, Donlan, Shenton, Owen, Wainwright, Dorn, Sherwin, Higgins, Henderson, Korkidas, Huby, Lupton, Westerman
Replacements: Thackeray, Boyle, Hlad, Catic

Wigan squad
Mathers, Calderwood, Phelps, Carmont, Richards, Barrett, Leuluai, Fielden, Higham, Coley, Bailey, Hansen, J Tomkins
Replacements: Palea'aesina, Colbon, McIlorum, Prescott

Wigan's Iafeta Palea'aesina gives a demonstration of brute force.

Wigan's hopes of staying in the top six would have been lifted by the visit to bottom club Castleford but they knew they couldn't take them too lightly as the boys from the Jungle were keen to add another scalp to their two wins over Leeds and Saints on home soil. Both teams were desperate for a win, and it was evident early on when plenty of errors were on show. But Wigan topped that error table and not surprisingly the Tigers went ahead from a neat kick from Brent Sherwin that put Ryan McGoldrick over near the posts. Craig Huby added the extras leaving Wigan wondering when they could hold onto the ball. Wigan just couldn't get it together and from yet another knock-on the home side drove downfield to allow Andrew Henderson to cross from close range, Huby again popped over the conversion and sent the Tigers fans into a frenzy. No doubt Warriors' coach Brian Noble was frothing at the mouth too as his side looked jaded and lost for ideas until George Carmont, Wigan's best player on the day, combined with Pat Richards who kicked deep into the corner and regathered to give them some hope. The extra two points scored from out wide took the frown off Noble's face for a few minutes at least. Craig Huby kicked a penalty midway through the first half to stretch the lead to 14–6 but despite the Tigers having the glut of possession and position Wigan somehow kept them out with last gasp defensive tackles.

The half time hooter couldn't have come at a better time for Noble's men. The coach tried to inject some fire and pace into his charges in the dressing sheds and it appeared to have worked when

Trent Barrett suddenly burst into action with a fine sidestep to go in under the sticks leaving Richards an easy conversion to make it 14–12. With Sherwin calling the shots Castleford had most of the play for the next 15 minutes but Wigan's defence managed to get back several times to stop what looked like certain tries. Against the run of play, Carmont's run took him close to the line and somehow he managed to off load to Mickey Higham who dived under the sticks to leave Richards with yet another simple two pointer and give them the lead at 14–18. Three minutes later though the Tigers struck back with more neat work from Sherwin, his flick inside pass gave Peter Lupton a chance to dive over. Huby slotted over the conversion to give the home side the lead yet again at 20–18. Amazingly Castleford lost concentration from the kick off, forcing them to drop out from under their own posts and it could have proved costly

when Colbon sent hooker Higham racing towards the line only for referee Thaler to call it a forward pass. Wigan were not going to be stopped a few minutes later when Thomas Leuluai crossed out wide. This proved too much for Richards to add the extras but it was enough to give the Warriors the lead again with just seven minutes left on the clock. Referee Thaler had been given the 'bird' throughout by both sets of fans but the home supporters put him back on their Christmas card list when the merry whistle blower gave a penalty against Wigan for obstruction with just minutes to go to full time. Huby made no mistake in slotting over the ball and tied up the match at 22–22, and that's how it ended with both coaches far from impressed. 'We had little ball and what we did have we dropped,' said Noble. 'We haven't got many points this season so at least we will take one point today,' commented Matterson.

Michael Korkidas drives for the line despite the attentions of Wigan's Paul Prescott.

engage
Mutual Assurance

Friday 27 June 2008

Kick off: 19.30, Venue: JJB Stadium, Att: 11,453, Match official: I Smith

Wigan (18) 38
T: P Richards 1, D Goulding 2, T Leuluai 1, M Higham 1, J Tomkins 1, G Hock 1
G: P Richards 5

Harlequins (16) 20
T: T Clubb 2, J Mbu 1, L McCarthy-Scarsbrook 1 **G:** H Paul 2

Wigan squad
Richards, Calderwood, Goulding, Carmont, Colbon, Barrett, Leuluai, Coley, Higham, Fielden, Hansen, J Tomkins, Hock
Replacements: Palea'aesina, Phelps, Mossop, O'Carroll

Harlequins squad
Melling, O'Callaghan, Clubb, Sharp, Bryan, Hill, Orr, Haggerty, Randall, Ward, Worrincy, Mbu, Paul
Replacements: Heckenburg, Grayshon, Tootill, McCarthy-Scarsbrook

Wigan found themselves at home for the first time in six weeks and looked confident and happy with the new pitch. When Mickey Higham scooted over for a neat solo try it left the fans wondering if this could be the day that Wigan piled up the points. That they did, 38 in fact, but it was a struggle at times and full credit went to Harlequins for taking full advantage of some silly errors in the first half and scoring no less than three tries in the space of 16 minutes. Louie McCarthy-Scarsbrook came off the bench to stun Wigan with his first real touch of the ball to power over, Henry Paul obliged with the extras to tie it up at 6–6 and soon after Joe Mbu latched onto a Scott Hill grubber kick and Wigan looked shaky.

More pain was to come when hooker Randall neatly off loaded to Tony Clubb who brushed aside Hansen's defensive effort to charge over and leave Brian Noble's men with plenty to do at 6–16 down and only seven minutes remaining of the first half. Amazingly, and with a touch of luck, Wigan bounced back with two tries in just three minutes to go into the sheds with a two point lead at 18–16. Thomas Leuluai kicked towards the posts and got the bounce that fooled the Quins defence and fell nicely into Pat Richards' hands to score an easy four pointer. Richards added the two and slotted over the conversion after Trent Barrett's kick found Goulding who in turn slipped an inside ball to Joel Tomkins to fall over the line.

Wigan boss Noble had plenty to say in the dressing rooms and was looking for a vast improvement although he could not have expected such an easy start to the second half where Mbu knocked on from the kick off allowing the position for Gareth Hock to cross from Palea'aesina's pass. He stretched the lead to 24–16 and when Darrell Goulding crossed four minutes later it was all over. Man of the match Thomas Leuluai added another before Goulding grabbed his second to leave Quins 38–16 down with 10 minutes to go, although Tony Clubb's race away try just before the end did little to lift the spirit of coach Brian McDermott who was loath to offer much in the press room after the match. 'We had far too many unforced errors and soft defence,' was about all he could say. It was easy to tell he was far from impressed with his young side who to be fair had little experience between them against a fired up Wigan outfit in the second stanza. Noble was more forthcoming, 'We made it tough for ourselves early and gave away penalties but we showed enough quality in the end and the try just before half time lifted us.'

Saturday 28 June 2008

Kick off: 18.00, Venue: Headingley Carnegie, Att: 17,619, Match official: P Bentham

Leeds (0) 18
T: L Smith 1, B Webb 1, M Diskin 1
G: L Smith 3

Castleford (6) 12
T: R Owen 1, J Westerman 1
G: C Huby 2

Leeds squad
Jones-Bishop, Hall, Jones-Buchanan, Smith, Donald, Allan, Webb, Leuluai, Diskin, Burgess, Lauitiiti, Bailey, Worrall
Replacements: Williams, Kaye, Haley, Chandler

Castleford squad
Donlan, Fletcher, Shenton, Owen, Wainwright, Dorn, Sherwin, Huby, Henderson, Korkidas, Lupton, Catic, McGoldrick
Replacements: Thackeray, Westerman, Higgins, Boyle

Leeds decided to rest all their England players and throw into the fray a bunch of youngsters to take on Castleford at Headingley Carnegie. For most parts the league leaders looked to be heading for a defeat against a spirited Tigers outfit who led by eight points going into the final quarter. The seven England internationals sitting in the stands must have thought the move by coach Brian McClennan was going to turn into disaster because Castleford deserved their lead. It took some magic from experienced players Brent Webb and Matt Diskin to turn the tide, grab two valuable league points and keep the chasing duo of Saints and Catalans at bay.

Matt Diskin, captain for the day, put in his best showing all season and enjoyed the responsibility of urging his young squad to bigger and better things and they responded throughout yet the Tigers looked to have it all sown up. Strong Castleford defence hardly allowed Leeds any room to move and kept them scoreless in the first half, the only try coming from Richard Owen who took advantage of some hard work from Ned Catic who set up Donlan and Dorn to handle before the centre dived over. Huby missed the conversion but added a penalty soon after to give them a 0–6 lead at half time. Joe Westerman again showed plenty of class in taking his side metres from the Rhinos line and after much pressure, the big forward leaped higher than the rest to accept Dorn's high bomb and stretch the lead to 0–10 against a struggling home side. Lee Smith finally got the scoreboard clicking for Leeds on 52 minutes when he crossed in the corner after fine work from youngsters Ben Kaye and Simon Worrall and the home fans started to think all was not lost at 4–10. With Castleford's defence looking shaky it was no surprise when experience came to the fore in Diskin and Webb. Diskin spotted a gap on the blindside and broke clear to off load inside to Brent Webb who crashed over near the posts, Lee Smith obliged with the conversion leaving Castleford hanging on to a two point lead at 10–12. Webb playing at scrum-half suddenly found another gap and repaid Diskin by sending him under the sticks just four minutes later to take the lead for the first time. Smith again popped over an easy conversion to give them a 16–12 lead with just 10 minutes to go. Castleford looked shattered and the heads went down when Lee Smith added a penalty four minutes from the hooter to shut out any chance of the Tigers snatching back the lead and a vital win. McClennan was more than pleased with his younger players. 'Thirteen players came through the Academy system, it's something they'll remember for a long time.' It was an amazing showing from Leeds and proved that the game is in good shape when so many youngsters were available to step up to the plate and handle pressure.

Sunday 29 June 2008

Kick off: 15.00, Venue: Grattan Stadium, Att: 9,741, Match official: B Thaler

Bradford (18) 40
T: M Platt 1, P Sykes 2, S Hape 1, I Harris 1, D Solomona 1, S Finnigan 1
G: I Harris 6

Hull KR (16) 20
T: B Cockayne 1, P Fox 1, M Dobson 1, P Cooke 1 **G:** P Cooke 2

Bradford squad
Platt, Evans, Sykes, Hape, Tadulala, Harris, Jeffries, Vagana, Newton, Lynch, Solomona, Finnigan, Langley
Replacements: Feather, Cook, Burgess, Godwin

Hull KR squad
Cockayne, Fox, Welham, Jake Webster, Fitzhenry, Galea, Dobson, Vella, Fisher, Mills, Gene, Chester, Cooke
Replacements: Crossman, Lovegrove, J Netherton, I'Anson

It was Shontayne Hape's last game for Bradford and a crowd of just under 10,000 bade farewell to a great servant of the Bulls. The New Zealand international didn't let the fans down either, scoring a typical try five minutes from the break to ensure his side went into the dressing rooms with a lead at 18–16. It had been a remarkable fight-back as they stuttered after a good start when David Solomona crossed after just six minutes for a converted try only to be outplayed by the Robins in a purple patch that allowed Hull KR to take control midway through the first half. Three tries in 12 minutes took the wind out of Bradford as Peter Fox the Rovers winger added a try on 14 minutes to go with the one he scored on his debut for England just two days previously, followed by Paul Cooke after 20 minutes and Michael Dobson after 26 minutes. Cooke added the extras to the last two to give them a commanding lead at 6–16.

Paul Cooke was in super form and was playing at loose forward for the first time for the Robins. His distribution was a telling factor on Bradford's defence, who took some time to regroup. When they did regroup Paul Sykes clicked into gear after Stanley Gene made an error from the kick off after Dobson's try. It proved to be costly for it lifted Bradford out of the doldrums and four minutes after Sykes' try it was Mr Hape himself who took the glory. He dived over from close range allowing Harris an easy conversion just before the break and left a stunned Rovers outfit paying the price for too many errors.

What had been a master class from Paul Cooke in the first half turned into a nightmare as the game went on and his influence soon faded as the Bulls started to run riot. Four unanswered tries in the space of 15 minutes broke the back of the tiring Robins as first Finnigan scored, soon followed by a four pointer from Sykes, his second of the game. Harris and Platt took the scoreboard to 40–16 whilst Ben Cockayne added a late consolation try to give coach Justin Morgan something to build on. He was encouraged by what he saw, 'I don't think we had much luck, they worked hard and we kept going until the final whistle.' The trouble is the Rovers can produce some magic at times and then fade away for long periods. What began as a good start to the season looked set to end with a poor position on the league table at the season's end.

Kick off: 15.00, Venue: GPW Recruitment Stadium, Att: 8,597, Match official: A Klein

St Helens (28) 46
T: A Gardner 1, W Talau 2, F Meli 1, S Long 1, K Cunningham 1, J Roby 1, M Fa'asavalu 2 **G:** S Long 4, P Sculthorpe 1

Huddersfield (6) 16
T: T Hemingway 1, S Jones 1, D Kirmond 1 **G:** T Hemingway 2

St Helens squad
Wellens, Gardner, Gidley, Talau, Meli, Eastmond, Long, Graham, Cunningham, Hargreaves, Gilmour, Clough, Sculthorpe Replacements: Wilkin, Roby, Fa'asavalu, Thompson

Huddersfield squad
Hodgson, Aspinwall, Wild, Whatuira, Lawrence, Hemingway, Robinson, Mason, Hudson, Griffin, Jones, Lolesi, Raleigh Replacements: Crabtree, Snitch, Jensen, Kirmond

With England thrashing France 56–8 down in Toulouse most fans of St Helens and Leeds were left wondering how many, if any, of their players would brush up and play for their clubs two days later. Saints opted only to rest Leon Pryce but threw in their other internationals against Huddersfield who perhaps had thoughts of catching the red and whites somewhat weakened. Sadly for the Giants that wasn't going to be the case as the home side blasted them away to the tune of 46–16. Saints again were in top form. They had too much strength and speed for the visitors who time and time again gave away silly penalties, a formula that did little for their health when the likes of Maurie Fa'asavalu started charging through like a wild bull. Not surprisingly the England international displayed some amazing passages of play that left the crowd gasping and wondering how he could have backed up from that torrid match in France two days earlier.

The Giants welcomed back Luke Robinson and Ryan Hudson and were expected to test the home side's resolve but when Keiron Cunningham finally broke the solid early defence midway through the first half it began to look like there was only going to be one winner. Cunningham's bust from dummy-half appeared to blow the wind out of Huddersfield's sails and predictably Saints added another four pointer five minutes later. Meli took advantage of Kyle Eastmond's long pass out wide to stroll over at the corner, and with Huddersfield again giving away penalties it looked like they were going to collapse in a heap. Yet Tom Hemingway took advantage of a stray pass from Gilmour and raced half the length of the field to score and raise their hopes. The try scorer added the extras to make it 10–6. The mistake appeared to have spurred on Saints to lift the momentum and that they did shortly after when man of the match Fa'asavalu stormed over just seconds after coming off the bench. Long slotted over the extra two and when Rod Jensen earned a spell in the sin-bin for a late tackle on Sculthorpe just a minute before it looked likely heads would go down in the Giants ranks and that's what happened. Ade Gardner and Fa'asavalu crossed within a space of one minute to send in the home side in charge at 28–6 on the break.

Acting assistant coach Keiron Purtill needed no explanation for their poor showing, 'If you give Saints that much possession they'll come up with tries.' The second half offered no respite to the Giants as St Helens drove home their superiority, Willie Talau setting it all going again with a smart touchdown. This was followed soon after by tries from Long, Roby and Talau (2) to rattle up a score of 46–6 with still a quarter of the match remaining. It became obvious that the home outfit took their foot of the gas allowing Danny Kirmond and Stuart Jones to touch down in the space of 10 minutes and giving some sort of encouragement for the Giants but it was all over well before the fat lady had even cleared her throat never mind started singing! Saints boss Daniel Anderson again had plenty to smile at, 'We looked sharp in the first 60 minutes and lost a bit of punch in the closing minutes.' Considering their England stars played on Friday night it wasn't surprising they ran out of steam slightly. The race to drag back league leaders Leeds was definitely on the cards despite Anderson saying it didn't matter if they picked up the silver top-of-the-table salver or not, finishing second would fit the bill.

Sunday 29 June 2008

Kick off: 15.15, Venue: The KC Stadium, Att: 11,988, Match official: S Ganson

Hull FC (12) 22
T: J Broughton 1, K Yeaman 1, S Berrigan 2 **G:** D Tickle 3

Warrington (6) 24
T: M King 1, K Penny 2, L Briers 1
G: C Hicks 4

Hull FC squad
Sing, Briscoe, Broughton, Yeaman, Raynor, Washbrook, Dykes, Dowes, Berrigan, Carvell, Manu, Tickle, Radford Replacements: Thackray, Houghton, Wheeldon, Burnett

Warrington squad
Hicks, Riley, Grix, King, Penny, Briers, Monaghan, Parker, Clarke, Rauhihi, L Anderson, Blythe, Harrison Replacements: Morley, Westwood, Cooper, Martin Gleeson

New Warrington coach Jimmy Lowes was pleased his team were now showing some self belief.

The players and fans hold an ovation in memory of former Hull captain David Topliss.

There's been little to get thrilled about at the KC stadium this year and again the Hull FC boys struggled to take the spoils at home. Coach Richard Agar knows they are getting better but a knockout punch from Matt King spoilt the party in the dying seconds when it looked likely the black and whites would hang on for a vital uplifting boost for their confidence.

The home side showed enough in the first half to suggest they are getting back into the groove and when Shaun Berrigan swapped passes with Yeaman to score the home fans were in good voice. Yet five minutes later the home crowd were silenced by the speed of Kevin Penny who may have a few faults in defence but give him a clear run and few in Super League will catch him. Hull's defence never got close as he scorched over from 85 metres to level the scores at 6–6. It set the scene for a bitter battle between two sides that have been in yo-yo mood this season and failed to put together a good showing on a regular basis for the full 80 minutes and this match proved to be no different. Both sides had chances with the final pass

going astray on a far too regular occurrence until Berrigan again crossed on 28 minutes. Tickle added the extras and that's how it stayed up to the break despite Warrington's prop Paul Rauhihi earning a 10 minute sin-binning for dissent, a factor that failed to impress Hull coach Agar, 'We should have had a bigger lead in the first half but our completion rate was poor, seven from 14 tells its own story.' Five minutes into the second half Warrington squared it all up again after good play from hooker Jon Clarke who offered up the ball to Lee Briers to crash over, Hicks added the two and it was game on despite having only 12 men out on the paddock. Hull dug deep and got good field position before Lee Radford found the youngster Jodie Broughton (on loan from Leeds) who took his chance well to give the home side a four point lead at 16–12. Tickle failed with the conversion, a miss that would prove costly.

To their credit, Warrington found some extra energy and after a good kick and chase near the Hull goal line Lee Briers produced an amazing ball steal from Tickle who could only watch Briers' long pass out to the winger Penny in horror. This allowed the speedster to stroll over without a finger touching him, Hicks missed the conversion but he would step up to the plate later and become a hero for the Wolves fans. Hicks and Warrington looked doomed when Raynor latched onto a pass from Matt Sing who had chimed into the backline beautifully to score and when Tickle added the vital two extra points six minutes from time it looked all gloom and doom for the visitors. But, under new coach James Lowes, the Wolves found a little bit of self belief and charged back to overcome the 22–18 deficit. With only seconds remaining the drama unfolded when Monaghan put King over for Warrington to level the scores at 22–22 leaving Chris Hicks to add the conversion and win the match. The hooter sounded before Hicks started his run up and the crowd watched in shock or amazement (depending on who you supported) as the ball flew over the cross-bar for a dramatic win for Warrington.

Lowes was delighted and praised Lee Briers for his effort, 'When Lee plays the ball there's no better half back in the game—he's a fantastic player.' The Hull fans drifted out of the stadium stunned and left wondering if the upcoming Challenge Cup semi final had yet again taken their mind off the job as it was a game they could have won.

Matt King gets over the line in Warrington's win at The KC Stadium.

Kick off: 20.00, Venue: Belle Vue,
Att: 5,479, Match official: A Klein

Wakefield (14) 14
T: S Gleeson 1, D Blanch 1
G: D Brough 3

Catalans (10) 30
T: S Raguin 1, Y Khattabi 2, C McGuire 2
G: T Bosc 5

Wakefield squad
Blaymire, Gleeson, Martin, Atkins,
Blanch, Drew, Brough, Wilkes, Obst,
Moore, Golden, MacGillivray, Demetriou
Replacements: Rooney, Sculthorpe,
Henderson, Bibb

Catalans squad
Greenshields, Murphy, Wilson, Raguin,
Khattabi, Mogg, Bosc, Chan, McGuire,
Elima, Mounis, Fakir, Carlaw
Replacements: Ferriol, Casty, Duport,
Touxagas

Wakefield had to play their home game against Catalans on a Tuesday night because Catalans had no less than eight internationals playing for France the previous Friday and one wondered how the boys from Perpignan could handle the problem of fatigue so soon after a tough encounter against England. The answer that they were going to struggle was borne out by the sluggish start that allowed Wakefield to produce some scintillating play in the opening 20 minutes that blasted the French side away. The Wildcats had the advantage of having 10 days to prepare for this clash and when Sean Gleeson dived over from Brad Drew's cut-out pass, most in the ground expected a bucketful of tries. MacGillivray passed a cream of an off load to set Atkins clear, who in turn sent Damien Blanch over. Nobody would argue at the expectation that the home

Olivier Elima comes in for attention from Oliver Wilkes in Catalans' win at Belle Vue.

side would do well but it proved to be the visitors who would keep the scoreboard man working overtime.

At 10–0 things were rosy as Drew and Brough made a mockery of Catalans' defence by producing top flight rugby be it with ball in hand or boot to ball, yet a huge high bomb turned the game on its head. Wakefield allowed the ball to bounce deep in Catalans' half and what looked like danger for Catalans soon became a problem for Wakefield's defence who allowed Casey McGuire the room to move. Sadly for the Wildcats their defence failed to do just that and allowed the hooker to break clear with a swerving run to avoid poor tackling from Blanch and Blaymire and race under the sticks to bring the score to 10–6. Brough tried to steady the ship with a penalty goal soon after to stretch the lead 12–6. He added another just before the break but not before some more poor defence allowed Younes Khattabi to score and see the visitors only 14–10 down in a half that was dominated by the home side early on. Catalans coach Mick Potter admitted after the game that he was surprised Wakefield hadn't taken them apart in the first 40 minutes, 'We were poor and they should have got more points but we hung in and changed things about in the second half,' and boy what a change it was.

Suddenly the confidence that Brough and Drew were showing in the opening stanza had gone and they opted for words rather than action to try and get back into the match but it never came as players argued with each other and spent more time talking to referee Richard Silverwood. Good, solid, hard work and no frills play from Catalans soon squared the board when Raguin crossed to make it 14–14 and then Younes Khattabi got the nod from the

Casey McGuire evades the Wakefield defence to race in for a try.

video referee for a controversial touchdown on 58 minutes. This upset fans and players alike as Wakefield's Blanch had one turned down in similar circumstances just a few minutes before. What followed was not pretty for Wildcats fans and their coach John Kear who had to witness some feeble defence which allowed the visitors to take charge. Again sheer power and hard work got Catalans another try three minutes later, Casey McGuire, who had a fine game of distribution at dummy-half, sealed it all when Blaymire made a mess of Mogg's kick to cross for his second and easy try. It was an amazing comeback for what should have been a tired outfit but Wakefield looked somewhat dusty and could hardly expect a pat on their backs from either coach Kear or their fans. Kear was far from impressed, 'It was the worst 40 minutes we've played for a long time and that's a concern.' It sure was John!

engage
Mutual Assurance

Friday 4 July 2008

Kick off: 20.00, Venue: JJB Stadium,
Att: 22,000, Match official: A Klein

Wigan (17) 23
T: D Goulding 1, C Phelps 2, L Colbon 1
G: P Richards 3   **DG:** P Richards 1

Leeds (0) 22
T: R Hall 1, G Ellis 1, K Senior 1,
D McGuire 1
G: R Burrow 1, K Sinfield 2

Wigan squad
Richards, Calderwood, Goulding,
Carmont, Phelps, Barrett, Leuluai,
Fielden, Higham, Coley, Hansen,
J Tomkins, Hock
Replacements: Colbon, McIlorum,
O'Carroll, Tuson

Leeds squad
Webb, Hall, Ellis, Senior, Donald,
McGuire, Burrow, Leuluai, Diskin,
Peacock, Jones-Buchanan, Lauitiiti,
Sinfield
Replacements: Bailey, Burgess, Allan,
Smith

They were calling it the best game of the season. And who could argue after watching a thrilling exhibition of rugby league from a Wigan side that bewildered the Leeds outfit in the opening 40 minutes with the Rhinos staging a great fight-back in the second half that set the nerves jangling.

It took just one minute for Wigan to show their intentions of giving the league leaders a scare after good work from Hock sent Pat Richards through a huge gap, Barrett quickly assessed the opening and after receiving the ball stabbed in a kick to the corner for young Aussie winger Cameron Phelps to pounce. Richards slotted over the extras from wide out to send the Warriors' fans wild.

If that wasn't enough, Phelps again scored in the corner through quick hands from Leuluai and Carmont just eight minutes later and one sensed the Rhinos were in deep trouble as they started to drop the ball and give away

Liam Colbon evades the Leeds tacklers as he goes over for a try.

Brent Webb finds his progress halted by Wigan's Trent Barrett.

penalties allowing Wigan to boss the match in the first 20 minutes. Leeds did at last get into some rhythm and had two video decisions turned down when first Ryan Hall and then Matt Diskin looked set to put them on the scoreboard but even those two efforts were against the run of play as the Wigan forwards dominated.

It had taken Stuart Fielden a long time to find some form and whilst he showed patches this term, this was to be his night as he crunched into the opposition with gusto and flair to produce the stuff that made him the best forward in the world three years ago. His 'bust up' with Jamie Peacock early in the game was the spark that ignited him back into action and the look in his eyes made it clear nobody was going to mess about with him on this night. With such dominance

up front it wasn't surprising that Wigan scored their third try, Leuluai's angled kick to the corner was snapped up by Liam Colbon who scrambled over to make it 16–0. Richards failed to add the conversion leaving Leeds with a slim chance to fight back. However, the Warriors' fullback decided to drop a goal with only seconds remaining of the first half to take the tally to 17–0, a move that bemused plenty in the crowd yet proved to be a smart tactic that eventually separated the two sides at full time.

Leeds just didn't have the possession to challenge Wigan's onslaught in the first 40 but rugby league can be a funny game at times and even the cock-a-hoop fans in cherry and white knew that the Rhinos would fight back and that they did. You sensed it wasn't going to be an easy stroll when Matt Diskin had his second attempt at scoring turned down by the video ref again just four minutes into the second half. Not for the first time Rob Burrow provided the inspiration and skills to get the Rhinos back into the match. His 50 metre burst took him past five would be defenders on a swerving run before off loading to Danny McGuire who carried the ball over the extra 10 metres to give Sinfield an easy conversion making it 17–6. But Leeds' hopes were soon shattered when Darrell Goulding crossed shortly after a Richards' penalty to maintain a strong lead at 23–6.

Predictably a few of the visiting fans started to look for the exits but soon turned around when Kylie Leuluai pinched the ball deep inside Wigan's half and from the resulting pressure the Rhinos stand off McGuire produced a neat dummy to break clear and send in Ryan Hall. Unfortunately Sinfield couldn't convert but at 23–10 and 15 minutes remaining the home side looked concerned. And so they should, especially when McGuire broke clear allowing his half back partner Burrow to launch a high kick which Donald palmed back to send in Senior out wide. This time Sinfield hit the target to make it 23–16 and game on.

Sadly the revival looked doomed when Sinfield was taken off with a knee injury shortly after but Leeds showed great resolve to launch yet another attack through the strong running of Ali Lauitiiti. The attack allowed a McGuire pass to bounce neatly into the arms of Gareth Ellis who touched down with nobody near him, Burrow took over the kicking duties and added the extras to leave the match in the balance at 23–22.

With just seconds remaining and Leeds eager to play the ball quickly they received a penalty from referee Ashley Klein after prop Andy Coley was adjudged to have not cleared the ruck, even though he appeared to be injured, leaving Burrow the difficult task of winning the game from 38 metres out. But Burrow's attempt agonisingly veered away at the last moment to slip outside the upright and send the Wigan supporters into a frenzy.

It was a classic encounter, and certainly a game of two halves. Relieved Wigan coach, Brian Noble, spoke after the game, 'They really ripped into us in that second half but we held on.' Leeds boss McClennan wouldn't point the finger at Burrow for missing that last gasp kick, 'It shouldn't have been like that—we could have done better at the start.'

Player of Round 20

Stuart Fielden, Wigan

Glimpses of his world's best tag, Fielden was awesome in defence and grafted like a man possessed.

Saturday 5 July 2008

Kick off: 18.00, Venue: Twickenham Stoop, Att: 4,276,
Match official: B Thaler

Harlequins (0) 0

St Helens (22) 54
T: A Gardner 1, W Talau 1, F Meli 1, L Pryce 1, J Graham 1, J Wilkin 1, J Roby 2, P Clough 1, K Eastmond 1
G: S Long 6, P Sculthorpe 1

Harlequins squad
Sheriffe, Bryan, Purdham, Sharp, O'Callaghan, Rinaldi, Hill, Ward, Randall, Haggerty, Clubb, Worrincy, Paul

Replacements: Heckenburg, Tootill, Grayshon, McCarthy-Scarsbrook

St Helens squad
Wellens, Gardner, Gidley, Talau, Meli, Pryce, Long, Graham, Cunningham, Hargreaves, Sculthorpe, Wilkin, Roby
Replacements: Clough, Fa'asavalu, Eastmond, Thompson

There were rumours that the Saints camp were actually cheering on the Wigan outfit as they watched in their hotel the night before their clash with Harlequins at the Stoop. Nobody within the camp would confirm it but they must surely have realised the loss for Leeds left them needing to beat the London side by 32 points or more to go top of the league table. When Leeds were six points clear in the league table it looked all over but the Saints have taken full advantage of the Rhinos' slump and they were in no mood to be kind to the Quins on a bright clear Saturday night.

Amazingly the home side made the first break when Worrincy raced 40 metres clear from the kick off which appeared to irritate St Helens no end. When Willie Talau barged over after 11 minutes it was obviously going to be a long day at the office for Brian McDermott's men who struggled to get a top side out onto the paddock due to eight of their senior players being injured. Not that it bothered Saints who must have created some kind of record by not giving away one penalty or allowing the opposition to score a point during the full 80 minutes. Saints gave a master class in support play and quick thinking led by the magic tricks of Leon Pryce who on this showing must surely be playing himself into contention for the Man of Steel award. His pace, step and ability to run the angles and then off load was a joy to watch and had his coach Anderson

Leon Pryce displayed his 'magic tricks' as St Helens nilled Harlequins.

purring at his and the team's effort. 'We scored some brilliant tries,' he said which to be fair was an understatement.

Not that the home side didn't try, far from it, but they were outclassed by a side in a rich vein of form which prompted Quins coach Brian McDermott to say, 'They are white hot, and I fear for the rest of the competition.' This was St Helens' 13th straight victory, the bookies have made them odds on favourites for the title and with a 0–54 score line you can see why. The Saints were awesome throughout with Long and Pryce leading the band and leaving the others to play the tune, especially Roby who never stopped running although neither did Quins' skipper Rob Purdham who showed great character.

With such a one sided affair it was hard to pick out the highlight of the game but that fell to Quins' fullback Rikki Sheriffe who stopped a rampaging Maurie Fa'asavalu one metre from the line with the tackle of the season. Sheriffe dumped the big forward to the ground as though a building had collapsed on him! Magic!

Kick off: 12.00, Venue: The Jungle, Att: 7,771, Match official: R Silverwood

Castleford (18) 18
T: M Shenton 1, L Dorn 1, P Lupton 1
G: K Dixon 3

Hull KR (0) 10
T: J Steel 1, M Vella 1 **G:** P Cooke 1

Castleford squad
Donlan, Dixon, Shenton, Owen, Wainwright, Dorn, Sherwin, Higgins, Henderson, Korkidas, Lupton, Westerman, McGoldrick
Replacements: Leafa, Boyle, Moore, Catic

Hull KR squad
Fitzhenry, L Gommersall, Jake Webster, Welham, Steel, Galea, Dobson, Crossman, K Netherton, Mills, Gene, Chester, Cooke
Replacements: Vella, Fisher, Lovegrove, I'Anson

Six defeats on the trot left Hull KR coach Justin Morgan with one huge headache and the loss at the hands of bottom club Castleford must have been hard to take. After such a promising start to the season, Rovers faltered and found it hard to get any sort of combination going. Judging by the way Castleford blasted them in the first half, one wondered if the Tigers could run riot in the final 40. The fact they didn't did little to ease the pressure on the Rovers boss who would have left The Jungle happy over keeping the home side scoreless in the second stanza but still concerned over how poor they were in the first half. Rarely did the Robins threaten the Tigers' defence in the early exchanges and they failed to shut down Brent Sherwin who at long last has found his old form so it was no surprise when the scrum-half produced a neat kick for Luke Dorn to cross early.

Kirk Dixon added the two and Castleford looked confident, so much so that 10 minutes later Michael Shenton scored after Peter Lupton's break from a Sherwin delayed pass. Dixon again found the mark and at 12–0 the Rovers were in a slump yet again.

Peter Lupton added to the visitors' embarrassment when they allowed Sherwin's huge bomb to bounce allowing him an easy score. Dixon obliged again and at 18–0 at the break you wondered how on earth the Robins could stop the rot. The fact they did was down to a good old fashioned look in the mirror to find some pride and that certainly came out after the restart. Paul Cooke at last found some energy and started to combine with Dobson well. Both produced fine kicks to put the Tigers on the backward foot for the first time but a charging run from sub Michael Vella got the ball rolling as he scattered the defence to crash over. Cooke's conversion gave the Robins some hope at 18–6.

Castleford struggled repeatedly to reorganise their defence but they dug deep and worked hard to produce some last ditch tackles. So much so it wasn't until eight minutes from time that Hull KR finally snatched a second try when Michael Dobson's long pass allowed winger Jon Steel to dive in at the corner. The vital conversion proved too difficult for Cooke and the Tigers held on. 'It was a very frustrating performance. Our ball security left a lot to be desired,' claimed Justin Morgan but Castleford coach Terry Matterson was happy for his scrum-half Sherwin who created all three tries. 'He makes things happen and we laid the platform for him today and showed we'll get the best out of him next year.'

Sunday 6 July 2008

Kick off: 15.00, Venue: The Galpharm
Stadium, Att: 10,785,
Match official: S Ganson

Huddersfield (12) 25
T: R Jensen 2, C Thorman 1, P Jackson 1
G: C Thorman 4 **DG:** C Thorman 1

Bradford (16) 24
T: M Platt 1, T Newton 1, A Lynch 1,
S Finnigan 1 **G:** I Harris 4

Huddersfield squad
Cudjoe, Jensen, Lawrence, Whatuira,
Elford, K Brown, Thorman, Mason,
Jones, Raleigh, Wild, Lolesi, Snitch
Replacements: Griffin, Jackson,
Kirmond, Hudson

Bradford squad
Platt, Evans, Sykes, Nero, Tadulala,
Harris, Jeffries, Vagana, Newton, Lynch,
Solomona, Langley, Burgess
Replacements: Halley, Godwin, Finnigan,
Feather

James Evans and Rod Jensen battle in mid air to claim the ball.

Chris Thorman would be the first to say
he is not having the best of seasons yet
his last gasp drop goal was enough to
finish off a Bradford side that left the
game wondering what went wrong after
they held a 12–22 lead at one stage. It
was a scrappy contest and left all the
players frustrated at times, not that the
referee helped, as Mr Ganson sent four
to the sin-bin and sent off Paul Sykes
after the final hooter had sounded.
Bradford coach Steve McNamara was
perplexed over some of the decisions by
the official and so was the Giants'
caretaker coach Paul Anderson who took
a deep breath before announcing, 'I have
to choose my words carefully, but there
were issues.' The Bulls' boss was more
forthcoming. 'What happened out there
wasn't right, I thought it was a
pantomime.' If it was then Mr Ganson
wouldn't go to the ball and Thorman
found the golden slipper as he coolly
dropped the one pointer to add to his
tally of one try and four goals that
snatched the win.

Paul Sykes lost the plot when Ganson
blew for the end of the game whilst
Bradford thought they had set the scrum
down in enough time to at least give
them a last chance to go for a drop goal
themselves. Mr Sykes made it clear to the
man with the whistle that he believed he
had made an error. Such was the
outburst from Sykes it forced the RFL to
send out a letter to all the clubs a week
later to inform them they would not
tolerate such behaviour and they would
punish severely. It would have had little
effect on McNamara's attitude at a time
when his side are going through a horror
patch and they know they are hanging
on to sixth spot by points difference only.

Michael Platt opened the scoring on five minutes but Harris missed the goal and it was the former Welsh star that sent out the pass for Jensen to intercept soon after, Thorman converting to take the lead 6–4, only for the heavily bandaged Terry Newton to swing it back Bradford's way after a fine off load from Solomona. Lynch took the Bulls further ahead only a few minutes after Cudjoe and Hudson had been shown the yellow card and at 6–16 the Bulls looked a good bet only for Paul Jackson to score just before the hooter sounded. Thorman added the two to take them to lemons at 12–16.

Three minutes after the restart James Evans became the third player to take a stint in the sin-bin but Bradford held out under enormous pressure before Simon Finnigan latched onto a huge bomb from Ben Jeffries to race 30 yards to stretch the lead even more. No sooner had Evans returned to the fray, then Ben Jeffries got the yellow card for dissent and was sent to a sin-bin that by this time was getting warmer by the minute!

At this stage things were at boiling point and Thorman started the comeback with a fine try off a Steve Snitch pass. He added the extras to bring it back to 18–22 with 15 minutes to go. Then in an amazing passage of play three incidents were put on report within six minutes, Terry Newton, twice (late challenge, reckless tackle) and Michael Platt (alleged biting). Two minutes from time Rod Jensen crossed after great footwork from Paul Whatuira and when Thorman goaled it looked like the Giants would hold on at 24–22. Yet from the restart Tadulala was held down and Bradford were more than happy to take the two and hopefully settle for a draw until Mr Thorman stepped up to the plate and swung over the one pointer.

Sunday 6 July 2008

Kick off: 15.00, Venue: Halliwell Jones Stadium, Att: 9,290,
Match official: P Bentham

Warrington (34) 60
T: C Riley 2, Martin Gleeson 1, M King 2, K Penny 3, M Monaghan 1, J Clarke 1, S Grix 1 **G:** C Hicks 8

Wakefield (18) 24
T: M Blaymire 1, J Demetriou 1, M Petersen 1, R Moore 1 **G:** D Brough 4

Warrington squad
Hicks, Riley, Martin Gleeson, King, Penny, Briers, Monaghan, Morley, Clarke, Rauhihi, L Anderson, Westwood, V Anderson
Replacements: Cooper, Parker, Grix, Harrison

Wakefield squad
Blaymire, Gleeson, Demetriou, Atkins, Petersen, Drew, Brough, Wilkes, Obst, Moore, Ferres, MacGillivray, Golden
Replacements: Reilly, Sculthorpe, Bibey, Ferguson

The tension of a close game clearly shows on the Huddersfield bench.

When Aussie Michael Monaghan landed on these shores it was all hope and joy that his linking with huge centre Matt King would bring out the best of Warrington and provide the thrust to take them to the top. Early in the season that hope was turning into fruition but then the Wolves hit the wall big time and slumped to such an extent it forced coach Paul Cullen to walk away from the job and leave the fans wondering where it had all gone wrong.

It may be a coincidence that the appointment of caretaker coach James Lowes has helped turn the corner but one can't avoid the fact Mr King and Mr Monaghan have started to click again. And so it proved against Wakefield, a side who appear to be thinking Wembley rather than pulling together, who suffered at the hands of the scrum-half's skills. There was little doubt the dry conditions helped Monaghan find top gear and when King opened the scoring on three minutes, his confidence returned, but Wakefield's new Aussie signing Matt Petersen crossed on his debut to show his worth soon after. The crowd knew this was going to be a high scoring game; 84 points indicated the defences from both sides needed tweaking but for all that, the entertainment value was high with ball in hand.

At 12–12 it looked anyone's game until Chris Riley started a purple patch for the home side where they scored three tries in just over a quarter of an hour, Monaghan and Grix stretching the lead to 28–12. But like many teams, Warrington made a mess of the restart to give Wakefield possession and good field position from which Brough's nice pass sent in fullback Blaymire for a converted try to leave the Wildcats just 10 points adrift. Then with just seconds remaining of the first half Warrington's speecy winger, Kevin Penny, swooped on a loose ball to race the length of the field to score an easy touchdown and leave the task for the Wildcats near impossible.

Nine minutes into the second half Matt King collected his second try to push the lead out to 40–18 ensuring his side would sneak into the fifth spot on the league table. Wakefield tried hard and were rewarded with tries from Brough and Demetriou but were put in the shade by Kevin Penny rounding it all off for Warrington with a hat trick. Mr Penny received a few words of wisdom from boss Lowes who was upset over his 'showboating' when he crossed for his third. 'It's not my sort of thing. I think t's disrespectful to the opposition, he's got to learn.' Lowes has handled the job well and one wonders if he can convince the powers that be at Warrington he's got what it takes to become a top coach? If he keeps winning like this he could just get the nod. Wakefield must be glad they're in with a chance of going to Wembley because on this form any prospect of a play-off spot looks doomed unless John Kear can find that magic touch yet again.

Sunday 6 July 2008

Kick off: 15.15, Venue: The KC Stadium, Att: 11,006, Match official: I Smith

Hull FC (0) 18
T: T Briscoe 1, S Berrigan 1, G Carvell 1
G: D Tickle 3

Catalans (12) 30
T: C Greenshields 1, J Murphy 1, O Elima 1, G Mounis 1, J Fakir 1
G: T Bosc 5

193

Hull FC squad

Sing, Briscoe, Yeaman, G Horne, Raynor, Washbrook, Berrigan, Dowes, Houghton, Carvell, Manu, Tickle, Radford

Replacements: Thackray, Broughton, Wheeldon, Hall

Catalans squad

Greenshields, Murphy, Wilson, Raguin, Khattabi, Mogg, Bosc, Chan, McGuire, Elima, Mounis, Fakir, Carlaw

Replacements: Casty, Ferriol, Touxagas, Quintilla

Ten wins from their last 11 matches is a record any coach would boast about but when it comes from the Catalans you really have to get excited over the transformation this club has gone through in just three years. The French outfit must be sad to lose their coach Mick Potter to St Helens next season for he has turned them into a solid side capable of going on to bigger things. Many thought the trip to Wembley last season was a flash in the pan but they have built on last season so much with such an improvement of their home grown talent that they must have been thinking Old Trafford would not be such a dream anymore. Despite Hull FC's low position in the table, to win at the KC is still a hard task but Catalans displayed great patience to grind out a good victory that left them just one point behind Saints and Leeds in the engage Super League table.

The Dragons opted to stay in England after playing against Wakefield the Tuesday before and it certainly worked to help lift what must have been a tired outfit. Yet on this showing the fitness levels at the club must be huge for they held off a rugged start from the home side to squeeze out a try from Elima on 12 minutes then battled bravely to keep Hull out for the rest of the half whilst adding another touchdown from Justin Murphy just before the break.

Graeme Horne's return to play his 100th game for Hull should have boosted the home sides' chances but it made little difference to their attacking force in the first stanza. However their defence was solid for most of that time, a boost of some sorts for coach Richard Agar who was confident they could get back into the match in the second half. But the optimism was short lived as back to form big forward Jamal Fakir crashed over soon after the restart. Finally Garreth Carvell, who stunned the club by asking for a transfer the day after signing a three year contract, scored a try that sparked Hull into action. When the black and whites' best player Shaun Berrigan crossed for another eight minutes later they found themselves just six points adrift at 12–18.

At last the home crowd found their voice but were soon silenced when Younes Khattabi accepted a long pass from Greenshields to score the visitors' fourth try amidst complaints from the Hull players that it had gone forward. Thomas Bosc, again in fine form, kicked the conversion to add insult to injury as far as the home crowd were concerned. At 12–24 Hull might have been expected to capitulate but they did fight back with a Tom Briscoe try with less than 10 minutes left only to watch man of the match Clint Greenshields seal the win before the hooter sounded to make it a convincing 18–30 result. Mick Potter was impressed with his charges whilst Hull boss Agar admitted they had played erratic football at times, surely knowing his team were out of the frame for a play-off spot with games now running out.

engage
Mutual Assurance

Friday 11 July 2008

Kick off: 19.30, Venue: GPW Recruitment Stadium, Att: 8,430, Match official: P Bentham

St Helens (46) 68
T: A Gardner 1, M Gidley 1, F Meli 2, S Long 1, L Gilmour 1, J Wilkin 1, P Sculthorpe 2, J Roby 1, C Flannery 1, P Clough 1
G: S Long 8, P Sculthorpe 2

Castleford (0) 12
T: K Dixon 1, M Shenton 1
G: K Dixon 2

St Helens squad
Wellens, Gardner, Gidley, Talau, Meli, Pryce, Long, Graham, Cunningham, Hargreaves, Gilmour, Wilkin, Sculthorpe Replacements: Roby, Flannery, Clough, Fa'asavalu

Castleford squad
Donlan, Dixon, Shenton, Owen, Wainwright, McGoldrick, Sherwin, Higgins, Henderson, Korkidas, Catic, Lupton, Westerman
Replacements: Dorn, Leafa, Boyle, Moore

Thirteen wins on the trot didn't prove to be an unlucky number for St Helens who were eager to make it 14 in a row at the expense of visitors Castleford, the side who had inflicted on them their last defeat way back in April. That 30–24 loss stunned the Super League never mind St Helens, but from that day on the Saints had become a formidable outfit that looked invincible. Any thoughts of the Tigers producing another upset was never on the cards after Matt Gidley scored just after the start of the match. This was followed by another seven tries in the first half to leave Castleford reeling at 46–0 as they left for the dressing rooms at half time.

Castleford had no answer to some superb play. Neat passes and sound defence never left any room for the Tigers to enter into the scheme of things as the home outfit simply took them apart. Long, Gilmour, Gardner, Clough, Flannery, Wilkin and Meli blitzed a poor Castleford side with amazing combinations and skills. Saints had good news for their fans too, their chairman Eamon McManus announced before the kick off that the new stadium had been given planning consent and the green light to start building in the not too distant future. The players wanted to turn this game into a celebration and that they did with an outstanding display.

Characteristically, Saints eased back in the second stanza and Castleford showed guts and determination to make some sort of game out of it. Such a commanding lead was hard to overcome although Castleford did score two tries through Dixon and Shenton partly due to some good work from Peter Lupton who tried his best against a strong tide in red and white. One particularly pleasing aspect was Paul Sculthorpe who seems to improve with each game, hopefully at last overcoming his run of serious injuries once and for all. His distribution was reminiscent of his former glory days when he won the Man of Steel twice adding even more pain towards those teams who have to face up to what is becoming such a difficult task—facing the mighty Saints.

There was still a way to go before the end of season party and the champagne corks could start popping but who could match a side that scored over 300 points in their last six games? Coach Anderson was pleased with his team's performance and delighted about the new ground announcement which could make the St Helens club even bigger. 'The club is going to be enormous, it's going to be an inspirational place to work and play.'

Friday 11 July 2008

Kick off: 20.00, Venue: Headingley Carnegie, Att: 14,739,
Match official: T Alibert

Leeds (18) 46
T: B Webb 1, R Hall 2, K Senior 1, S Donald 1, D McGuire 2, J Jones-Buchanan 1 **G:** K Sinfield 7

Huddersfield (2) 8
T: M Aspinwall 1 **G:** C Thorman 2

Leeds squad
Webb, Hall, Toopi, Senior, Donald, McGuire, Burrow, Leuluai, Diskin, Peacock, Jones-Buchanan, Ellis, Sinfield
Replacements: Lauitiiti, Bailey, Burgess, Ablett

Huddersfield squad
Cudjoe, Aspinwall, Elford, Whatuira, Jensen, Robinson, Thorman, Mason, Jones, Raleigh, Snitch, Wild, K Brown
Replacements: Jackson, Griffin, Hudson, Kirmond

It's nearly 50 years since Huddersfield last won at Headingly and on this showing—as the Rhinos ripped the Giants apart—that record could go on for another 50 years yet! A 46–8 score line suggested it was all too easy and at times it looked that way as the Rhinos shrugged themselves out of the lethargic state they've been in for the past few weeks.

A solid win does wonders for the confidence and this victory put them in fine mood for the up coming semi clash with St Helens as the much maligned forwards laid the platform for success. Gareth Ellis showed that his recent stint at centre did little to help the Leeds cause and in moving back to his second row position he was more than just good, he was inspirational as he ripped into the Giants' with great agility. The switch back to his normal position allowed Clinton Toopi to return from an

Ryan Bailey caused problems for the Huddersfield defence.

Danny McGuire touches down as Leeds blitz Huddersfield.

injury he sustained in the World Club Challenge way back in February and he played his part too.

Jamie Jones-Buchanan was another in top form and he blitzed the Giants defence time and time again providing much more off loading skill than we have seen from Leeds for quite some time. He off loaded for Webb to feed Burrow who took it on further to produce the kick that allowed Donald to cross for the first try. McGuire and Jones-Buchanan added two more before the break and at 18–2 it looked like there was no way back for Huddersfield who had taken the lead after just two minutes with a Thorman penalty and which was to prove the Giants only score for 60 minutes. Martin Aspinwall finally crossed the try line going into the final quarter but it was all over soon after the second half got underway when Sinfield's kick confused the Giants defence and they just stood watching as McGuire slid over in waterlogged conditions.

Hall, Webb, Senior and Hall again added more pain to the Giants who looked out of sorts right from the start which left stand in coach Keiron Purtill to comment that they were disappointing. 'It's tough for us; we just have to keep working hard. The only positive is that they didn't get 50.' With the likes of McGuire, Webb and Burrow enjoying the space allowed it was pleasing for coach McClennan who liked what they did in the first half but felt they needed to improve for the full 80. 'The first half went pretty well, the second half was really poor.' Either way Leeds were a much happier side with this solid win under their belts as the race for the engage Super League crown heated up. It looked like it was going to be a tight finish.

Kick off: 20.00, Venue: Halliwell Jones Stadium, Att: 8,158, Match official: B Thaler

Warrington (12) 32
T: C Hicks 1, Martin Gleeson 2, M King 1, L Anderson 1 **G:** C Hicks 6

Bradford (18) 28
T: M Platt 1, C Nero 1, S Tadulala 1, B Jeffries 1, A Lynch 1 **G:** P Deacon 4

Warrington squad
Hicks, Riley, Martin Gleeson, King, Penny, Briers, Monaghan, Morley, Clarke, Rauhihi, L Anderson, Westwood, V Anderson
Replacements: Parker, Grix, Harrison, Cooper

Bradford squad
Platt, Halley, Evans, Nero, Tadulala, Jeffries, Deacon, Vagana, Harris, Lynch, Solomona, Finnigan, Langley
Replacements: Cook, Godwin, Kopczak, Feather

The return of scrum-half Paul Deacon was a huge lift for the Bradford Bulls as they travelled to Warrington eager to keep in touch with the top six. When he converted two early tries from Andy Lynch and Chris Nero within the first 10 minutes it looked likely that the Wolves were back into yo-yo form yet again. Putting together a winning run has been Warrington's problem for most of the year and whilst new coach James Lowes has tightened up the defence in his short tenure, one had to wonder what he could do to get his outfit into the game at 0–12 down.

Centre Martin Gleeson set things into motion, and what a try it turned out to be. He took advantage of a smart break from Matt King deep within his own quarter who off loaded to the supporting Gleeson who showed amazing speed and agility to confuse the defence and then side step Michael Platt and race under the posts to score a 90 yard special. The score livened things up as both sets of forwards charged into each other with gusto. Each side could have scored but for some great defence and Bradford were unlucky to have a try disallowed for obstruction when Kopczak crashed over. It took a high kick from Deacon to set the scoreboard ticking again as his high bomb allowed Semi Tadulala to pinch the ball out of Chris Riley's hands and go in at the corner. Deacon added the extras and the Bulls were once again in charge at 6–18. It should have stayed that way at the break but with just seconds remaining the try scoring hero Tadulala knocked on which gave Warrington the chance to form the scrum just before the hooter. And it came up trumps as Gleeson crossed for his second after good work from Briers at the scrum base allowing Hicks an easy conversion to send them into the changing rooms just six points adrift at 12–18.

The Bulls started the second half with the same enthusiasm as the first where they took an early lead. When Platt took advantage of some poor marking near the line it appeared Bradford would kick on at 12–24. Most coaches will tell you that no side should waste a 12 point lead in the second half but this is Super League and things happen so quickly these days that two converted tries just isn't enough. And so it proved as Warrington slowly started to hit top form courtesy of an error from Dave Halley. This allowed Man of the Match Jon Clarke to be involved twice in a seven man movement that brought a try to Chris Hicks who added the extras. Matt King soon followed with a barging lunge for the line after a quick pass from Monaghan confused the defence; Hicks again added the two to make it all square midway through the second half.

Louis Anderson made it three tries in the space of 10 minutes to put the home side in front for the first time, Hicks made it five from five with the conversion and it was all Warrington from there on in. Bradford struggled to stay with the pace and weren't helped by the sin-binning of David Solomona who was adjudged to have hit Briers late whilst in the act of kicking. Referee Ben Thaler took a touch judge report and showed the big forward the yellow card, a decision that infuriated Bulls boss Steve McNamara. 'I don't blame the ref, it was the touch judge at fault and it's the second week running that an official has done us.' Chris Hicks eagerly kicked the resulting penalty to take James Lowes' men into a 32–24 lead. Bradford did hit back with a try to Ben Jeffries but Deacon was off target and the home side held on to take a victory that secured fourth spot on the table. Coach Lowes refused to be carried away with the result. 'We still have work to do and once we get it right we will become a force.'

Saturday 12 July 2008

Kick off: 18.00, Venue: Belle Vue, Att: 5,379, Match official: R Silverwood

Wakefield (12) 18
T: D Blanch 1, J Rooney 1, B Drew 1
G: D Brough 3

Hull FC (6) 26
T: T Briscoe 1, K Yeaman 1, D Houghton 1, C Hall 2 **G:** D Tickle 3

Wakefield squad
Blaymire, Blanch, Gleeson, Henderson, Petersen, Rooney, Brough, Moore, Drew, Wilkes, Ferres, Golden, Demetriou
Replacements: Bibey, Ferguson, Cbst, Sculthorpe

Hull FC squad
Sing, Briscoe, G Horne, Yeaman, Raynor, Washbrook, Berrigan, Dowes, Houghton, Thackray, Manu, Radford, Tickle
Replacements: Broughton, Hall, Wheeldon, Cusack

The rehearsal for the Challenge Cup semi final never seemed to excite the players and it was clear to everyone that both teams had their eyes on Wembley rather than a run out at Belle Vue stadium. To say this match lacked spice is an understatement as neither side appeared willing to try something different—like hard work for a start! Both coaches agreed the semi was a telling factor and neither would have found much to shout about when watching the replay. Although to be fair to Hull they sparked up in the second half and scored four tries to add to Danny Houghton's early score in the first half.

Houghton's effort was tinged with a slice of luck as his kick forward bounced off the posts to allow him to score. In fact all three tries in the first half came from kicks. Brad Drew stabbed the ball twice before Rooney snapped it up to cross, then when Danny Brough lofted a high kick skywards, the Hull defence allowed it to bounce into the arms of Damien Blanch to give Wakefield a 12–6 lead at the break.

Most in the crowd were hoping for a huge improvement after the restart and were rewarded with the best move of open play in the match so far when six passes gave Kirk Yeaman his chance to cross. Five minutes later another bout of quick hands saw Craig Hall touchdown to give the visitors a 12–16 lead. This extended after yet another kick and dribble produced a try for Tom Briscoe that took the game away from the Wildcats. Tickle had failed to convert the

Gareth Raynor battles with Matthew Petersen for the ball.

two previous tries but slotted over Briscoe's effort to make it 12–26 with just 10 to go. It looked like the game would fizzle out as minds drifted towards Wembley yet again so it was with some surprise that the best moment of the game came near the end when Craig Hall scored an 85 metre solo try to get the visiting fans worked up. It was a fine effort as he took an inside off load from Tom Briscoe who was heading towards the touchline and produced some neat footwork and speed to evade the defence racing in an arc towards the sticks.

Wildcats coach John Kear admitted his side had dropped their standards and it would take a big effort to get them back on track. 'You've got to question our mental fortitude.' Hull boss Richard Agar wasn't too concerned about their play at times and was happy with a win, stating, 'It was a gutsy effort.' Both sides know they will have to improve if they get to Wembley in the last week in

August. Sadly the game didn't live up to expectations especially after both sides paid their respects to the sad loss of Dave Topliss before the match with a fine clapping tribute. Oh how both sides would have loved to have a man of Topliss's pedigree playing today.

Ewan Dowes readies himself for the tackle on Kevin Henderson.

Kick off: 19.00, Venue: Stade Gilbert Brutus, Att: 6,225,
Match official: A Klein

Catalans (14) 32
T: C Greenshields 2, A Chan 1,
C McGuire 1, O Elima 1 **G:** T Bosc 6

Harlequins (0) 26
T: R Sheriffe 1, T Clubb 1, S Hill 1,
L McCarthy-Scarsbrook 1, C Randall 1,
G: R Purdham 3

Catalans squad
Greenshields, Murphy, Wilson, Raguin, Khattabi, Mogg, Bosc, Chan, McGuire, Elima, Croker, Mounis, Carlaw
Replacements: Guisset, Casty, Quintilla, Touxagas

Harlequins squad
Sheriffe, Wells, Clubb, Howell, Sharp, Hill, Orr, McCarthy-Scarsbrook, Randall, Ward, Purdham, Worrincy, Paul
Replacements: Heckenburg, Grayshon, Tootill, Barker

The one thing the English clubs hate is a trip to the South of France at the height of summer. Hot weather and humidity can be a huge advantage for Catalans yet when the Harlequins arrived at the Stade Gilbert Brutus they couldn't believe their eyes as the rain tumbled down leaving the pitch awash with water.

It was a telling factor for both sides who struggled to keep the ball, and at times, their tempers under control, especially after Casey McGuire had sneaked over after 10 minutes to allow Bosc an easy conversion to take a 6–0 lead. A clumsy challenge from Tony Clubb on Younes Khattabi left tempers frayed and the home crowd incensed. Referee Klein did well to restore order but the incident lifted the Dragons who soon made the scoreboard attendant earn his money. This time Alex Chan barged over, not long after Bosc had kicked a penalty goal, and the talented scrum-half had no trouble kicking the conversion to stretch their lead to 14–0, giving them high hopes of an easy win.

Full credit went to the London outfit for digging in before the break although it could have been worse if the video referee had not turned down Justin Murphy's try close to the hooter. What coach Brian McDermott said at half time certainly worked and to everyone's surprise the visitors took the lead through three tries within the first 10 minutes to stun the home fans. Henry Paul's kick gave Scott Hill the chance to post their first score followed by touchdowns from Clubb and Sheriffe, the former taking a length of the field intercept whilst the latter scored a controversial try when it bounced off Hill's chest for what appeared to be a knock-on.

Both sides upped the anti, charging into each other with no fear and again tempers became frayed. Things calmed down a little after a neat pass from Bosc sent in man of the match Clint Greenshields for a converted try. But Catalans just couldn't close the game down and another intercept, this time from Chad Randall, brought the scores level again when Purdham failed to add the extras, leaving the game in the balance at 20–20.

Ten minutes before full time Purdham had the chance to take the lead but his penalty attempt fell short and it stayed that way until Olivier Elima latched onto another Bosc grubber kick to score. When the provider booted over the extra two, Harlequins looked doomed until they were awarded a penalty for obstruction just three minutes from time. McCarthy-Scarsbrook took full advantage of the attacking position to dive over near the posts. Purdham added an easy conversion to bring it level again at 26–26. With only seconds remaining Bosc missed with a field goal attempt but the French outfit knocked on from the deep kick downfield allowing Harlequins to rush to form the scrum and drive towards the posts for a drop goal attempt.

Sadly for the visitors, David Howell got involved with Justin Murphy in a scuffle instead of packing down. This resulted in an all-in brawl as the hooter went. Referee Klein took an age to calm things down and one wondered who would get the penalty. The home side got the nod and instead of putting the ball up the jumper they opted to kick for touch and from the tap Bosc chipped over a stunned Quins defence to give Greenshields the winning try well after the hooter had sounded. Bosc made it six from six for a well earned 32–26 win. The visitors displayed poor defence but full credit went to the home outfit for being inventive despite the rain falling throughout.

Kick off: 15.00, Venue: New Craven Park, Att: 8,481, Match official: I Smith

Hull KR (10) 39
T: J Steel 1, R Lovegrove 1, M Dobson 4, K Netherton 1 **G:** P Cooke 5
DG: M Dobson 1

Wigan (16) 22
T: P Richards 1, G Carmont 2, J Tomkins 1 **G:** P Richards 3

Hull KR squad
Fitzhenry, Steel, Welham, Jake Webster, Lovegrove, Galea, Dobson, Crossman, K Netherton, Mills, Vella, Gene, Cooke
Replacements: I'Anson, Aizue, J Netherton, Fisher

Wigan squad
Richards, Calderwood, Goulding, Carmont, Phelps, Barrett, Leuluai, Fielden, Higham, Coley, Hansen, J Tomkins, Hock
Replacements: McIlorum, Colbon, O'Loughlin, Palea'aesina

Wigan, buoyed by their great win over Leeds the week before, were odds on to put one over on a Rovers side that had lost their last six games. They were almost immediately put on the back foot when Kirk Netherton scored for Rovers after just four minutes. Joel Tomkins replied five minutes later as Wigan clicked into gear after some fine handling and set the scene for a ding-dong battle with the crowd on edge throughout.

George Carmont, yet again in good form, put the visitors in charge when he crossed, giving Richards an easy conversion to go 4–10 up midway through the first stanza, leaving the Robins looking down the barrel of another loss. But to Rovers' credit they clicked into gear with some fine play from scrum-half Michael Dobson who amazingly turned the game on its head in the second half. Carmont chimed in for his second touchdown five minutes from the break to give Wigan a 10–16 lead going into the sheds.

When Pat Richards scored within the first minute of the restart it looked all doom and gloom for the home side with seven regulars still out injured. Surely they couldn't drag themselves back from 10–22 down. Or could they? Rovers coach Justin Morgan had plenty to say to his charges at the break and obviously Mr Dobson realised some drastic action was needed and boy, did he produce the magic to snuff out Wigan's hopes. Six

Jake Webster crosses the try line in Hull KR's win over Wigan.

minutes into the second half Dobson went over for his second try after his shrewd kicking game had forced the visitors back into their own quarter. Four minutes later, another teasing kick from Dobson into the in goal area allowed them the position and possession to send Jon Steel flying in at the corner. Cooke's wonderful touchline conversion put the Rovers level at 22–22 and suddenly the home fans found their voices again.

It was a remarkable turn around and even the most ardent fan couldn't have foreseen such a change in fortunes in the Rovers play and when Dobson scored his hat trick on 60 minutes, Wigan looked tired and shell shocked. The Warriors just couldn't get their hands on the ball as Dobson teased them time and time

again with a kicking display that his coach Morgan rated one of the best he'd seen. Dobson was superb in all departments. So was the old stager Stanley Gene who worked tirelessly all day and proved yet again age is no concern to those who train hard and have a never say die attitude—a factor that Wigan coach Brian Noble was quick to acknowledge. 'We just didn't touch the ball in the second half and Dobson's kicking game was outstanding, I thought he and Stanley Gene were superb.'

It was amazing to see a side like Wigan having to withstand so many consecutive plays; not surprisingly the man of the match cheekily added a drop goal for good measure and scored his fourth try to sink the Warriors without a trace. With such ball control, boss Morgan was happy with the win. 'I'm very proud, we played with a lot of energy and Michael Dobson was outstanding.' The win couldn't have come at a better time considering the injury crisis at the club, although the forced introduction of youngsters like Chaz I'Anson and Kris Welham auger well for the future. This was a great team effort that deserved a victory. Dobson has taken a little while to settle back into Super League and has at times tried to do too much with ball in hand, a factor that perhaps has proved a little negative to his side since his return to the big time. Yet in this game he appeared more relaxed and didn't overplay things and a continuation of this form could well see the Robins sneak into the play-offs.

Player of Round 21

Michael Dobson, Hull KR
Four tries and a field goal gives some indication of Dobson's skills. Amazing in defence and attack.

ROUND 22

engage
Mutual Assurance

Friday 18 July 2008

Kick off: 20.00, Venue: JJB Stadium, Att: 19,958, Match official: A Klein

Wigan (6) 12
T: T Leuluai 1, M Higham 1
G: C Phelps 2

St Helens (22) 46
T: A Gardner 2, M Gidley 1, S Long 1, K Cunningham 1, L Gilmour 1, J Wilkin 1, J Roby 1
G: M Gidley 1, S Long 6

Wigan squad
Mathers, Colbon, Goulding, Carmont, Phelps, Barrett, Leuluai, Fielden, McIlorum, Coley, Hansen, Tomkins, Hock
Replacements: Palea'aesina, O'Carroll, Mossop, Higham

St Helens squad
Wellens, Gardner, Gidley, Talau, Meli, Pryce, Long, Graham, Cunningham, Hargreaves, Gilmour, Wilkin, Sculthorpe
Replacements: Roby, Cayless, Flannery, Fa'asavalu

Wigan fans have been faithful to the cause for many years, despite the fact they've struggled to drag back the glory days when the likes of Edwards, Hanley and Offiah were strutting their stuff. But they turned up in droves despite the weather to encourage the cherry and whites, so it was even more embarrassing to see so many heading towards the exits early when St Helens, their local rivals, thrashed them yet again to the tune of 12–46.

The Saints have put Wigan to the sword three times this term and scored an amazing 149 points! That in itself is enough to turn the fans off but it was a poor performance from the home side and they could hardly blame the sending off of Michael McIlorum for their demise. The young hooker lost his head and his high swinging arm did little to enhance Ade Gardner's looks; referee Ashley Klein had no option but to show

Sean Long races through the gap to score in Saints' defeat of Wigan.

Gareth Hock loses the ball in the tackle.

him the red card. Wigan coach Brian Noble was unimpressed with the decision and stated it left his men with a hard task after just six minutes. 'It's difficult enough to play against Saints with 13 men, never mind with 12.' And so it proved to be the case as St Helens yet again displayed such a high skill factor that they crushed Wigan into submission and offered some great tries that were a pleasure to watch.

At the heart of it all was Sean Long who was here, there and everywhere throughout and steered his side into fantastic field position before unleashing astute passes to create the gaps. It was just reward to Long who was clapped onto the field by his team mates before the kick off as he made his 300th appearance for the red and whites and what a showing it was. Saints' boss Anderson was full of praise for the veteran half back, 'He has a great sense of the big occasion and he played up to that billing tonight…we played well and handled the wet conditions, I can't

remember the last time we played in wind and rain.'

The JJB Stadium could have been six feet underwater but St Helens wouldn't have been stopped in this form. Fifteen straight wins says it all and they must have been confident about going into the semi final of the Challenge Cup next week against Leeds. But whilst the other semi finalists—Hull FC and Wakefield—have been holding back, this Saints outfit were on fire and when Lee Gilmour burst through on two minutes to open the scoring one wondered when the floodgates would open.

The sending off didn't help but Wigan didn't get going and when Fielden lost his temper and gave away a penalty, Cunningham made them pay as he charged over from close range on 11 minutes. From there on in it was the Long show! His short passes created a few chances that amazingly St Helens threw away, Gardner and Meli squandering try opportunities, and when Sculthorpe went off with a hamstring problem half way through the first half one wondered if Wigan could get back into the match. They were helped by the emergence of Palea'aesina from the bench who added some fight to the home side with some strong surges forward which allowed Hock and Leuluai to combine and send the half back over. And when Phelps converted it looked likely the Warriors might start to regain confidence at 6–12. Hopes were soon shattered when James Roby stepped through from dummy-half to put Saints in charge again at 6–18, Long slotting over his third from three on the half hour. This was soon followed by Gardner who scored out wide after Hock had lost possession close to his own line to leave Saints well in charge at the break at 6–22.

More problems were to come in the second half for Wigan who couldn't handle the ball. Another error, this time from Higham's wild pass, gave Wilkin his chance to kick downfield twice and regather for the try that closed out the match at 6–28. A neat kick from Flannery on the short side allowed Gidley to score out wide and Sean Long added to the scoreboard to stick the knife in even further. Gardner grabbed another before Higham went over for a consolation try just before the end but most of the Wigan fans had left the stadium by this time as the travelling Saints fans sang their hearts out content with another thrashing of their closest rivals.

Noble's face said it all and new Wigan chairman, Ian Lenagan, didn't look too happy either but he at least created a historic breakthrough by entertaining the Saints board to a meal after the match, something that hasn't occurred at the Wigan camp for nearly nine years. Not surprisingly the St Helens bosses obliged!

Kick off: 18.00, Venue: The Galpharm Stadium, Att: 5,033,
Match official: R Silverwood

Huddersfield (18) 18
T: L Cudjoe 3 **G:** C Thorman 3

Warrington (6) 19
T: S Grix 1, P Rauhihi 1, B Westwood 1
G: C Hicks 3 **DG:** L Briers 1

Huddersfield squad
Cudjoe, Aspinwall, Brown, Whatuira, Hodgson, Thorman, Robinson, Mason, Hudson, Raleigh, Lolesi, Wild, Kirmond
Replacements: Jones, Jackson, Snitch, Griffin

Warrington squad
Hicks, Riley, Grix, King, Penny, Briers, Monaghan, Morley, Clarke, Rauhihi, Anderson, Westwood, Martin Gleeson
Replacements: Parker, Bracek, Harrison, Cooper

The fortunes of new coach James Lowes took a turn for the best as his Wolves outfit 'pinched' a win at the expense of Huddersfield at The Galpharm Stadium. For the first 40 minutes the Giants had this game wrapped up. Warrington started with centre Gleeson at loose forward in an amazing change of tactics by Lowe and one that he quickly revised after watching the Giants race to a commanding 18–6 lead at the break.

Young fullback Leroy Cudjoe was the star of the show in those first 40 minutes, displaying some amazing skills and field positioning to score a hat trick and set up what should have been a convincing win over the Wolves. Cudjoe's first came after winger Riley fumbled a high Thorman kick which allowed the fullback to stroll over from a Hudson grubber to the corner. His second was more spectacular after some neat quick passing and so was his third which left no doubt the youngster was well in the running for man of the match.

Thankfully for Warrington, Ben Westwood crossed on 30 minutes to give them some hope but at 18–6 down it was going to take plenty words of wisdom from Lowes to shake the Wolves back into action. The former Great Britain hooker admitted to some 'industrial language' in the sheds and gave them the 'haircryer' treatment. This certainly did the trick as Warrington came out looking more determined and soon showed the Giants they were not getting a win handed on a plate. Simon Grix led the way with a strong burst downfield that produced a rugged try a couple of plays later. The big centre handed off both Wild and Cudjoe to charge over and wake the sleeping dog. Chris Hicks slotted over the two extras and suddenly the Giants looked shaky— Warrington sensed it and they started to play a more open style of football with Gleeson starting to get more involved as he'd slipped back into the centre position. Lee Briers suddenly sparked into action, his neat break and pass to Morley sent the skipper racing away. Morley in turn found Rauhihi who charged over the line big time. Hicks converted to bring the scores level at 18–18 with just 30 minutes to go.

Full credit went to Huddersfield for hanging on against the tide and producing some solid defence to keep Warrington at bay. In fact they could have won the game if two controversial video decisions had gone their way. But the luck went to Warrington, borne out by the fact Robinson knocked on under no pressure when looking to go for the drop goal. The Wolves didn't fluff their chance, Briers slotting the one pointer

eight minutes from the hooter to snatch an amazing victory.

Giants' stand in coach Paul Anderson admitted they'd started the game well but faded. 'I give them A for effort but we have to improve a bit in terms of smartness.' Lowes was sure his side would fight back even at 18–6 down. 'I knew we would create some chances, we were slightly off this week but we scraped a win.' There's little doubt Warrington have improved under Lowes and one wondered when or if he would be given the job full time.

Adrian Morley had to rally the team in Warrington's narrow win over Huddersfield.

Kick off: 19.00, Venue: Stade Gilbert Brutus, Att: 9,880,
Match official: I Smith

Catalans (18) 24
T: S Raguin 1, O Elima 2, C Stacul 1
G: T Bosc 4

Leeds (10) 37
T: L Smith 1, R Hall 2, S Donald 1,
D McGuire 1, R Burrow 1, A Lauitiiti 1
G: K Sinfield 4 **DG:** K Sinfield 1

Catalans squad
Greenshields, Stacul, Wilson, Raguin, Pelo, Bosc, McGuire, Chan, Gorrell, Elima, Croker, Mounis, Carlaw
Replacements: Guisset, Casty, Quintilla, Touxagas

Leeds squad
Smith, Hall, Toopi, Senior, Donald, McGuire, Burrow, Leuluai, Diskin, Peacock, Ellis, Jones-Buchanan, Sinfield
Replacements: Lauitiiti, Scruton, Kirke, Ablett

You could see it on the face of Leeds coach Brian McClennan that this win in the South of France was a huge relief not only for himself but the Rhinos club as a whole. Not many face Catalans and score over 30 points so the 24–37 score line was reward in itself and the ploy of flying down early to prepare for this match proved vital. Leeds had trained hard the evening before in hot conditions as they knew the game would be won in the final quarter and that stamina would play a key role. It proved to be the case with Catalans racing away to an 18–6 lead within the first 25 minutes through fine tries from Cyril Stacul, Olivier Elima and Sebastien Raguin.

The Rhinos got off to a flying start when Lee Smith scored in a good position for Sinfield to kick the two extra points and lead 0–6 after just a few minutes. The hot conditions certainly helped the French outfit as they fought back with some rugged play from the pack of forwards and Leeds did well to keep them down to three tries. The Dragons showed such dominance up front that Leeds were delighted to snatch a late first half try from Ryan Hall to take them to the break just eight points adrift but a hamstring injury to Jamie Jones-Buchanan did little to settle the Rhinos' nerves.

Undeniably the ploy of taking Jamie Peacock and Kylie Leuluai from the field of play early proved a winner as both came back in the latter part of the game to stamp their authority alongside Ali Lauitiiti who was nothing short of brilliant in the second half. Once the sun had gone down Leeds looked more at ease. With the forwards now bossing the middle of the park, the likes of McGuire and Burrow started to weave their magical skills. They both combined for the stand off to cross three minutes after the restart for a vital touchdown which Sinfield goaled to leave them just two off the pace at 18–16. Catalans bounced back with another Elima try. They knew by the way both Rhinos half backs were playing that the game was still in the melting pot. So it proved when Burrow again combined sweetly with his number 6 who crossed for his second try of the day. Sinfield missed the conversion but Leeds fired up again and looked to overturn the 24–20 deficit.

Lady luck shined on the visitors when Mounis had a try waved away by the video referee and before the home crowd had finished booing, the Rhinos had slipped into the lead as Ali Lauitiiti barged over to give Sinfield an easy task

Mick Potter rued the fact that his team let slip a good lead.

line on 75 minutes gave them some breathing space—more oxygen was added when Sinfield dropped a one pointer just a few minutes from the end. It looked likely that Leeds would hang on at 24–31 but Ryan Hall made sure with a try in the dying seconds.

It was proof that Leeds had at last returned to top form and left coach McClennan happy. 'We showed a lot of character, they made it tough for us.' Catalans maestro Mick Potter rued the fact that his team let slip a good lead but they again showed the Dragons are far from out of this competition and on their day could be in with a chance to make a Grand Final for the first time. Such was the energetic showing from all the players that fans from both sides applauded the teams off the field of play.

Kick off: 12.15, Venue: The KC Stadium, Att: 21,283, Match official: S Ganson

Hull FC (16) 44
T: M Sing 1, C Hall 1, G Horne 1, K Yeaman 2, T Briscoe 2, S Wheeldon 1
G: D Tickle 6

Hull KR (18) 18
T: B Cockayne 1, B Galea 1, C I'Anson 1
G: M Dobson 3

Hull FC squad
Sing, Hall, Horne, Yeaman, Briscoe, Washbrook, Berrigan, Dowes, Houghton, Thackray, Manu, Tickle, Radford
Replacements: Lee, Broughton, Wheeldon, Cusack

Hull KR squad
Cockayne, Fox, Lovegrove, Welham, Steel, Galea, Dobson, Vella, K Netherton, Crossman, Gene, J Netherton, I'Anson
Replacements: Aizue, Mills, Chester, Fisher

of adding the two to leave Catalans stunned and behind 24–26. Again the rub of the green went the Rhinos way as Carlaw had another try turned down by the video referee. This decision sent the home fans into a frenzy of rage and like before Leeds hit back whilst the French were thinking about what might have been. It came from a deep kick downfield where Donald, who had switched to fullback, took it easily and with a poor chase in place sidestepped in and out past Gorrell and raced away 75 metres for an amazing try that turned the game on its head. Despite Sinfield not adding the extras, the 24–30 score

With Hull KR holding a three successive win tally over rivals Hull FC, not many black and white fans were looking forward to this derby clash and when the Robins opened up the scoring early on it looked likely new Hull FC coach Richard Agar would have to wait for his first victory over the old enemy. Jason Netherton carved out the chance for Ben Galea to score after just 10 minutes and Dobson had little problems adding the extras to make the home side look nervous.

Young Tom Briscoe finally brought them back into the match with a fine try out wide but Tickle couldn't add the conversion. There was more trouble for the home side when Ben Cockayne scored off Dobson's fine off load, the provider kicking an easy conversion to make it 4–12 midway through the first stanza with Hull FC struggling to get their defence in order. Wheeldon's try half an hour in at least gave the home fans some hope at 10–12 but the Rovers were bossing things. It didn't help matters when Agar's men made a mess of a Dobson grubber kick into the in goal area allowing Chaz I'Anson to dive on the ball before they could react. Dobson again added the extra two to stretch the lead to 10–18 coming up to the break leaving the black and white fans silent. They did have something to cheer about four minutes later when Kirk Yeaman, playing his best game all year, shrugged off a couple of would be defenders to cross for a vital four pointer to send the sides into the sheds at 16–18, and game on.

Sadly for Rovers they didn't show the same spirit as in the first 40 and were swamped by a ruthless showing from the home side that lifted their spirits for the following week's clash with Wakefield in the Challenge Cup semi final. Hull scored six tries without reply, leaving Robins' boss Justin Morgan a confused man. 'We

Paul Cooke was dropped for the match against local rivals Hull FC.

showed good signs in the first half but lacked discipline and didn't put enough pressure on their kickers.' Rovers just collapsed and many of their fans were left wondering why Paul Cooke had been omitted from the starting line up. Rumours suggest he was dropped for disciplinary reasons, either way they certainly missed his guile but it would have been hard for anyone to stop the black and whites in this mood in the second half. It took only six minutes of the second half for Hull FC to gain control when Graeme Horne took advantage of a huge Washbrook bomb to take the lead for the first time at 22–18 after Tickle slotted over the extras. When Matt Sing scored another try from yet another kick, this time from Tommy Lee, the writing was on the wall. Rovers were doomed and never looked likely to get back on the horse.

Yeaman added his second, so did Tom Briscoe, and Craig Hall rubbed salt into the wounds by scoring the last of the day to make it 44–18 at the final whistle, leaving Rovers wondering where it all went wrong. Hull FC coach Richard Agar knew the lads hadn't played well at times despite chalking up a convincing win. 'The players know we have a very important seven days ahead of us…we ironed out a few things at the break and it showed up well.'

Kick off: 15.00, Venue: Grattan Stadium, Att: 9,429, Match official: P Bentham

Bradford (0) 24

T: B Jeffries 1, P Deacon 1, I Harris 1, T Newton 1 **G:** P Deacon 4

Wakefield (6) 10

T: D Blanch 2 **G:** B Drew 1

Bradford squad

Platt, Evans, Sykes, Nero, Tadulala, Jeffries, Deacon, Vagana, Harris, Lynch, Solomona, Finnigan, Langley
Replacements: Newton, Cook, Burgess, Kopczak

Wakefield squad

Reilly, Blanch, Demetriou, Gleeson, Petersen, Rooney, Drew, Wilkes, Obst, Moore, Golden, Ferres, Sculthorpe
Replacements: MacGillivray, Henderson, Bibey, Ferguson

The semi final blues yet again brought about Wakefield's downfall despite going into the second half with a 0–6 lead over the Bradford Bulls at the Grattan Stadium. It was a better showing in the second half from the Bulls who lacked ideas in the first 40 but awoke in time to put the Wildcats to the sword.

Wakefield have been thinking about the clash with Hull FC in the Challenge Cup for weeks now and despite what coach John Kear says, it appears their only outlook on life is Wembley. On this showing that will just be another dream in the heads of those loyal Trinity fans who crave for the glory days of Fox, Brooke and Turner. Not that Bulls coach Steve McNamara was worried, he had been bewildered by his side's recent showings and was glad to grab a win and stay in with a chance of a play-off spot come the season's end.

It all looked promising for Wakefield when Damien Blanch took advantage of Bradford kicking off out on the full to score from the first set of the game giving them a flyer, but it all went a bit scrappy after that. In fact the only real excitement came near the end of the first stanza when an all-in brawl erupted, earning Sam Burgess a yellow card. Burgess surprised everyone as it was rumoured he would miss the World Cup for England with a bad shoulder injury but there he was sat on the bench, ready for action.

Not many games at this stage of the season see only one try scored in the first half and the shortage of tries was an indication of the lack of energy on the pitch. Astonishingly, Wildcats boss John Kear was pleased with his team's showing. 'It was a much better performance than the previous two. We looked after the ball, kicked reasonably well and played some good field position rugby.' This probably gives an idea of the problems Wakefield have had of late. Bradford sensed they may have their minds on other things and Wakefield allowed Terry Newton and Paul Deacon the chance to take over in the second half with a try from Deacon which he converted to level the scores after 48 minutes.

It was a lift for Coach McNamara who had watched his side lose twice in close encounters in successive weeks. 'It was a poor game, lacked intensity but we were a lot better in the second half,' he added. Four minutes after Deacon had squared it all up Terry Newton showed his guile to cross over the try line and when Jeffries also scored to make it 18–6 it looked all over with just a quarter left to play. Blanch gave Wakefield some hope 10 minutes from the end but that was nullified with Iestyn Harris' try soon after. Wakefield certainly missed the prompting of scrum-half Danny Brough but Kear was certain he would be fit for the semi final. I hoped so because they would certainly need him.

Kick off: 15.00, Venue: Twickenham Stoop, Att: 2,112,
Match official: B Thaler

Harlequins (12) 12
T: C Melling 1, J Grayshon 1
G: R Purdham 2

Castleford (28) 66
T: S Donlan 1, R Owen 3, M Shenton 3, M Wainwright 1, L Dorn 3,
R McGoldrick 1, N Catic 1
G: K Dixon 7

Harlequins squad
Melling, Bryan, Sharp, Purdham, O'Callaghan, Hill, Paul, Temata, Randall, Ward, Barker, Grayshon, Haggerty
Replacements: Skee, Heckenburg, Tootill, Mbu

Castleford squad
Donlan, Owen, Shenton, Dixon, Wainwright, Dorn, Sherwin, Higgins, Moore, Huby, Guttenbeil, Lupton, McGoldrick
Replacements: Westerman, Henderson, Boyle, Catic

With Harlequins missing five first team regulars through injury and suspensions after the previous game against Catalans, Castleford proved too good for the London side. There was little hope of success with the odds stacked against them but they at least gave it their all in trying to stem a Tigers outfit that clicked into gear early.

It took less than 10 minutes for former London player Luke Dorn to prize open the Quins defence to send in Stuart Donlan and from there on in it was one way traffic. Despite Melling dragging one back soon after Donlan's effort, three tries in six minutes left the home side in disarray, so it was no surprise to find the score 12–28 at the half time hooter. The first half was scrappy despite the free flowing scoring as both sides struggled to hold onto the ball. It soon became obvious that when Ned Catic scored barely seconds from the restart, the Quins were looking down the barrel of a huge gun. Castleford produced some heavy shells to blitz the home side away. Eight tries in the last stanza didn't tell the story of the Quins' effort but to be fair Castleford combined well to score some delightful four pointers which delighted coach Terry Matterson. 'The forwards laid the platform and the backs got the rewards. I was pleased, especially with "Shenny" [Michael Shenton]. He's sharp and there aren't a lot of quality English centres around—he wouldn't let England down.'

Shenton and Owen both grabbed hat tricks whilst Luke Dorn was amazingly handed his bag of three thanks to his interception of a long pass from Scott Hill after the hooter had sounded, leaving him an easy stroll to the line. Harlequins boss Brian McDermott wasn't too despondent after the match and praised his youngsters for having a dig. 'It wasn't great but I'm not going to say anything negative, there was no lack of effort.' The sad part was not just out on the field of play either, only 2,112 turned out to support both teams. Harlequins needed a win to bolster the hopes and future of the club, although the five missing players did little to help the cause of a club short on depth.

Player of the Round 22
Michael Shenton, Castleford
A hat trick of tries from Shenton helped the Tigers blow away the Quins. A solid game that must have caught the attention of England coach Tony Smith.

Friday 1 August 2008

Kick off: 20.00, Venue: New Craven Park, Att: 8,074,
Match official: R Silverwood

Hull KR (12) 30
T: B Cockayne 1, K Welham 1,
B Fisher 1, M Vella 1, C I'Anson 1
G: M Dobson 5

Catalans (10) 16
T: Y Khattabi 1, G Mounis 1, V Duport 1
G: T Bosc 2

Hull KR squad
Cockayne, Fox, Welham, Lovegrove, Steel, Galea, Dobson, Crossman, Fisher, Mills, Vella, Gene, Chester
Replacements: Aizue, I'Anson, K Netherton, J Netherton

Catalans squad
Greenshields, Wilson, Mogg, Raguin, Khattabi, Bosc, McGuire, Chan, Gorrell, Elima, Mounis, Croker, Carlaw
Replacements: Guisset, Duport, Touxagas, Casty

Mick Vella added to the score line against Catalans to keep hopes up for a top six finish.

Hull KR produced a second half blitz against high flyers Catalans to bring off a shock 30–16 win to keep their slim hopes of a play-off spot going. In reality they would have to win all their remaining games to trouble the top six. It was a superb performance from Justin Morgan's men, who again started the match without Paul Cooke, who remained stood down after his off field antics upset the Rovers coach. Both sides battled it out over the first quarter and a neat piece of play from Catalans' Gorrell sent in Gregory Mounis. Bosc converted and it looked likely that the under strength Robins would be ripped apart by the French outfit that had been in outstanding form. But to the home side's credit they muscled up and tightened their defence to hold out wave after wave of attack from the visitors.

Kris Welham again showed great promise and his try midway through the first stanza lifted Rovers back into the match. It was a much needed touchdown after they had lost Chris Chester to a bad neck injury minutes before. Welham dribbled the ball downfield to score after Dobson's short kick confused the Catalans defence. Dobson added the two to square it all up. Just before half time Gorrell's 40/20 paved the way for Younes Khattabi to score from the scrum, although it was a while before the video referee awarded the try, 'Benefit of the doubt' was the call. Bosc couldn't add to the score from out wide, the ball hitting the post and bouncing out. Stanley Gene was again in top form and his charging run enabled Rovers to hit back and take them to the sheds with a two point lead. The PNG international slipped the ball to another up and coming youngster, Chaz I'Anson to crash over, Dobson easily slotted over the extras to make it 12–10 at the interval.

Rovers had a scare when Gene got put on report for a late tackle soon after the restart but he provided the push for Ben Fisher to take advantage of some crafty play from Galea and Netherton who sent in the crafty hooker. Dobson's conversion made it three from three for the scrum-half and the home side had their tails up. Fullback Ben Cockayne added another within minutes and when Mick Vella took advantage of the strong burst from David Mills it was little wonder the home fans were screaming for more with a score line of 30–10. Three tries within 15 minutes broke Catalans' hearts and whilst Duport crossed the try line with a quarter of the half remaining the Robins defence made sure they took the spoils.

Morgan was pleased with their performance, 'Dobson gave us some direction and Gene was outstanding as usual.' Catalans' boss Mick Potter stated it was one of their worst showings, 'I was disappointed with our handling.'

Kick off: 20.00, Venue: JJB Stadium, Att: 12,842, Match official: B Thaler

Wigan (28) 66
T: C Phelps 1, G Carmont 2, P Richards 2, T Leuluai 1, M Higham 1, J Tomkins 3, I Palea'aesina 2
G: R Mathers 1, P Richards 8

Hull FC (0) 6
T: J Thackray 1 **G:** J Thackray 1

Wigan squad
Mathers, Calderwood, Phelps, Carmont, Richards, Barrett, Leuluai, Fielden, Higham, Coley, Bailey, Hansen, Tomkins
Replacements: Palea'aesina, Colbon, O'Carroll, Smith

Hull FC squad
Hall, Sing, Horne, Yeaman, Raynor, Washbrook, Lee, Dowes, Berrigan, Carvell, Radford, Tickle, Manu
Replacements: Cusack, Briscoe, Houghton, Thackray

Wigan were blasted by their own chairman at a midweek fans forum where Ian Lenagan claimed his side were lacking leadership and passion. The claim hit home and the players responded in the best possible manner by thrashing Wembley-bound Hull FC at the JJB Stadium. A three match losing run was hard to take for Wigan fans and many would have taken sides with their chairman; that was until they witnessed the way their team ripped Hull apart. Trent Barrett was one of the players singled out for poor form and he produced a cracking display reminiscent of his Australian international days where his creativity broke down defences with ease. He laid on no less than six tries for the Warriors. Wigan's performance proved that sometimes it takes not only a few words of wisdom from the coach

'We did some good things tonight,' said Brian Noble of his charges.

but also from the chairman to inspire the players!

Sometimes a good kick up the backside doesn't hurt and Hull FC just couldn't handle the magic thrown at them. Maybe Richard Agar's men did celebrate a touch too hard after their semi final win that would take them to Wembley but he would have been cringing at some of his defenders' attempts to tackle the rampaging Warriors. Agar was quick to point out it had been a tough few weeks for the club with injuries and all but admitted they were not at their best. 'It was a pretty shocking effort,' he added.

Not that the Wigan fans complained. Pat Richards set the scene soon after the kick off, Barrett's kick allowing the fullback to score. Mickey Higham chimed in from dummy-half; Tomkins added another and went on to score another three! Four

tries in any match is something to be remembered and the big forward enjoyed every minute of it.

With a half time score of 28–0 one would have expected Wigan to slow things down but they upped the anti and went for broke with some delightful team play that brought them another seven tries in the final 40. Hull were never at the races having just one chance in the first half and not many more in the second. This gave boss Agar cause to state, 'I might be wrong but I reckon if you check the stats Wigan did the least number of tackles ever in a Super League match.' Wigan's coach Brian Noble was delighted for the players: 'Some of the things that were said about them were a bit unfair. We did some good things tonight but there are some other things to do better.'

Kick off: 19.30, Venue: Halliwell Jones
Stadium, Att: 9,150,
Match official: S Ganson

Warrington (4) 22
T: C Hicks 2, M King 1, J Clarke 1,
L Mitchell 1 **G:** C Hicks 1

Leeds (6) 12
T: K Leuluai 2 **G:** K Sinfield 2

Warrington squad
Hicks, Riley, Martin Gleeson, King, Penny,
Briers, Monaghan, Morley, Clarke,
Rauhihi, L Anderson, Westwood, Grix
Replacements: Mitchell, Parker, Cooper,
Harrison

Leeds squad
Tansey, Smith, Ablett, Senior, Jones-
Bishop, McGuire, Burrow, Leuluai,
Diskin, Peacock, Ellis, Kirke, Sinfield
Replacements: Scruton, Lauitiiti, Worrall,
Anselme

Just a few weeks ago Warrington were
out of the top six, had lost their coach
and appeared to be doomed for yet
another poor season then along came
James Lowes and the guys start to click.
Many felt it could be a case of 'a change
is as good as a rest' and they wondered
if the outspoken former hooker had the
brains and the energy to pull the Wolves
out of the doldrums. But any doubters
were quickly convinced after watching
them crush a strong Rhinos outfit that
battled to the end. The announcement
from the club that Lowes had signed a
new contract to coach them for next
season was a huge lift to the side and it
showed with a sparkling performance
against the mighty Rhinos.

The win left them firmly in fourth spot
on the table and what was once just a
dream now looked a possibility in that
they really could press for a chance to

walk out onto the Old Trafford pitch on 4
October. Since Lowes took over,
Warrington looked a more settled outfit,
and whilst one has to respect the hard
work put in by the former coach Paul
Cullen the fact is the Wolves have a
different look about them now,
especially in defence.

A tweak here and there has ensured the
defence is more solid and it showed in
the first half as they battled it out to
negate most of what the Champions
threw at them. Both defences were
working overtime and unsurprisingly it
took half an hour before the first try was
recorded. Big prop Kylie Leuluai lunging
over from close range gave the visitors
the edge on one of the few occasions
that Leeds made a break. Sinfield's
conversion made it 0–6 and that's how it
stayed until just before the half time
break when Matt King finally scored
after a long period of pressure from
Warrington's forwards. The try came
after a wonderful run by young
substitute Lee Mitchell who burst
through for 20 metres before off loading
to another star performer Chris Hicks
who sent in King at the left hand corner.
Hicks missed the extras as the half time
hooter sounded but this provided a
confidence boost for Warrington to kick
on in the final stanza.

So it proved and with the Wolves pack in
superb shape, they started to take
control. Rauhihi's strong burst put
Warrington in a great position. Then
Briers' went on a run supported by
Morley who ran on the angle before
turning the ball back inside to hooker
Jon Clarke who raced away under the
sticks. Hicks took an easy conversion to
give the Wolves the lead for the first time
at 10–6.

With the forwards in such an aggressive

mood, the likes of Briers and Monaghan started running the show and a bit of Briers magic sent Hicks charging towards the posts only for Sinfield and Scruton to deny the fullback with a great dual tackle. Quick hands stretched the Rhinos defence before Hicks couldn't be stopped. This time he squeezed in at the corner flag to make it 14–6 after the try scorer failed with the conversion attempt. Hicks made up for his miss with the boot seven minutes later when he finished off a great break from Kevin Penny who raced away 40 metres to give his side a good position for the fullback to boost the scoreboard to 18–6. Another strong 45 metre run from Lee Mitchell earned him a great try as he shrugged off the defence to dive in at the corner and wrap up a wonderful victory for the home side. Leuluai scored a late consolation try, his second of the match, with just two minutes remaining but it was far too late.

Warrington coach Lowes was full of praise for skipper Morley's effort, 'Moz has been doing that all year. A lot of names have been bandied around for Man of Steel and his ought to be up there with them.' It was a superb performance from the captain and augers well for the upcoming World Cup. Rhino's boss Brian McClennan suggested his side was a touch flat but praised Warrington's showing. 'Hats off to them, their defence was good. We've got to re-ignite ourselves for the run-in. We just need to get our rhythm back,' he added.

Kick off: 15.00, Venue: Twickenham Stoop, Att: 2,534, Match official: A Klein

Harlequins (22) 36
T: C Melling 1, W Sharp 3, D Howell 1, T Clubb 1, R Sheriffe 1 **G:** R Purdham 4

Bradford (0) 24
T: S Tadulala 1, B Jeffries 1, A Lynch 1, S Finnigan 1 **G:** I Harris 4

Harlequins squad
Melling, Sharp, Howell, Clubb, Sheriffe, Hill, Orr, Haggerty, Randall, Ward, Grayshon, Purdham, Paul
Replacements: Rinaldi, Temata, Mbu, Heckenburg

Bradford squad
Platt, Halley, Sykes, Evans, Tadulala, Jeffries, Harris, Vagana, Newton, Lynch, Solomona, Finnigan, Langley
Replacements: Cook, Nero, Godwin, Kopczak

Bradford's hopes of hanging onto the sixth play-off spot took a savage blow with a loss to the Harlequins at the Twickenham Stoop on a sunny Sunday to the tune of 36–24. The Quins were unstoppable in a 20 minute period as they crossed for four unanswered tries to leave the pitch at the break with an incredible 22–0 lead. Former Aussie star Scott Hill was the star of the show and his guile and ball distribution was top class. He struggled with injuries over the season and at times looked off the pace but on this occasion you couldn't point the finger, he was all quality and confused a lacklustre Bulls outfit in the first half. Chris Melling got the ball rolling when he finished off some good work from Danny Ward on 17 minutes. Soon after Will Sharp got in on the act by scoring a brace in quick succession and squeezed in between was David Howell's touchdown to leave the Bulls looking doomed.

What was said in the Bradford dressing room at half time was probably not for printing. Steve McNamara obviously got the message across as the Bulls bounced back with such strength they actually took the lead midway through the second half in an incredible fight-back that left the Quins reeling. At 22–24 Bradford had the momentum and looked certain to break away from what looked like a tiring home side.

Simon Finnigan scored soon after the restart, followed shortly by Semi Tadulala who accepted a beauty of a pass from Solomona. Ben Jeffries added to the score sheet on 40 minutes and when Andy Lynch carried four tacklers over near the posts the game had turned on its head. Harris slotted over all four conversions and a sigh of relief could be heard from the travelling Bulls fans and players alike. Bradford then had to

A touchdown by David Howell left the Bulls looking doomed.

defend like madmen as Quins threw everything at them and with just seven minutes remaining it looked likely the Bulls would hang on. But Quins found some belief and scored an incredible three tries in those remaining minutes. Danny Orr's grubber kick found Rikki Sheriffe and then man of the match Scott Hill created the space for Tony Clubb to cross. And when Sharp went in for his hat trick the visiting fans had already gone for the exit gates.

Quins boss Brian McDermott was happy that the senior players had come to the rescue late in the game, 'We'd lost all momentum in the second half and again some key players came up with some great plays.' He also added that they still had an outside chance of making the play-offs. Bradford still held a two point league table lead over seventh place Wakefield, although this proved little consolation for Steve McNamara. 'We're far better than that,' was his assessment of their performance in London.

Sunday 3 August 2008

Kick off: 15.30, Venue: The Jungle, Att: 6,935, Match official: R Silverwood

Castleford (14) 14
T: R Owen 1, L Dorn 1
G: C Huby 1, J Westerman 2

Huddersfield (14) 40
T: P Whatuira 1, D Hodgson 1, C Thorman 1, R Hudson 1, D Griffin 1, J Lolesi 1 **G:** C Thorman 8

Castleford squad
Donlan, Owen, Shenton, Lupton, Wainwright, Dorn, Sherwin, Higgins, Henderson, Huby, Guttenbeil, Westerman, McGoldrick
Replacements: Korkidas, Boyle, Sargent, Arundel

Huddersfield squad
Cudjoe, Aspinwall, K Brown, Whatuira, Hodgson, Thorman, Robinson, Mason, Hudson, Griffin, Wild, Lolesi, Raleigh
Replacements: Crabtree, Jones, Jackson, Kirmond

Huddersfield, with hopes of scraping in to the top six, posted their first back to back wins of the season, thrashing Castleford 14–40 at The Jungle. It was another high tally for Chris Thorman who bagged 20 points in a top class showing for the Giants.

The first half was even throughout and a half time score line of 14–14 left the fans still wondering who would take the spoils. Huddersfield had raced away to a 2–12 lead in the first quarter only for the Tigers to claw their way back into the match with tries from Richard Owen and Luke Dorn. Craig Huby got the home side moving with a three minute penalty. But tries from David Hodgson and Jamahl Lolesi put Huddersfield in charge within the first quarter whilst Castleford struggled, which was no surprise due to a 'flu bug that had ravaged the club all week.

To their credit the Tigers showed some spirit to go in all square at the break and had a good chance after the restart only for them to squander the opportunity. Dorn's 60 metre interception should have brought them a score but Sherwin lost the ball with the Giants struggling to get back in defence. It was to prove costly, even though they defended well to keep the Giants out until the final quarter when former Tigers star Ryan Hudson dived over from dummy-half to break the deadlock. Thorman failed to add the extras but it was to be his only miss of the game. Again Castleford threw away chances to equalise and when Korkidas got sin-binned for a high tackle on Robinson only seconds after coming off the bench the writing was on the wall; Thorman kicked the penalty. Not long after tempers flared and players came flying in from everywhere which earned both Darrell Griffin and Ryan McGoldrick a yellow card which appeared to take the wind out of the Tigers sails. Thorman kicked another penalty to make it 14–22 then three quick tries in 10 minutes from Paul Whatuira, Darrell Griffin and Chris Thorman blasted Castleford away.

It was a strong performance from the Giants with Whatuira and Cudjoe showing up well but the Tigers made them work hard for the spoils with Luke Dorn again hitting the high spots. Tigers' coach Terry Matterson admitted the sin-binning of Korkidas didn't help: 'It was a silly thing from one of my players at a crucial time.' Stand in coach for the Giants Paul Anderson still believes they could make the play-offs: 'Until it becomes a mathematical impossibility we're looking up not down.'

Sunday 3 August 2008

Kick off: 15.30, Venue: Belle Vue, Att: 5,781, Match official: P Bentham

Wakefield (0) 10
T: B Drew 1, B Ferres 1 **G:** D Brough 1

St Helens (30) 42
T: K Eastmond 1, J Graham 1, K Cunningham 1, J Wilkin 1, C Flannery 1, J Roby 1, P Clough 1
G: M Gidley 1, K Eastmond 6

Wakefield squad
Blaymire, Blanch, Demetriou, Atkins, Grix, Brough, Drew, Bibey, Obst, Sculthorpe, Ferres, MacGillivray, Golden
Replacements: Leo-Latu, Moore, Gleeson, Wilkes

St Helens squad
Wellens, Gardner, Gidley, Gilmour, Meli, Pryce, Eastmond, Graham, Cunningham, Hargreaves, Wilkin, Flannery, Sculthorpe
Replacements: Roby, Cayless, Clough, Emmitt

Many fans feel St Helens are not the same side without Sean Long, but try telling that to youngster Kyle Eastmond

Ricky Bibey gets to grips with James Graham.

Oliver Wilkes is unable to escape from Keiron Cunningham and Paul Clough.

who produced some magical touches to help blast the Wildcats away on their own ground. Wakefield perhaps could look to that semi final loss as some excuse for their display but it was never going to be easy for them when Chris Flannery opened the scoring after just 13 minutes.

Saints again showed what they are made of with some outstanding combinations and support play—the speed and swerving of Eastmond is a joy to watch. The youngster dashed away for a length of the field intercept and had a hand in two other scores. Wilkin, Roby, Graham and Clough added more tries to take the visitors back to the changing rooms with a comfortable 0–30 lead and even the most ardent Wildcats fan had no thoughts of a second half fight-back. Brett Ferres lifted their spirits soon after

the restart with a solid try off Brough's pass but energy soon ran out as Eastmond's solo long range effort snuffed out any hope.

Brad Drew dived over from dummy-half late in the match but Cunningham matched that soon after and the home fans were looking for the exits. Another low key performance from John Kear's men led the coach to admit, 'It was very poor.' Saints coach Anderson wasn't getting carried away with their win or the showing of youngster Eastmond. 'He kicked well and scored a nice try but there are plenty of areas where he can improve.' Deep down though one suspects Anderson is pleased with the way all of his youngsters are coming through the ranks and Eastmond is certainly a kid to watch for the future.

engage
Mutual Assurance

Kick off: 20.00, Venue: Headingley Carnegie, Att: 17,508,
Match official: B Thaler

Leeds (16) 28
T: C Ablett 1, D McGuire 1, N Scruton 1, L Burgess 1, J Tansey 1
G: R Burrow 1, K Sinfield 3

Bradford (12) 18
T: P Sykes 1, J Evans 1, W Godwin 1
G: I Harris 3

Leeds squad
Webb, Smith, Ablett, Senior, Donald, McGuire, Burrow, Peacock, Diskin, Leuluai, Kirke, Ellis, Sinfield
Replacements: Scruton, Burgess, Tansey, Worrall

Bradford squad
Platt, Halley, Sykes, Evans, Tadulala, Jeffries, Harris, Vagana, Newton, Lynch, Cook, Finnigan, Langley
Replacements: Johnson, Nero, Godwin, Kopczak

Several years ago a Leeds versus Bradford clash would ensure a full house and a thriller but sadly these days the Bulls are in yo-yo mode and their fans turn up not knowing if they will witness good or bad. The fact that this Leeds win was their ninth out of the last 10 clashes with the old foe indicated the problems Bradford were facing in finding their lost glory but the Bulls showed tremendous fortitude in pushing the Rhinos to the limit. In fact the result was still in doubt right up to the last minute when Danny McGuire held onto a difficult pass and put the game out of reach of the Bulls at 28–18. This was

indicative of the visitors' huge effort despite playing without stars Deacon and Solomona, although the replacement, Matt Cook, showed up well in a hard working pack that ensured Leeds had to dig deep throughout.

Matt Diskin and Rob Burrow found top form as both controlled the ruck area with great aplomb and again a terrific showing from Jamie Peacock ensured they deserved the victory. It didn't start well for Leeds as winger Donald injured

Kevin Sinfield wraps up Semi Tadulala in Leeds' win over Bradford.

a rib and had to be taken from the field. This was followed by a nasty incident involving Platt and Webb which earned the Bulls fullback a sin-bin stint. Rob Burrow joined in the fracas earning his first-ever yellow card for his effort and left the field with blood streaming from his face. The crowd were in no doubt this was going to be a crunch match with no love lost between the two sides. Seconds later Bradford took the lead with a fine effort from Sykes, Harris' goal taking it to 0–6 and Leeds did not look good at all.

Despite the errors Leeds hit back with a try from substitute Jordan Tansey on the quarter hour mark. This was soon followed by a charging effort from Luke Burgess who beat Tadulala to stretch the lead to 10–6, leaving Bradford struggling to get possession. Eight minutes before the break Nick Scruton scored to leave Sinfield an easy conversion and at 16–6 it looked

unlikely the Bulls could spark a revival. But to their credit Bradford fashioned a fine try for James Evans who stole the ball away from McGuire to give them hope, leaving them adrift by just four points at the break, 16–12.

Leeds boss Brian McClennan was unhappy with their first half showing and was left with more problems soon after the restart when Wayne Godwin took advantage of another error from McGuire who lost the ball under pressure from Evans. Harris converted to put them in front again 16–18. The final quarter saw Leeds at their best as they stepped up a gear against a Bulls outfit that started to look tired. It came as no surprise when Ablett scored to leave it 22–18 and despite the video referee turning down two claims for tries from first Burrow and then McGuire, Leeds looked confident, yet couldn't breathe easy against a spirited Bradford side until McGuire sealed it.

Jordan Tansey scores despite Simon Finnigan's tackle.

Kick off: 19.00, Venue: Stade Gilbert Brutus, Att: 9,535,
Match official: S Ganson

Catalans (10) 16
T: C Greenshields 1, J Wilson 1,
A Gorrell 1 **G:** T Bosc 2

Wigan (4) 16
T: P Richards 2, H Hansen 1
G: P Richards 2

Catalans squad
Greenshields, Khattabi, Wilson, Raguin, Pelo, Mogg, Bosc, Casty, Gorrell, Elima, Mounis, Fakir, Carlaw
Replacements: Ferriol, Guisset, Duport, Touxagas

Wigan squad
Mathers, Calderwood, Phelps, Carmont, Richards, Smith, Leuluai, Fielden, Higham, Coley, Hansen, Bailey, J Tomkins
Replacements: Palea'aesina, Colbon, McIlorum, O'Carroll

Another hot day in the South of France did little to help Wigan in their quest to rise up the league table and as expected, before the shadows lengthened, Catalans made good use of possession to take an early lead. Gorrell went over on the quarter mark of the first half, then man of the match Clint Greenshields came on the angle from the blind side of a scrum win to breeze over for an easy touchdown. The Warriors must have been wondering where they could find some leadership out on the park for it had been a poor showing from the visitors up to this point. The introduction of Palea'aesina once again did the trick, his charging runs lifted the spirits and at last Wigan looked dangerous. The visitors were rewarded with a try before the break when Leuluai found Richards unmarked out wide to stroll in. The try

scorer failed to add the extras but it was just what Wigan needed.

With the sun going down and the temperature dropping it was expected the Warriors would come out refreshed and firing but Noble's men were stunned when John Wilson snatched a high kick to dive over making it 16–4 just seven minutes into the second half. Wigan then had a stroke of luck when 10 minutes later Thomas Bosc had a try turned down by the video ref for obstruction, a decision that was dubious at best. The home crowd made their feelings clear but were soon silenced when Thomas Leuluai broke clear from his own 25 before sending in Pat Richards for his second of the match. Richards easily added the extras to leave them just six points adrift at 16–10. Amazingly, Bosc missed a sitter that probably would have won the match after Mathers had been penalised but his attempt went wide. That gave Wigan the impetus to strike back and that they did although they too suffered at the hands of the video referee who turned down Liam Colbon's touchdown, stating there had been a little knock on in the scoring process. Again it looked marginal but the Warriors shrugged off the disappointment and charged forward to get in a good position. Leuluai then off loaded to Harrison Hansen who scored with seconds remaining leaving Richards with a pressure conversion. He obliged with bells on to earn a point that surely had now cemented Wigan in a play-off spot.

Player of Round 24
Thomas Leuluai, Wigan
Leuluai turned up the heat when it looked like Catalans had taken control, some fine solo breaks that turned the match for Wigan to grab a draw.

Wigan boss Brian Noble was happy to get a point, saying, 'We showed great improvement.' Catalans were happy with the league point as it looked likely they would secure third spot on the table and a vital home ground advantage in the play-offs.

Kick off: 19.00, Venue: GPW Recruitment Stadium, Att: 10,258, Match official: R Silverwood

St Helens (10) 17
T: A Gardner 1, K Cunningham 1, L Gilmour 1 **G:** S Long 2 **DG:** S Long 1

Warrington (10) 16
T: C Riley 2, M King 1 **G:** C Hicks 2

St Helens squad
Wellens, Gardner, Gidley, Flannery, Meli, Pryce, Long, Cayless, Cunningham, Graham, Gilmour, Wilkin, Roby
Replacements: Fozzard, Hargreaves, Clough, Eastmond

Warrington squad
Hicks, Riley, Martin Gleeson, King, Penny, Briers, Monaghan, Morley, Clarke, Rauhihi, Mitchell, Westwood, Grix
Replacements: Parker, Bracek, Cooper, Blythe

The business end of the season always throws up dramatic games after a long and hard season. And the St Helens versus Warrington clash proved beyond doubt that Super League is becoming faster and more nerve racking for both players and fans, not to mention coaches. New Wolves coach James Lowes was left wondering what on earth they have to do to break the hoodoo that Saints have had over them over the past few years.

Leading 10–16 with less than five minutes to go, Lowes must have felt the victory was his but never underestimate the boys from the GPW Recruitment Stadium when it comes to snatching a last gasp win. Once again Keiron Cunningham supplied the pass to send Gilmour over the try line after good build up work from Roby and Graham. Long's easy conversion levelled the scores with just a few minutes left on the clock and the crowd were treated to a battle royal as each side tried to get position for the drop goal. Briers had first chance but his attempt drifted wide and with just three seconds remaining, Sean Long banged over a 40 metre one pointer to send the home side into raptures and the visiting fans to their knees. Warrington should have won the game and paid the price of not attempting an earlier drop goal when several chances presented themselves within the last 10 minutes. Saints were stunned and looked down and out but they had so much belief in their own ability. Little wonder then that Warrington coach Lowes was quick to point out, 'You just can't give Saints a sniff.'

This win extended Saints winning run to 18 and in sight of a record for the club. Long's cool head was just one advantage the St Helens side brought to their game. The guile of Cunningham coupled with rugged forward play offered their backline many chances. But to be fair to Warrington, on this occasion their defence snuffed out most of the talent on show, which must surely suggest Wolves may just be more than a side making up the numbers in the play-offs. Morley, Westwood and Clarke had outstanding games matching anything Saints produced and even when Cunningham scored early to give them a 6–0 lead it was obvious this was going to be one tough encounter.

After a quarter of an hour, Saints added a second through Gardner who dived into

Adrian Morley attempts to break through the Saints defence.

Warrington's Chris Riley scores in a tense game.

the corner from another fine flick pass from centre Gidley and despite St Helens making unusual handling errors, in most parts down to some solid Wolves defence, one expected the red and whites to forge ahead even more. Matt King found some form at last for the Wolves and scored a fine try by brushing aside three would be defenders to squeeze in at the corner flag. Hicks' fine touchline conversion made it 10–6 and a buzz went around the ground that Warrington were not going to fold, a fact borne out when Chris Riley scored from a magnificent slip pass to level the scores with just two minutes remaining of the first half. Hicks couldn't add the extras and the teams went to the sheds all square.

Warrington came out for the second

stanza on fire and battered the Saints defence for long periods. They finally got their rewards midway through the half with Riley bagging his second four pointer to give the visitors the lead for the first time. Hicks didn't fail to add the extras this time. Saints looked confused at being six points adrift, and that was how it should have stayed until the home side clicked into gear and pulled off a remarkable comeback.

Daniel Anderson admitted his side had dropped the ball far too often and added, 'We were classy for the final minutes or so but scrappy for the rest because Warrington tackled very well.' They did but it still left them with nothing but heartache.

Kick off: 15.00, Venue: New Craven Park, Att: 8,284,
Match official: P Bentham

Hull KR (0) 16
T: P Fox 1, J Steel 1, M Dobson 1
G: M Dobson 2

Harlequins (28) 40
T: W Sharp 1, D Howell 1, S Hill 1,
C Randall 1, G Haggerty 1, H Paul 1
G: R Purdham 8

Hull KR squad
Briscoe, Fox, Jake Webster, Welham, Steel, Galea, Dobson, Crossman, Fisher, Mills, Vella, Gene, Cockayne
Replacements: K Netherton, Cooke, J Netherton, Aizue

Harlequins squad
Melling, Sharp, Clubb, Howell, Sheriffe, Hill, Orr, Ward, Randall, Haggerty, Grayshon, Purdham, Paul
Replacements: Rinaldi, Temata, Heckenburg, McCarthy-Scarsbrook

Harlequins kept their slim top six hopes alive with a stunning performance at Craven Park and in the process left the Robins wondering if their dream of being involved in the final shake up had gone out of the window. On this form one would presume the home fans went home despondent to say the least.

Chad Randall set the scene with a try after just five minutes with a fine run from dummy-half. Three more tries followed for Harlequins as Rovers looked well off the pace both with ball in hand as well as in defence. The home fans looked on in disbelief with a score line at the break of 0–28. Sharp, Howell and Henry Paul crossed whilst Purdham kicked six from six.

Before the game there was a buzz around the ground when Paul Cooke was named in the starting 17 following his apology to the club for his off field behaviour. Unfortunately there was no buzz at all from the players. Harlequins were outstanding as each player supported with gusto and left defenders clutching thin air. The normally shrewd play from Michael Dobson was not on display and Hull KR suffered badly by missing tackle after tackle, a complete contrast to Rob Purdham who ensured the Quins were a solid team when he steered them about the park.

Despite a more encouraging start to the second half where Jon Steel scored soon after the kick off it wasn't long before Harlequins reached top gear again,

'I think it was one of our best away performances,'
said Brian McDermott. © Harlequins

Haggerty diving through some poor defence to get the scoreboard clicking once more. This was soon followed by Scott Hill's touchdown which took it to 4–40 with 20 minutes remaining. The Rovers did at last score two more through Fox and Dobson but the cue had been taken home, never mind put on the rack, by then. Brian McDermott was pleased after the match, 'I think it was one of our best away performances.' It was and halted a record seven away straight losses for the London outfit.

Sunday 10 August 2008

Kick off: 15.30, Venue: Belle Vue, Att: 6,498, Match official: I Smith

Wakefield (12) 22
T: S Gleeson 1, R Atkins 1, S Obst 1, B Ferres 1 **G:** D Brough 3

Castleford (24) 48
T: S Donlan 2, L Dorn 1, S Moore 1, C Huby 1, A Henderson 1, J Westerman 2 **G:** K Dixon 8

Wakefield squad
Blaymire, Blanch, Gleeson, Atkins, Grix, Rooney, Brough, Sculthorpe, Obst, Wilkes, Ferres, Golden, Demetriou
Replacements: Leo-Latu, Bibey, Bibb, Henderson

Castleford squad
Donlan, Owen, Shenton, Dixon, Wainwright, Dorn, Sherwin, Higgins, Moore, Huby, Guttenbeil, Lupton, McGoldrick
Replacements: Henderson, Westerman, Catic, Sargent

When a home side leads 12–0 within the first quarter playing against the bottom side in the league you have every right to think the win is there for the taking. So it would have been unwise to stand in the way of Wildcats coach John Kear after this encounter with arch rivals Castleford at Belle Vue.

Wakefield crashed to their seventh straight loss which left them with no chance of making the play-offs. Kear was livid at the collapse as the Tigers swamped in for eight tries in a remarkable showing that indicated to their coach Terry Matterson that it's not all gloom and doom down the Jungle way despite being odds on for the wooden spoon. The Tigers may look towards their wins over Leeds, St Helens and Warrington for satisfaction this season but this win over their near neighbours would have given them much better cause for celebration.

Two tries from Gleeson and Obst within 15 minutes had the home side crowd in raptures with Brough clicking into gear. But the clutch soon blew up and left them in reverse as Castleford ripped them apart with some scintillating moves that brought two tries each for Donlan and Westerman. Ryan McGoldrick was in fine form and he steered the Tigers about the park like a traffic cop. Not that Wakefield got anywhere near him to arrest him and put him under the cosh because his guile and off loading was superb, a point not missed by his coach Matterson. 'We controlled the ball in the second half, I was frustrated at the beginning but all credit to the guys. Ryan McGoldrick has been doing a really good job for us.'

Kear was far from impressed. 'It's pointless blaming other people, we all need to go away and I hope we all have sleepless nights.' After watching the Tigers race away to a convincing 22–48 win it wouldn't be too easy for any Wildcats fan to find a restful night's sleep either and they, like many in our game, were left wondering what happened to a side that showed so much promise early in the year.

Kick off: 18.00, Venue: The KC Stadium, Att: 11,921, Match official: T Alibert

Hull FC (14) 24
T: T Briscoe 1, G Horne 1, S Berrigan 1, D Houghton 1 **G:** D Tickle 4

Huddersfield (18) 30
T: M Aspinwall 1, P Whatuira 2, J Lolesi 1 **G:** C Thorman 5, L Robinson 2

Hull FC squad
Sing, Briscoe, G Horne, Yeaman, Raynor, Washbrook, Dykes, Cusack, Berrigan, Carvell, Manu, Tickle, Radford
Replacements: Houghton, Lee, Thackray, Dowes

Huddersfield squad
Cudjoe, Aspinwall, K Brown, Whatuira, Hodgson, Thorman, Robinson, Jackson, Hudson, Griffin, Wild, Lolesi, Raleigh
Replacements: Crabtree, Jones, Kirmond, Faiumu

Hull FC's run into the Challenge Cup final gained momentum when they raced away to a 14–0 lead over visitors Huddersfield after just 15 minutes. This should have given their coach Richard Agar a huge morale boost but sadly within minutes after the kick off he had lost Adam Dykes with a quadriceps injury that ruled him out for Wembley. It was yet another tale of woe for the men from The KC Stadium and by the time the game had finished Agar faced even more injury worries as Carvell, Tickle and Cusack all left the field at some point during the match.

Danny Houghton, who had substituted Dykes, soon put the home side ahead after 10 minutes. When Berrigan added another a few minutes later it looked likely that the Giants' slim hopes of a top six spot had gone, even more so when Tickle kicked a penalty goal midway through the first half to give them a convincing 14–0 lead. But full credit to the Giants who rallied with some rugged forward play that enabled Paul Whatuira to score from a smart pas from debut boy and New Zealand hooker David Faiumu. There was more to come from the Giants with Jamahl Lolesi who beat the defence to touchdown a well placed Thorman kick. From the restart, Hull kicked out on the full and Robinson put the Giants in striking distance to allow Aspinwall to dive over Raynor into the corner. Thorman added the conversions to both tries and Huddersfield went to the dressing rooms 14–18 up.

The black and whites regained the lead shortly after the restart when Graeme Horne slid over to give Tickle an easy conversion and take the score to 20–18. Thorman's penalty squared it up again before Whatuira went over for his second try of the match. Thorman again was on target to make it five from five attempts and a 20–26 lead, which he extended a few minutes later with a long range penalty. Huddersfield appeared to have the game won with an eight-point cushion with as many minutes remaining but Hull bounced back into contention with a Tom Briscoe try. With Tickle off the field with an injury, Berrigan took over the kicking duty but couldn't add the conversion. By this time Thorman had left the playing area with concussion so it was left to Robinson to kick a long range penalty to steer the Giants to safety at 24–30 just before full time. Afterwards, Richard Agar stated they had started well as in so many games this year, 'Things went against us and then there's the inability to change that momentum.'

engage
Mutual Assurance

Friday 15 August 2008

Kick off: 20.00, Venue: Headingley
Carnegie, Att: 17,354,
Match official: T Alibert

Leeds (24) 54
T: B Webb 1, L Smith 1, C Ablett 1,
A Gibson 1, D McGuire 1, R Burrow 1,
A Lauitiiti 1, J Tansey 3
G: G Ellis 1, K Sinfield 6,

Castleford (6) 12

Leeds squad
Webb, Smith, Ablett, Senior, Gibson,
McGuire, Burrow, Leuluai, Diskin,
Peacock, Ellis, Kirke, Sinfield
Replacements: Lauitiiti, Scruton, Burgess,
Tansey

Castleford squad
Donlan, Owen, Shenton, Dixon,
Wainwright, McGoldrick, Dorn, Higgins,
Moore, Huby, Guttenbeil, Lupton,
Westerman
Replacements: Leafa, Henderson, Catic,
Sargent

Leeds' last home game in the regular
rounds proved a bit of a damp squib as
they entertained bottom club Castleford.
In past times, the Wheldon Road outfit
would often have given Leeds a fright but
the Rhinos were back into the swing and
raced away for a 54–12 win without really
getting into top gear.

Not that the Tigers didn't try, far from it.
They held their own for the first 20
minutes despite having Scott Moore sent
to the sin-bin after a couple of minutes
play. Ashley Gibson got things started for
the home side and soon after Rob Burrow
scampered over and it looked easy but the
Tigers bounced back with a try from

Richard Owen to make it 10–6. Castleford
were gaining in confidence only to see
Smith cross out wide soon followed by a
further two tries in as many minutes that
blew Castleford out of the water; Ablett
and Lauitiiti touching down. Whilst
Sinfield could only add one conversion
from his last three attempts, at 24–6 the
game was effectively over as the teams
left the field for the half time break.

Jordan Tansey and Brent Webb scored
during the third quarter against an
improved Castleford defence. The Tigers
even scored a try from Luke Dorn who
again is having a great season. But the
tiredness started to take its toll and Leeds
just pulled away without clicking into top
gear and added three more tries to keep
Castleford rooted to the bottom of the
table. Jordon Tansey completed his hat
trick with only seconds remaining to leave
Leeds still in with a chance of finishing top
of the pile, provided St Helens slipped up.

McClennan hailed his side for their
discipline, 'We did well in that area and
we came up with some good things.'
Tigers coach Matterson was still confused
over the sin-binning of Moore after just
two minutes on the advice of a touch
judge. 'I'm still trying to work out why we
got a man sent to the sin-bin,' he added.

Friday 15 August 2008

Kick off: 20.00, Venue: JJB Stadium,
Att: 12,319, Match official: B Thaler

Wigan (16) 32
T: C Phelps 1, T Smith 1, T Leuluai 1,
M Higham 1, J Tomkins 1
G: P Richards 6

Wakefield (4) 22
T: O Wilkes 1, D Sculthorpe 1,
D MacGillivray 1 **G:** D Brough 5

Wigan squad
Mathers, Calderwood, Phelps, Carmont,
Richards, Smith, Leuluai, Fielden,
Higham, Coley, Bailey, Hansen, Tomkins
Replacements: Palea'aesina, Colbon,
McIlorum, O'Carroll

Wakefield squad
Grix, Blanch, Gleeson, Atkins, Petersen,
Rooney, Brough, Wilkes, Drew, Moore,
Demetriou, Golden, Sculthorpe
Replacements: MacGillivray, Bibey,
Leo-Latu, Bibb

Stuart Fielden had two objectives during
Wigan's clash with Wakefield Wildcats:
lead by example as the skipper; and
prove to those in charge that he was
ready to break back into international
football. He came up trumps on both
counts and worked like a Trojan, never
mind a Warrior, as he carried the ball
time and time again to give his side good
positions to launch their attacks. Yet this
wasn't the only topic on the supporters'
minds as a group of Warriors fans asked

for signatures on a petition notice to
keep Mickey Higham at Wigan. It does
seem weird that this talented hooker is
being shown the door, not for the first
time either as Wigan wanted to dump
him at the end of last season too.
Thankfully, if you are a Wigan fan he,
like Fielden, provided enough skill and
determination to ensure they came out
on top of a Wakefield side desperate to
find some form.

Tim Smith scored the first try of the game
and his first for the Wigan club having
thrown a huge dummy and a swerve to
wipe out two penalty goals from Danny
Brough. The trusty boot of Richards
converted Smith's effort and pushed
Wigan in front at 6–4 after 15 minutes'
play. Half way through the first half
Leuluai forced a goal-line drop out from
his huge bomb and on receiving the ball
sidestepped and jinked his way for a
great solo try. Richards added the two but
failed with the conversion after Cameron
Phelps scored, but at 16–4 the Warriors
looked good until Richie Mathers was
dismissed just before the break. The

Pat Richards goals as Wigan take the points against Wakefield.

Damien Blanch and Pat Richards leap to compete for the ball.

sending off of Mathers looked harsh, although the officials had no problems giving him the red card for what they had decided was a bad forearm in the face of Wildcats' Demetriou.

Obviously the Wildcats had plenty to play for after the restart and were rewarded with a try from Danny Sculthorpe soon after. Brough converted to make it 16–10 and Wigan looked rattled. They suffered more pain when Brough broke clear to enable McGillivray to dive over out wide and Brough banged over the difficult kick to level the scores at 16–16. Sculthorpe's late tackle enabled Richards to post a penalty to ease Wigan in front again but hooker Mickey Higham did some quick thinking when he forced his way over from dummy-half to give them

breathing space. Wakefield made use of the extra man with 15 minutes left when Oliver Wilkes scored a try. Brough converted to bring his side just two points adrift. Then Richards slotted over a penalty to give Wigan a four point lead and in the final minutes Joel Tomkins sealed the win by pouncing on Smith's grubber kick. Richards obliged with the extras and Wigan claimed a difficult win 32–22. Brian Noble was impressed with the showing from his squad. 'We were well in control, we kept believing.' Despite the loss, John Kear was pleased his side had turned things around after the poor show against Castleford the week before. 'The attitude was 100 percent better.'

Kick off: 19.30, Venue: The Galpharm Stadium, Att: 12,127,
Match official: A Klein

Huddersfield (12) 20
T: M Aspinwall 1, D Hodgson 1, D Kirmond 1 **G:** C Thorman 4

Catalans (10) 22
T: J Murphy 1, A Mogg 2, A Gorrell 1
G: T Bosc 3

Huddersfield squad
Cudjoe, Hodgson, Wild, Whatuira, Aspinwall, Brown, Thorman, Robinson, Jones, Griffin, Hudson, Crabtree, Raleigh Replacements: Kirmond, Faiumu, Lolesi, Jackson

Catalans squad
Greenshields, Murphy, Pelo, Mogg, Wilson, Mounis, Raguin, Bosc, Elima, Fakir, Gorrell, Carlaw, Guisset Replacements: Duport, Ferriol, Chan, Touxagas

Northern rugby league fans love a bargain and when Huddersfield announced they would open their gates for free when Catalans visited The Galpharm Stadium, a bumper crowd was expected to click through the turnstiles. Just over 12,000 witnessed a tough encounter which would decide the fate of the Giants' play-off chances whilst the French side needed a win to secure the third spot in the table. The fact that they did must have pleased coach Mick Potter, who must be a hot favourite to pick up coach of the year following the Perpignan-based outfit's reversal of fortunes.

Catalans finished 10th last term, so the improvement was easy to see but they had to fight hard to overcome a Giants side who were starting to play some good football. Martin Aspinwall got the huge crowd roaring when he finished off a fine kick from Kevin Brown after just six

Gregory Mounis and Olivier Elima halt the progress of Eorl Crabtree in Catalans' narrow win.

minutes but Thorman failed to add the extras. Huddersfield could have gone further ahead if the touchdown from Whatuira a few minutes later had been given but the video referee declared a 'no try'. Justin Murphy levelled the score from a wide pass from Adam Mogg to leave it at 4–4 and soon after it looked likely the same player would produce Catalans' second try. Unfortunately the ball was intercepted by David Hodgson who raced away 70 metres to score an unlikely try. Thorman again failed with the conversion but added a penalty on 30 minutes to ease the Giants away to the tune of 10–4. In slippery conditions, fast open play was rare but when Huddersfield tried to keep the ball alive, Aaron Gorrell intercepted it and waltzed over for an easy try that Bosc converted to level the score. Thorman's boot just before the break added an extra two that took them to lemons 12–10 ahead.

It was a far cry from the 48–0 thrashing the Giants suffered at the hands of the French way back in May, a result that saw the demise of coach Jon Sharp. The team showed much improvement under the guidance of stand-in coaches Anderson and Purtill who must have been confident they could stunt the visitors' ambitions of securing third spot. It seemed likely this would happen when Thorman again slotted over a penalty to stretch the lead even more. But Catalans have demonstrated a different attitude to away games this year and showed they are worthy of such a high position in the league by bouncing back. This they did with a superb try from Adam Mogg after a sweeping run by fullback Greenshields. Bosc surprisingly failed to convert but with the scores level at 14–14 it was anyone's match.

Danny Kirmond became the hero for the

Ashley Klein has a word with Catalans' prop Jerome Guisset.

home side when on 61 minutes he dived over after some nice footwork giving Thorman an easy conversion. However, Mr Mogg had other ideas with his second try of the game—and it was a belter, although he appeared to hurt his shoulder whilst scoring. Bosc added the two to level again at 20–20 with a quarter of an hour left and whilst both sides struggled to get in a good position to score it looked like the conditions had taken their toll. Doubtless both sides would have been happy with a draw but a silly penalty from Stuart Jones who upended John Wilson without the ball gave Bosc a chance to swing it Catalans' way, he promptly booted it over to take the spoils.

Giants' Paul Anderson was disappointed they didn't get the win, 'We were not patient enough.' Potter was delighted yet realised there was a long way to go before they could keep their thoughts on a play-off at home, 'We still have work to do.'

Kick off: 15.00, Venue: Grattan Stadium, Att: 9,181, Match official: I Smith

Bradford (12) 42

T: J Evans 1, B Jeffries 1, P Deacon 1, J Vagana 1, T Newton 1, M Cook 1, W Godwin 1 **G:** P Deacon 7

Hull FC (10) 14

T: M Tony 1, M Sing 1, K Yeaman 1 **G:** C Hall 1

Bradford squad

Halley, Evans, Sykes, Nero, Tadulala, Jeffries, Deacon, Vagana, Newton, Lynch, Cook, Finnigan, Langley
Replacements: Johnson, Godwin, Solomona, Kopczak

Hull FC squad

Tony, Sing, Yeaman, Hall, Briscoe, Washbrook, Berrigan, Cusack, Houghton, Dowes, Manu, G Horne, Radford
Replacements: Wheeldon, Thackray, Lee, Burnett

England coach Tony Smith knows only too well that he would be struggling to find a replacement in the National side if Rob Burrow got injured. But the return of the old stager Paul Deacon for Bradford may have just given Smith a reminder that he still has the class and nouse to play at the top level. He showed that in abundance during Bradford's 42–14 hammering of Challenge Cup finalists Hull FC.

Deacon's return was a huge boost for Bulls coach Steve McNamara and he was glowing in praise over Deacon's all round performance. 'Paul was really good for us today. His try will be good for his confidence.' And what a try it was as the former Great Britain star sidestepped past three players to score and then became provider for two more in a man

of the match showing that Hull just couldn't compete with. Hull were all at sea right from the kick off when the ball went out on the full giving Bradford the position for Evans to cross. Deacon's conversion made it 6–0. Poor Hull suffered again from the next kick off. This time the ball stayed in the field of play but Jeffries' break clear had the black and whites defence in such a mess it allowed Newton to dive over from close range. Deacon obliged and the Bulls were sailing away without the opposition touching the ball!

It looked easy but Bradford suffered with an injury to Newton soon after his try. The Bulls just lost a bit of shape and gave Hull the green light to fight back. Hull did this through Motu Tony but Hall couldn't add the two extras. Tempers flared soon after and Thackray and Tadulala got yellow cards after a mini-brawl that tested referee Ian Smith's patience. Then Matt Sing finished off a great piece of work from Manu and Hall to take Hull into the dressing rooms just two points adrift at 12–10. The first 15 minutes after the restart were neck and neck with Godwin scoring and Yeaman replying in kind. Then it became the Paul Deacon show as the scrum-half instigated a Matt Cook touchdown before going solo seven minutes later to take them 30–14 ahead. Deacon again showed great skills to give Vagana a rare four pointer four minutes from time and Jeffries added more woe to the men from The KC Stadium to wrap it all up with a nice solo number.

Bulls coach McNamara had little to smile about but was happy with the showing whilst Hull's Richard Agar was quick to point out that his team needed to play better against Harlequins the following

Here seen scoring a try, Paul Deacon made a superb comeback against Hull FC for Bradford.

week to give his side confidence before the Wembley showdown. 'We need to have a good performance. Some of our errors are schoolboy stuff and it's the second week running.' Hull were in poor shape and injury worries again reared their head after the match with plenty of his players bruised and battered. It would take something special if Hull were to trouble Saints at Wembley.

Sunday 17 August 2008

Kick off: 15.00, Venue: Twickenham Stoop, Att: 3,629,
Match official: S Ganson

Harlequins (16) 16
T: S Hill 1, R Purdham 1, J Rinaldi 1
G: R Purdham 2

St Helens (6) 32
T: A Gardner 1, W Talau 2, J Cayless 1, J Graham 1, P Clough 1
G: M Gidley 1, K Eastmond 3

Harlequins squad
Melling, Sharp, Clubb, Howell, Sheriffe, Hill, Orr, Ward, Randall, Haggerty, Temata, Purdham, Paul
Replacements: Rinaldi, Heckenburg, McCarthy-Scarsbrook, Grayshon

St Helens squad
Wellens, Gardner, Gidley, Talau, Meli, Pryce, Eastmond, Cayless, Cunningham, Graham, Gilmour, Wilkin, Flannery
Replacements: Hargreaves, Fozzard, Roby, Clough

St Helens had to battle hard and dig deep to turn over a Harlequins side that held sway for over an hour of a game and the final 16–32 score line did little justice to the London side's efforts. Saints coach Daniel Anderson admitted they were flat in the first half. 'We were lucky to be just 10 points down at the break.' Quins have a habit of lifting their game each time they take on St Helens and the table toppers soon realised it was going to be tough to snare a win in the capital given the London sides' impressive defence which forced errors from Anderson's men.

Rob Purdham again showed his class by scoring after just five minutes from a Howell inside pass but the try scorer failed with the extras. Ten minutes later Scott Hill set the alarm bells ringing when he scored after a great break from the improving Will Sharp who raced 30 metres clear before sending the Aussie star over the line. Saints looked to be suffering with the absence of Sean Long as they struggled to find any shape but the injection of sub James Roby paid dividends as his long break allowed Paul Clough to grab a vital four pointer. Young Kyle Eastmond converted and it appeared to settle the visitors but French hooker Julien Rinaldi soon restored the Quins' lead when he squeezed over just before half time.

Willie Talau soon got Saints back in the match after the restart but Eastmond missed the conversion to make it 16–10 and it stayed that way until midway through the half. Then James Graham, the best for Saints by a mile, latched onto a slip pass from Cunningham to cross. Gidley added the conversion to level the scores. Cunningham again was the provider just a few minutes later; his pass this time seeing Jason Cayless barge over. Eastman restored to kicking duties had no problem with the conversion and ensured Saints took control at 16–22. Gardner and Talau added two more touchdowns against a tiring home side but it had been a hard tussle for the league leaders. Quins coach Brian McDermott thought they had cracked under pressure, 'We should not have been chasing the game.'

Kick off: 15.00, Venue: Halliwell Jones Stadium, Att: 8,530,
Match official: P Bentham

Warrington (22) 34
T: C Hicks 1, Martin Gleeson 1, L Briers 1, B Westwood 1, S Grix 2 **G:** C Hicks 5

Hull KR (12) 36
T: P Fox 2, K Welham 2, Jake Webster 1, B Cockayne 1 **G:** M Dobson 6,

Warrington squad
Hicks, Riley, Martin Gleeson, King, Penny, Briers, Monaghan, Morley, Clarke, Rauhihi, Mitchell, Westwood, Grix
Replacements: Cooper, Parker, Blythe, Wood

Hull KR squad
Briscoe, Fox, Welham, Jake Webster, Steel, Galea, Dobson, Aizue, Fisher, Mills, Vella, J Netherton, Gene
Replacements: Cooke, Crossman, Cockayne, K Netherton

Seven minutes remaining and a lead of 34–18 is enough for any coach to think he's home and dry. That is what Warrington coach James Lowes must have felt when his team had completely outplayed the visiting Hull Kingston Rovers and looked set to secure another two vital league points to keep them in the top four in the table. But rugby league has a habit of pulling shock results and fight-backs out of the hat. After last week's loss to Saints, courtesy of Sean Long's last second drop goal that left the fans in a depressed state of mind, it was hard for a Warrington fan to watch their side throw away a game they had in the bag. Those loyal fans at the Halliwell Jones Stadium must have found it a bitter pill to swallow when, in the space of eight days, they witnessed their heroes fall at the last hurdle once again.

To say they were stunned was an understatement as their team controlled the match for most of the second half, yet let in 18 points in the space of the final eight minutes. Chris Hicks continued his top form by scoring soon after the kick off by taking an inside switch pass from Gleeson to dive over the whitewash. Unfortunately the try scorer couldn't add the extras. Rovers' scrum-half Dobson slotted over a penalty soon after to keep them in the game and when Jake Webster crossed after good work from Galea a shock was on the cards. Warrington doggedly dragged themselves back into the match on 20 minutes when Briers sidestepped his way under the sticks to leave Hicks an easy conversion and a lead of 10–8. Morley was showing out well for Warrington but again defence became a problem giving Kris Welham a nice try from Dobson's neat kick into the corner. The try provider failed to add the extra two but Rovers held a slim two point advantage at 10–12. Ten minutes before the break Warrington hit a purple patch when Ben Westwood crashed over and two minutes later Gleeson did the same to offer Hicks two easy conversions and a healthy 22–12 lead at the hooter.

Both sides suffered from lack of ball control and lapses in defence but it was an exciting contest which started to look lopsided soon after the restart with Grix scoring early to make it 28–12. But the Robins wouldn't lie down, Galea's well placed kick finding Cockayne, Dobson obliged with the extras to make it 28–18 leaving the game open. With 15 minutes to go Warrington appeared to have sealed the win when Briers kicked a 40/20 which allowed Simon Grix to go over for his brace of tries, Hicks' goal leaving Hull KR a huge hill to climb to overcome a 34–18 scoreboard. Actually it was more than a hill, the deficit was of Everest proportions but Paul Cooke put in a smart kick to the corner which gave Peter Fox his chance. Dobson's fine touchline conversion still appeared to be nothing more than a consolation effort. At 34–24 and just three minutes to go there should have been no nerves in the home ranks but surprisingly that's what Warrington did, opting to keep the ball alive instead of shutting up shop. Gleeson tried a hurried pass out wide that went to ground, Kevin Penny fumbled the ball and Peter Fox snatched it up to race away and dive in the corner. Dobson slotted over yet another fine conversion and the crowd started getting restless at 34–30.

Now there was panic all over the place as Warrington's defence went on holiday. It was no surprise to see Paul Cooke stab the ball into the corner with just seconds left on the clock for Welham to dive in and score out wide. That left Dobson with a kick to win a remarkable match and the little Aussie didn't fold under pressure. He even waved away Cooke who perhaps thought he would take the vital kick. But Dobson was on fire and gleefully connected cleanly and watched the ball sail between the posts to send the travelling fans into ecstasy and the home supporters looking for the nearest cliff!

Wolves coach Lowes admitted they had played dumb at times, 'That's how you throw away a game,' he added. Rovers' boss Morgan smiled and suggested, 'We learned a couple of things today, not least "Keep the faith".'

Player of Round 25
Peter Fox, Hull KR
Amazing two try hero, Fox turned a certain defeat into an amazing win for the Robins showing great speed and determination.

engage
Mutual Assurance

Friday 22 August 2008

Kick off: 19.30, Venue: The KC Stadium, Att: 12,269, Match official: T Albert

Hull FC (14) 26
T: M Tony 1, K Yeaman 1, E Dowes 1, G Horne 1 **G:** D Tickle 4, L Radford 1

Harlequins (0) 6
T: C Melling 1 **G:** R Purdham 1

Hull FC squad
Tony, Briscoe, Byrne, Yeaman, Raynor, Washbrook, Lee, Cusack, Berrigan, Dowes, Manu, Tickle, Radford
Replacements: Houghton, Thackray, G Horne, Wheeldon

Harlequins squad
Wells, Sharp, Clubb, Howell, Sheriffe, Hill, Orr, Haggerty, Randall, Ward, Temata, Grayshon, Purdham
Replacements: Melling, Williams, McCarthy-Scarsbrook, Rinaldi

Hull at last found some confidence and form to overpower below par Harlequins at The KC Stadium. But coach Richard Agar whilst pleased at the performance was left with yet more injury problems especially concerning Motu Tony who picked up a leg injury just after half time. It was another tale of woe for the club who have struggled all season to get a full fit squad out on the park each week and Agar knew his side had to register some points to give them a lift before the Wembley clash with hot favourites St Helens. 'Much better,' was the claim by the black and whites coach but the team would have to improve further to have any chance in the Challenge Cup final.

At least Hull defended well and kept the visitors to just one try, something that has been hard to do this term considering they've conceded 663 points; an average that does little to scare opponents even at home with a huge crowd behind them. The FC supporters are a loyal bunch borne out by the fact over 12,000 turned up in the hope they would see a flicker of improvement before heading for London town and Wembley. They did see an improvement mainly due to a solid performance from the defence. The return of Raynor and Tickle helped but hooker Berrigan showed the way, his promptings from the play the ball area were highlights that proved too much for the Quins.

Ewan Dowes scored after just eight minutes and, when Tickle added the conversion and then later a penalty, the home side looked in good shape. After this the defences dominated with neither side looking likely to score until a mistake by Quins late into the first half when they failed to defuse Tommy Lee's kick into the corner allowing Motu Tony to touch down.

With a lead of 14–0 at the break Harlequins needed to make a quick response. It looked like they may get their chance when Motu Tony was carried from the playing area leaving the Hull team looking despondent. Then another piece of fine work from Berrigan enabled Graeme Horne to cross for Hull's third try midway through the second half snuffing out any chance of the London outfit getting back into the match. Kirk Yeaman's try made certain of victory just before the end to take it to 26–0. Harlequins did get on the score sheet just before the hooter sounded when Purdham created a chance for Chris Melling to grab some sort of consolation.

Friday 22 August 2008

Kick off: 20.00, Venue: JJB Stadium, Att: 14,778, Match official: A Klein

Wigan (10) 16
T: M Calderwood 1, C Phelps 1, E O'Carroll 1 **G:** C Phelps 2

Leeds (24) 52
T: B Webb 2, L Smith 2, K Senior 1, K Leuluai 1, A Lauitiiti 1, L Burgess 1, K Watkins 1 **G:** K Sinfield 8

Wigan squad
Mathers, Calderwood, Phelps, Carmont, Colbon, Barrett, Leuluai, Fielden, Higham, Palea'aesina, Hansen, Coley, J Tomkins
Replacements: Prescott, O'Carroll, Mossop, Smith

Leeds squad
Webb, Smith, Ablett, Senior, Tansey, McGuire, Burrow, Leuluai, Diskin, Peacock, Ellis, Lauitiiti, Sinfield
Replacements: Scruton, Burgess, Worrall, Watkins

They often say it's not how you start but how you finish. If that's the case then Leeds Rhinos showed they were more than capable of holding onto the Super League trophy after blitzing a Wigan outfit that had also showed top form over the past few weeks. The Rhinos were still smarting over their loss to the Warriors in July by that odd point 23–22 and were obviously out for revenge in a big way. Even the most ardent Leeds fan could not have foreseen what was to unfold at the JJB Stadium as the boys from Headingley rattled up a 16–52 victory that did heaps of good for their title defence.

The return of Trent Barrett to the Warriors ranks was a bonus, but injuries to both Pat Richards and Phil Bailey put pressure on the home side. The game had hardly settled down before Richie Mathers, who had escaped any punishment for his forearm lunge the week before, was put on report for kicking out in the tackle. The incident brought blood to Rob Burrow's face, an act that certainly contributed to cranking up the tough encounter that was to follow.

The game also had a touch of controversy, none more so than the Calderwood opening try which took video referee Steve Ganson no less than four minutes to decide to give the Wigan winger the nod. Time and time again Ganson watched replay after replay to see if Barrett had knocked on from a high McGuire bomb which allowed Calderwood a clear race to the line. Eventually the scoreboard posted the points with Phelps adding the extras and stopped all at the ground from yawning and falling asleep!

Defences were well on top until the midway mark when Brent Webb wriggled over after some sustained pressure from Leeds. The Rhinos had previously gone close from attempts from Smith, Ablett, Peacock and Ellis but some desperate Wigan defence stopped them from scoring. The floodgates opened as Leeds started to rip through with ease, Ellis and Peacock again showing great strength. Luke Burgess went over on 24 minutes, Sinfield's goal making it 6–12, yet Brian Noble's men refused to lie down. Two minutes later George Carmont had a try turned down by the video referee but nothing could prevent Cameron Phelps from touching down out wide after Calderwood palmed the ball back to make it 10–12. Wigan again charged down field from the kick off and had the overlap but Tim Smith's pass went astray behind Carmont who could do nothing but watch as Lee Smith scooped up the ball to race away under the sticks for a 60 metre effort. Sinfield's conversion made it 10–18. The Rhinos extended their lead soon after when Lauitiiti's break enabled Kylie Leuluai to barge over to send them to the interval with a commanding lead of 10–24.

Wigan amazingly allowed Sinfield's second half kick off to bounce into touch for them to regain possession and Webb made short shrift of poor defence at the scrum to jink over after barely 30 seconds had gone by. Sinfield made it

five from five to leave Wigan with little chance to comeback. From there on in it was a procession to the line as Wigan faltered in defence against a rampant Rhinos side eager for points. Ali Lauitiiti and Senior took the score line to 10–42 before the Warriors got a consolation try from O'Carroll eight minutes from full time but even then Leeds refused to put the cue on the rack and secured two more tries from Lee Smith and Watkins. Sinfield's eight goals from nine attempts proved how important it was to take the field with a recognised kicker, something Wigan failed to do, but in the end skills from the Leeds attack proved the difference.

Rhinos coach McClennan claimed, 'We're getting there. That will give us some confidence, but we've still got a lot to do yet'. The score line said it all, Leeds looked good.

Brent Webb races for the line in Leeds' comprehensive beating of Wigan.

Kick off: 19.00, Venue: Stade Gilbert Brutus, Att: 8,320,
Match official: P Bentham

Catalans (10) 32
T: S Raguin 1, T Bosc 1, O Elima 1,
A Gorrell 1, J Baile 1, J Touxagas 1
G: T Bosc 4

Wakefield (26) 38
T: D Blanch 2, S Gleeson 1, R Atkins 1,
D Brough 1, T Leo-Latu 1
G: D Brough 7

Catalans squad
Greenshields, Murphy, Khattabi, Raguin,
Pelo, Mogg, Bosc, Elima, Gorrell,
Guisset, Baile, Carlaw, Touxagas
Replacements: Griffi, Duport, K Bentley,
Quintilla

Wakefield squad
Grix, Blanch, Gleeson, Atkins, Petersen,
Rooney, Brough, Bibey, Drew,
Sculthorpe, Wilkes, MacGillivray,
Demetriou
Replacements: Reilly, Watene,
Henderson, Leo-Latu

John Kear was pleased to see his side pick up the points in Perpignan.

It's not often anyone could say that Wakefield have been hot over the past few weeks—a trip to the South of France facing their ninth loss on the trot was a daunting experience for both players and the loyal fans who travelled to the land of frogs legs. With a temperature of over 30 degrees it was likely that yet another visitor would fall in a heap due to the humidity but the Wildcats stunned the home side with some fine attacking play and regained some of the form that made them top six hopefuls earlier in the year.

Danny Brough found his form too and teased the Catalans defence time and time again, so much so the visitors held a commanding lead of 10–26 at the break thanks to tries from Gleeson, Blanch,

Brough and Atkins. Brough also added three conversions and two late penalty goals to stun the home fans and leave Mick Potter, the Catalans coach, plenty to think about.

Thanks to Bosc and Mogg the home side created chances and were rewarded with tries to Touxagas and Gorrell that kept them in the match but they were guilty of keeping the ball alive far too much and forcing passes that went to ground. It may have been exciting to watch but Potter will probably reel in their exuberance in the play-offs. Not that Wakefield were complaining as it allowed them plenty of possession for Drew and Brough to start enjoying themselves.

Seven minutes into the second stanza Tevita Leo-Latu took a neat short pass from Drew to extend the lead even further at a time when Wakefield were under the cosh with Catalans going close three times in the opening five minutes. Yet another dropped ball gave the

Wildcats the possession and the position to score. The home side then rallied with three touchdowns in the space of 17 minutes, thanks to a heavy penalty count against Wakefield which sent the Wildcats into panic mode.

First Olivier Elima, then Jean Philippe Baile crossed and when Raguin took advantage of an excited defence to score out wide nerves were jangling in the Wildcats camp. Bosc added goals to the first two tries but couldn't add the vital conversion of Raguin's effort leaving just six points between the sides and 12 minutes to full time. More pressure saw Wakefield tackle like demons but Bosc grabbed up a loose pass from his own player and somehow charged under the sticks to give him an easy conversion to tie up the game at 32–32.

On the restart Brough put in a curving kick that Raguin fumbled and then for some unknown reason threw the ball back into empty space. Wakefield pounced on the free ball and Drew smartly took the blind side option to find Grix who in turn sent an inside pass to Blanch who made no mistake. Brough missed the conversion but he made amends when he kicked a penalty just before the hooter to seal a dramatic win.

Sunday 24 August 2008

Kick off: 15.00, Venue: The Galpharm Stadium, Att: 6,150,
Match official: B Thaler

Huddersfield (6) 22
T: P Whatuira 2, S Jones 1, D Kirmond 1
G: C Thorman 3

St Helens (18) 40
T: K Eastmond 2, W Talau 1,
D McGilvray 1, K Cunningham 1,
C Flannery 1
G: K Eastmond 5, S Long 3

Huddersfield squad
Hodgson, Aspinwall, Brown, Whatuira, Elford, Thorman, Robinson, Crabtree, Hudson, Mason, Jones, Lolesi, Wild
Replacements: Griffin, Raleigh, Kirmond, Faiumu

St Helens squad
Eastmond, Gardner, Gilmour, Talau, McGilvray, Wheeler, Long, Fozzard, Cunningham, Cayless, Flannery, Sculthorpe, Hargreaves
Replacements: Meli, Graham, Clough, Thompson

Wembley-bound St Helens looked likely to be without prop forward Jason Cayless after he suffered a knee injury in the opening minutes of their 22–40 victory at the Galpharm Stadium. It was a bitter blow to the league leaders who yet again showed their class in ripping the Giants apart, registering their 20th successive victory. St Helens went behind early in the match when Stuart Jones scored a try from a nothing kick which sliced off the boot of big Eorl Crabtree and confused the Saints defence enough for Whatuira to race 50 metres to create a shock touchdown. Thorman added the extras, but it just poked the visitors in the eye. They levelled the scores soon after when Cunningham produced one of his play the ball specials and barged over. Long converted, as he also did for Willie Talau's try a few minutes later to take it to 6–12.

Youngster Kyle Eastmond yet again displayed his talent by scoring on the 25 minute mark, although it looked like there had been a knock-on from Long before the fullback had chance to cross. But the scrum-half ignored the boos from the home fans to calmly add the conversion and send the visitors in at the break 6–18 in front.

The Giants looked a different side after

Willie Talau evades the Huddersfield defenders in Saints' victory at the Galpharm Stadium.

the restart and deservedly got back into the match through two tries in the first quarter of the second half from centre Paul Whatuira. The first of the two tries came from a Robinson kick, the latter after good work from Elford who kicked ahead from a Saints handling error to set up his centre partner. Thorman could only add the extras to one of the tries but at 16–18 the game was on the edge, that was until St Helens, like so often, clicked into gear. Kyle Eastmond took control as Long had been rested at half time and the new 'super kid' steered them home. Eastmond's five goals and two tries were too much for Huddersfield as he jinked and used amazing speed to irritate the defence. Tries from Flannery and Dean McGilvray ensured Saints kept Huddersfield at bay before man of the match Eastmond wrapped it up with a neat try two minutes from the hooter.

The Giants' effort wasn't up to standard according to coach Paul Anderson 'I thought we were poor,' although the club had some consolation from the try from youngster Danny Kirmond who showed amazing footwork to score with a great solo effort. Saints had rested five first teamers but Anderson was happy with the way the youngsters played, and that Paul Sculthorpe had come through the full 80 minutes. 'In a normal week I would have given him a rest but wild horses won't stop his making himself available for selection [at Wembley].'

Sunday 24 August 2008

Kick off: 19.30, Venue: The Jungle, Att: 5,902, Match official: I Smith

Castleford (22) 44
T: S Donlan 2, R Owen 2, K Dixon 1, M Wainwright 3, L Dorn 1, N Catic 1
G: K Dixon 1, C Huby 1

Warrington (12) 24
T: C Riley 2, L Briers 1, M Blythe 1
G: C Hicks 3, C Riley 1

Castleford squad

Donlan, Owen, Shenton, Dixon, Wainwright, McGoldrick, Dorn, Sargent, Henderson, Korkidas, Guttenbeil, Catic, Lupton
Replacements: Leafa, Higgins, Huby, Boyle

Warrington squad

Hicks, Riley, Martin Gleeson, King, Welch, Briers, Monaghan, Morley, Clarke, Parker, Mitchell, Westwood, Grix
Replacements: Blythe, Bracek, Cooper, Wood

Has the Warrington revival burst? This was the question asked by the Wolves fans who made the trip to The Jungle and endured a sad loss where defence seemed to have become a stranger to Warrington's tactics. Close encounters over the previous few weeks obviously had drained the Wolves both physically and mentally as they allowed Castleford to boss the game for most parts of the match. Luke Dorn again put in a top showing as did his half back partner Ryan McGoldrick. They completely overshadowed Monaghan and Briers who looked lethargic and confused for most of the 80 minutes.

Dorn set things in motion after five minutes with an intercept of a pass and raced away the length of the pitch to swerve out wide and score. Kirk Dixon missed with the conversion. In fact the Tigers only slotted over two conversions from 10 tries in the end, a factor that prevented Warrington from even more

embarrassment on the day. It became evident early that both Morley and Parker were not fully fit. This allowed Castleford to boss things in the forwards which gave Warrington little chance for success. Although for a brief period when Briers scored after seven minutes it looked likely they would weather the early storm but their confidence soon faded along with poor attempts at tackling which set the Tigers on a scoring spree. Wainwright grabbed a hat trick with the last play of the game but his two first half efforts cemented a Tigers win and not surprisingly the home side went in at the break 22–12 up.

James Lowes was a fierce looking Warrington coach as he left the playing area at the interval to take his troops to task. His words of wisdom appeared to do the trick when Matthew Blythe crossed on 47 minutes to give them hope at 22–18. However, the Warrington revival was soon quashed when Richard Owen scored twice within as many minutes. If Huby had been on target with the conversions it would have sunk the visitors out of sight but when Ned Catic strolled over with considerable ease to make it 36–18, coach Matterson must have felt safe. Castleford did have a small scare when Riley scored to drag the Wolves back to 36–24 but Dixon and Wainwright's third sank any hopes of a revival from Warrington. Michael Shenton was in fine form and played his opposite Matt King off the park and the fact the Tigers had rested Joe Westerman and had Brent Sherwin injured only added confusion as to why James Lowes' men performed so dismally.

'It was a full team effort,' said a pleased Castleford coach Terry Matterson, whilst Lowes went away wondering how on earth he could get his side back into the

Player of Round 26

Ryan McGoldrick, Castleford

Best game of the season for the creative Tiger. McGoldrick's combination with Dorn was superb and too hot for Warrington to handle.

swing for the play-offs. They would need a last round win at home against Huddersfield to give them a home tie in the top six showdown.

Monday 25 August 2008

Kick off: 14.15, Venue: Grattan Stadium, Att: 10,353, Match official: R Silverwood

Bradford (10) 42

T: P Sykes 1, D Halley 1, J Evans 1, C Nero 1, S Tadulala 1, T Newton 1, M Cook 1, D Solomona 1
G: P Deacon 5

Hull KR (18) 18

T: K Welham 1, M Vella 2
G: M Dobson 3

Bradford squad

Sykes, Halley, Evans, Nero, Tadulala, Jeffries, Deacon, Vagana, Newton, Lynch, Cook, Finnigan, Langley
Replacements: Johnson, Godwin, Solomona, Kopczak

Hull KR squad

Briscoe, Fox, Welham, Jake Webster, Steel, Galea, Dobson, Aizue, Fisher, Mills, Vella, Lovegrove, Gene
Replacements: Cooke, Cockayne, Crossman, K Netherton

When any player retires it becomes a nostalgic moment and the Bradford fans turned out in force to say farewell to prop forward Joe Vagana who after many years has decided to hang up his boots. There was a carnival atmosphere amongst the home crowd as they expected the Bulls to send the big fellow away with a victory and at the same time secure two points that could move them even further up the league table. They knew a win could grab the fourth spot, depending on other games in the final week, but after the first 20 minutes not many in the Odsal Grattan Stadium were having thoughts of a home tie in the play-offs. This was because Hull KR, who also had an outside chance to grab the sixth spot, played the Bulls off the park and raced away to a commanding 0–18 lead.

It was 20 minutes of sheer agony for the Bulls supporters. First they watched Kris Welham intercept Jeffries' pass to race the length of the pitch for a shock score. Dobson added the two points, and then soon after Mick Vella got into the act by handing off Sykes for another converted try. Vella then repeated the feat seven

Big Joe Vagana says farewell to the Grattan Stadium.

Matt Cook gets the ball down for the Bulls.

minutes later, this time crashing through the defence to silence the home crowd and give Dobson yet another easy two pointer. Bradford just weren't at the races and needed something special to fight back with. Thankfully the experience of Paul Deacon came to the fore and it was his kicking and passing game that turned the tide as Paul Sykes and Dave Halley crossed just before the break to give the Bulls some hope for the second half.

Bulls boss Steve McNamara was eager to change things at the break. He reverted back to their old defensive pattern rather than the new one they tried out in the first half, which obviously wasn't working. It did the trick and they started to force the errors from the Rovers with tough no nonsense tackles that stunned the visitors and lifted the home side. Three tries in 10 minutes blasted Hull KR off the park, Solomona burst over, followed by Tadulala who accepted Deacon's pass with glee and when Matt

Cook kicked through and regathered it was clear that the Robins had shot their bolt at 26–18 down.

Chris Nero cleverly got to Deacon's high kick to stretch them away even further and with Deacon adding the extras it was all over at 32–18. Rovers had no answer and were out on their feet trying to stem the tide but more heartache was to come from Evans and Newton who added two more four pointers. It was good to see the Bulls hooker Newton concentrate on the game rather than continue his battle with Stanley Gene who he claimed (to the referee) had bitten him. Newton retracted the claim after the match but his last minute try enabled Vagana the chance to slot over the conversion in a nice gesture to finish his career at Odsal but the big prop sent it wide. The players claimed they had dug deep for Big Joe and showed some great spirit in turning the game around but they needed to improve before they could challenge for glory.

Friday 5 September 2008

Kick off: 20.00, Venue: GPW Recruitment Stadium, Att: 13,500, Match official: A Klein

St Helens (6) 16
T: A Gardner 1, M Gidley 2
G: S Long 2

Wigan (12) 16
T: G Carmont 1, J Tomkins 1
G: P Richards 4

St Helens squad
Wellens, Gardner, Gidley, Talau, Meli, Roby, Long, Fozzard, Cunningham, Graham, Gilmour, Wilkin, Flannery
Replacements: Hargreaves, Clough, Fa'asavalu, Eastmond

Wigan squad
Mathers, Phelps, Goulding, Carmont, Richards, Barrett, Leuluai, Fielden, Higham, Coley, Hansen, Bailey, J Tomkins
Replacements: Palea'aesina, Colbon, Prescott, Smith

Not many Wigan fans turned up at the GPW Recruitment Stadium expecting a close contest as the previous three encounters this year had St Helens averaging nearly 50 points a game over the Warriors. This was crunch time and Brian Noble's boys had started their launch for play-off glory in the same fashion as last year and came with a much more intense defence than earlier in the season.

Not that Saints laid down, far from it, as both sets of forwards crunched into each other with no regard for their safety. Tempers were running hot and when Palea'aesina launched a late shoulder charge on Graham midway through the first half the entire game erupted with the Saints prop forward chasing after the big Wigan unit to square things up earning him a sin-binning for retaliation. Up until then

Saints snuff out the Wigan attack.

things were all square as defences were on top and few chances on offer yet it was no surprise with St Helens down to 12 men that the visitors took the lead.

Trent Barrett was again finding top form and his pass sent in centre Carmont for a neat try just a few minutes after Graham had left the field and it was soon followed by a try from Joel Tomkins who crashed over after fine work from Leuluai and the impressive Barrett. Richards' trusty boot converted both to make the score 0–12 to leave the home side facing an uphill battle. The return of Graham added extra incentive to Saints' play and at last they started to create space, helped by some silly penalties given away by Wigan that allowed them a chance to send Gidley in near the right corner. With three Wigan defenders swamped around the Aussie centre it was hard to establish if he had got the ball down but after a long wait Gidley was given the benefit of the doubt by video ref Ian Smith. Long added a vital conversion from out wide to send them into the break just six down at 6–12.

Pat Richards again proved that a solid goal kicker is worth his weight in gold when he thumped over a long range penalty to stretch Wigan's lead to 6–14 soon after the restart. It looked like Saints were getting tired as they struggled to get into the swing again and they looked thankful of yet another penalty given away by Wigan who started to lack discipline. Fa'asavalu was stopped short and from the play the ball Cunningham dashed down the short blind side to enable Gidley to feed Gardner who crossed for his 29th try of the season. Long converted again from out wide to bring them back to just two points adrift at 12–14.

Keiron Cunningham proudly displays the League Leaders Shield. © Bernard Platt

An hour into the game the home side took the lead for the first time as Gidley spun out of a tackle to touchdown after good work from Kyle Eastmond. Long missed the extras but it was turning out to be a thriller as the huge crowd of over 14,000 braced themselves for a thrilling finish. And so it turned out as Meli had a try turned down by the video ref before Pat Richards' boot squared things up at 16–16. Both sides went close before Wigan gained a penalty only for Richards to turn down an attempt to kick at goal on the half way line. He went for distance instead to set the Warriors up for a drop goal attempt which sailed wide past the posts with just two minutes remaining. But Wigan had their opposition stuck in their own half and ensured Saints never got a chance to go for a one pointer.

All in all it was a fair result with both outfits giving everything and nobody was upset as the draw enabled Saints to lift the League Leaders trophy for the fourth year on the trot with Wigan grabbing a home play-off. Brian Noble was far from disappointed over the decision of not going for goal, 'Keeping the Saints at their end of the field was the right decision, I wouldn't criticise them for that. There were plenty of things we did well and it was a good solid performance to take into the play-offs,' he added. Saints boss Anderson was upset over the Graham incident claiming that Palea'aesina should have been sin-binned too. 'James was hit high and late.' Either way it set up the league for a thrilling play-off series and fans left the ground thinking that maybe Wigan could be the dark horses yet again. The Warriors certainly looked in the mood, especially Barrett who made it clear he wants to leave these shores with a major trophy under his belt.

Friday 5 September 2008

Kick off: 20.00, Venue: Belle Vue, Att: 6,448, Match official: S Ganson

Wakefield (12) 12
T: S Grix 2 **G:** D Brough 2

Leeds (12) 30
T: B Webb 1, S Donald 1, J Tansey 1, A Lauitiiti 2 **G:** R Burrow 1, K Sinfield 4

Wakefield squad
Grix, Blanch, Martin, Atkins, Peterser, Rooney, Brough, Watene, Drew, Bibey, MacGillivray, Golden, Demetriou
Replacements: Sculthorpe, Wilkes, Leo-Latu, Henderson

Leeds squad
Webb, Smith, Ablett, Senior, Donald, McGuire, Burrow, Scruton, Tansey, Peacock, Lauitiiti, Ellis, Sinfield
Replacements: Jones-Buchanan, Burgess, Bailey, Kirke

The Leeds Rhinos arrived at Belle Vue in the knowledge they needed plenty of points to secure a convincing win and hoped Saints came unstuck against Wigan to secure the League Leaders position. The wet conditions didn't lift their spirits too much as they struggled to overcome a gutsy showing from the home side who pushed them all the way.

It was a tough opening and when Webb was put on report for a high shot it wasn't going to be easy for Brian McClennan's mob who finally broke through midway into the first half from a Jordan Tansey try which Sinfield converted. However Wakefield showed resolve despite having gone through a bad patch for a few weeks and took the lead when two quick tries from Grix stunned the Rhinos down to their boots. Leo-Latu's pass from close range earned the fullback his first whilst a trademark off load from Sculthorpe sent him in for his second to take a 12–6 lead.

Wakefield's kicking game this season has been out of the top drawer, if they could have matched that with a stern defence they would have contested the play-offs and whilst many of their fans were disappointed it looked likely they would end the season with a major scalp to give them hope for next year. Rooney showed some neat off loads whilst Drew and Brough provided them with good positions to launch the attacks that needed some brave defence, especially from Gareth Ellis who was eager to finish the regular season with a top game at his old stomping ground. He didn't disappoint and produced some crunching tackles.

The Rhinos needed something special and it came five minutes from the break in the shape of winger Donald who stepped inside and kicked through to the posts then beat the defence to the line leaving Sinfield an easy conversion. Wakefield should have taken the lead again just seconds before the hooter when Atkins made a clean break only for Drew to be taken out off the ball but Brough couldn't add the penalty so it was all square at 12–12 at half time.

It was stalemate for 20 minutes after the restart as both sides seemed more interested in offering big shots at each other in bone crunching exchanges. The game turned on its head when Leeds got a lucky bounce that confused Grix and allowed Lauitiiti to snap up the ball and send in the Rhinos' skipper Sinfield for a game breaking try. The conversion from the try scorer jumped them in front 12–18 with 20 minutes remaining.

The conditions were beginning to tell on both sides and power rather than skill was needed to win the match. Leeds found it in the rampaging runs of Lauitiiti who scored two touchdowns to see off a spirited effort from the Wildcats, a factor that their coach, John Kear, was only too pleased over. 'I'm disappointed with the result but delighted and proud of the effort.' Rhinos' boss Brian McClennan paid tribute to the home side, 'It was a tough game, Wakefield came out with much enthusiasm.' It was a good, hard run out for Leeds and they can now rest up for a fortnight before facing St Helens where the winners go straight to Old Trafford.

Kick off: 18.00, Venue: The Jungle, Att: 8,067, Match official: I Smith

Castleford (10) 16
T: R Owen 1, K Dixon 1, R Boyle 1
G: K Dixon 2

Bradford (10) 18
T: S Tadulala 3 **G:** P Deacon 1, I Harris 2

Castleford squad
Donlan, Owen, Shenton, Dixon, Wainwright, McGoldrick, Dorn, Sargent, Henderson, Korkidas, Guttenbeil, Catic, Lupton
Replacements: Leafa, Higgins, Huby, Boyle

Bradford squad
Sykes, Halley, Evans, Nero, Tadulala, Jeffries, Deacon, Vagana, Newton, Lynch, Cook, Finnigan, Langley
Replacements: Harris, Solomona, Godwin, Kopczak

Winger Semi Tadulala became the hero of the day at The Jungle helping to squeeze Bradford into the play-offs and earn a trip to Wigan but it was a desperate struggle and a controversial penalty that secured the win. The Bradford winger scored two tries; one after just two minutes into the match but it was his second on 70 minutes that allowed the Bulls to get back into the game when it looked like a home win was on the cards.

Bradford swamped the Tigers in their previous contests this year scoring just under a century of points, so it was more than likely they would ease past them

Stuart Donlan is stopped in his tracks by Bradford's Terry Newton and Jamie Langley.

this time around. Not so, and it took a brave referee to award the Bulls a last minute penalty that broke the Tigers' hearts. Referee Ian Smith won't expect any Christmas cards from the Castleford area after he penalised Ned Catic for holding down Simon Finnigan too long. That was after Harris had thrown the dummy and broke into open space before handing on to Finnigan who was halted by a thrilling tackle from Catic that should have seen the match end in a draw.

Understandably, Catic had more than a few words to say after the referee gave the penalty and was promptly shown the red card. As he trudged towards the dressing room Harris booted the ball over the cross bar to snatch victory. Harris proved to be a valuable substitution for Deacon as his sideline conversion of Tadulala's try kept them in the match and able to take advantage of those vital last minute two points. Castleford were heartbroken for they knew they had the game in the bag through some fierce defence and a tireless effort from hooker Andrew Henderson. With 10 minutes remaining and a six point lead they looked comfortable until Tadulala and Harris produced the magic. Tigers coach Terry Matterson was proud of his players, 'It's been a challenging year and it's been a credit to the players.' Bulls boss McNamara whilst pleased with the win knew they had to improve to push Wigan in the play-offs, 'We played well within ourselves, there's a lot more to come.'

Castleford celebrate as Ryan Boyle scores but to no avail as Bradford take the points.

Saturday 6 September 2008

Kick off: 18.00, Venue: Halliwell Jones Stadium, Att: 8,585,
Match official: B Thaler

Warrington (6) 20
T: C Riley 1, M King 1, K Penny 1, J Clarke 1 **G:** C Hicks 2

Huddersfield (24) 38
T: S Wild 2, C Thorman 1, D Faiumu 1, K Brown 1, R Hudson 1
G: C Thorman 7

Warrington squad
Hicks, Riley, Grix, King, Penny, Martin Gleeson, Monaghan, Morley, Clarke, Rauhihi, Mitchell, Westwood, Blythe
Replacements: Wood, Parker, Cooper, Bracek

Huddersfield squad
Hodgson, Aspinwall, Wild, Lawrence, Elford, Thorman, Robinson, Crabtree, Faiumu, Mason, Raleigh, Jones, Brown
Replacements: Hudson, Jackson, Griffin, Kirmond

Warrington knew that a win against Huddersfield would give them fourth spot and a home play-off so the local fans were keen to see them overcome a Giants side that were playing for nothing other than pride. Like so often this season the Wolves supporters witnessed a poor showing where again their defence just fell apart. When James Lowes took over from Paul Cullen they had a dream run of wins, followed by a shocking run of losses that left everyone in rugby league confused, including their coach.

What Warrington produced was nothing short of abysmal as the Giants displayed style, skill and determination to rock the Warrington defence and leave them knowing a trip to the South of France was on the cards if Bradford beat the Tigers. Stephen Wild had a field day, time and time again he broke through out wide to set up positions for his side to control the match. His first run allowed Crabtree to pass to Thorman who crossed after just three minutes. This score started some of the home fans booing and by the time the first half hooter sounded most of the Wolves faithful had joined in.

Lee Briers failed a fitness test so Martin Gleeson took the stand off role and it was clear that his skill factor was impeded by his new position—it was a gamble that didn't pay off—but despite Warrington having many top players injured they should have had the measure of Huddersfield. Adrian Morley again picked up an injury and Rauhihi, despite passing a fitness test before the game, looked to be struggling. The Giants were in no mood to offer sympathy and went into rampage mode to lead 6–24 at half time.

Warrington made too many errors to even think about giving the Giants a contest although Huddersfield took their foot off the pedal whilst coasting in the second stanza which allowed Warrington into the game and gave them some hope, King, Penny and Clarke crossing in a 20 minute purple patch that got them within six points. The Giants turned up the heat with scores from Faiumu and Wild to complete the victory. To make matters worse Rob Parker picked up an injury with just seconds remaining to add even further woe to a demoralised Wolves camp.

Coach Lowes was furious, 'I'm not very happy at all. It was a shocking game.' It might have been shocking for the Wolves but far from upsetting for Huddersfield who have finished the season with a flourish. They must feel confident of a huge improvement next term under a new coach.

Sunday 7 September 2008

Kick off: 12.00, Venue: New Craven Park, Att: 10,197,
Match official: P Bentham

Hull KR (18) 36
T: P Fox 1, J Steel 1, S Gene 1, M Vella 1, M Aizue 1, B Cockayne 1
G: M Dobson 5, B Fisher 1

Hull FC (4) 8
T: K Yeaman 2

Hull KR squad
Briscoe, Fox, Welham, Webster, Steel, Galea, Dobson, Mills, Fisher, J Netherton, Gene, Vella, Cooke
Replacements: Crossman, Aizue, Cockayne, Watts

Hull FC squad
Hall, Sing, G Horne, Yeaman, Raynor, Washbrook, Webster, Dowes, Berrigan, Cusack, Manu, Tickle, Radford
Replacements: Houghton, Lee, Thackray, Burnett

Normally a 'derby' match between the two Hull sides gains top billing but such has been the disappointment out on Humberside this year that the two rivals were left playing for pride alone. Whilst the Rovers can console themselves in finishing mid table it was hard for the black and whites to go to Craven Park knowing they would end the season next to bottom.

Whilst Hull FC look back on reaching Wembley they have to accept the fact they have under achieved this term even allowing for injuries to key players. Young coach Richard Agar was hoping for a fine display to take them into next year with some sort of confidence. Sadly for him and the fans the players failed to show up to their potential. In front of a record crowd the Robins took their rivals apart with some fine play. Michael Dobson was the key factor to success, his all round game was inspirational and playing behind a strong pack it was obvious to all that he would overshadow former KR star James Webster who was making his debut for the black and whites.

Not only was it a record crowd but it was the first time a video referee system was used at a non televised game and Ashley Klein was called to make three decisions, one a no try whilst two others were awarded. Either way it was all Rovers and when Jon Steel burst over after just 10 minutes it seemed it was going to be a long day at the office for Agar's men. Rovers coach Justin Morgan was proud of his team in the 36–8 win but praised Hull FC for their display at Wembley, 'It was always going to be difficult for them to back up and they did the city proud.' Deep down you sensed that Morgan expected more this season but they have beaten all the teams above them this year apart from Leeds so a seventh spot is not to be scoffed at. Hull FC on the other hand can feel disappointed with only eight league wins and Agar has made it clear a few players will be 'shipped out' this close season.

After Steel's try Hull FC tried hard to stop the free flowing Robins and scrambled back well before the floodgates opened on 30 minutes, Makali Aizue and Ben Cockayne flying over to send them into an 18–0 lead. Hull did get some relief when Yeaman, Hull FC's best player, accepted a pass from Hall to cross out wide to make it 18–4 just before the half time hooter sounded.

Yeaman scored again 10 minutes into the restart but Tickle failed at goal again and the miss appeared to take the wind out of the sails of the visitors, allowing Rovers to take charge again. Paul Cooke provided one of his trade mark long passes to send Peter Fox in out wide and then Michael Vella added another eight minutes later. Local favourite Stanley Gene brought more pain to the black and whites with a memorable score to which Dobson again

Stanley Gene dives in to claim the ball from James Webster and score in Hull KR's win over Hull FC.

added the extras to add to his successes from the previous two touchdowns. All in all it was a fine performance from the Rovers who made it 5–3 in their favour in Super League clashes.

Sunday 7 September 2008

Kick off: 15.00, Venue: Twickenham Stoop, Att: 2,447,
Match official: R Silverwood

Harlequins (22) 34
T: W Sharp 1, C Randall 2, R Purdham 1, J Rinaldi 2 **G:** R Purdham 5

Catalans (8) 24
T: D Pelo 2, A Mogg 1, C McGuire 1 **G:** A Gorrell 4

Harlequins squad
Sharp, Wells, Howell, Clubb, Melling, Hill, Orr, Ward, Randall, Haggerty, Temata, Purdham, Paul
Replacements: Mbu, Rinaldi, McCarthy-Scarsbrook, Heckenburg

Catalans squad
Greenshields, Pelo, Wilson, Raguin, Stacul, Mogg, McGuire, Elima, Gorrell, Guisset, Mounis, Croker, Carlaw
Replacements: Chan, Casty, Touxagas, Fakir

The Harlequins have not had much luck against the Catalans Dragons in the three previous encounters and justifiably have construed to throw away a win on each occasion. Their final throw of the dice this season proved far too much for a French outfit that appear to have had their eyes on the play-offs for quite some time. The visitors took the lead early when Mogg crossed on 13 minutes and when Gorrell converted to add to his earlier penalty it looked like they were not going to miss the injured and influential Thomas Bosc. That lead was soon pegged back when fullback Will Sharp scored to make it 6–8,

and then came a burst of three tries within six minutes, Randall bagged a brace whilst Purdham chased after Orr's grubber kick to touch down and leave Catalans stranded at 22–8 at the hooter.

Rinaldi celebrated his final game at the Stoop by squeezing through under several bodies to touch down with just a quarter of the match remaining and at 28–8 it should have been all over. The visitors found some space and shape to make a game of it and scored three tries in 10 minutes, McGuire and Pelo (2) made the home side look shaky yet a second try from Rinaldi against his old club sealed the win five minutes from the end.

It would be an insult to the Quins to suggest Mick Potter's boys had pulled the punches of late for it was a fine effort from the London club to finish in such a manner but it didn't please coach McDermott, 'I don't think we played well, we made some breaks but many errors'. Mick Potter, the Catalans coach, also shrugged his shoulders over a match that failed to excite 'It was a scrappy game where we overplayed things.'

Far too many mistakes took the edge off the game in wet conditions and it had an 'End of season' look about it. Despite this the two Quins hookers, Randall and Rinaldi, displayed solid performances and there was a fine farewell showing from Scott Hill who displayed touches of magic that reminded us how much of an influential player he has been over the past decade. The game was also a fitting tribute to Henry Paul who will ply his trade in the Union ranks next season and will be missed down the Twickenham Stoop way. The London outfit have a few up and coming youngsters and the future looks bright, yet they need to secure a talisman with experience for next season to help bring them on.

engage
Mutual Assurance

Friday 12 September 2008

Kick off: 20.00, Venue: The Stobart Stadium, Att: 6,806,
Match official: A Klein

Wigan (12) 30
T: M Calderwood 1, T Leuluai 1, H Hansen 1, J Tomkins 1, G Hock 1
G: P Richards 5

Bradford (8) 14
T: A Lynch 1, S Finnigan 1
G: P Deacon 2, I Harris 1

Wigan squad
Mathers, Calderwood, Phelps, Carmont, Richards, Barrett, Leuluai, Fielden, Higham, Coley, Hansen, Bailey, J Tomkins
Replacements: Palea'aesina, Hock, O'Carroll, Smith

Bradford squad
Platt, Evans, Sykes, Nero, Tadulala, Jeffries, Deacon, Vagana, Newton, Lynch, Solomona, Finnigan, Langley
Replacements: Harris, Morrison, Cook, Kopczak

Irrespective of what you say or feel about Brian Noble's coaching you can't deny the guy has what it takes when it comes to big game tactics and the ability to overcome off field difficulties beyond his control. Having a home advantage is a super boost to any sudden death encounter and the Warriors were happy to entertain Noble's former club, the Bradford Bulls, for the sudden death play-off.

Sadly they were forced to move away from the JJB Stadium and play at Widnes after the stadium owner Dave Whelan refused to let them play there! Whelan dropped the bombshell early in the week that left the fans frustrated and the players amazed they would give up home advantage and the huge following they normally receive from their loyal fans. It wasn't the best scenario but Noble dug deep to encourage his players to push it all to one side and begged the fans to turn The Stobart Stadium into their own. That they did and despite a few boycotting the place, the noise at the home of the Widnes Vikings was amazing and so was the match even though a tinge of controversy overshadowed a fine contest.

The 30–14 score line suggests Wigan won easily, far from it, in fact Bradford bossed the opening moments, took the lead from Deacon's penalty and should have been awarded a try to Nero soon after but the video referee Phil Bentham turned it down for a knock-on. A superb kick into the corner from Deacon allowed winger Tadulala a chance to flick the ball backwards which allowed Nero an easy touch down, yet Bentham took nearly four minutes to decide as he watched the slow motion replay over and over again and finally awarding the knock-on and no try. It amazed not only people at the ground but thousands of viewers watching on TV. It came at a crucial moment for Bradford who were in full control against a nervous Warriors defence thanks to their rugged start amongst the forwards where Lynch and Vagana were awesome.

An eight point lead would have been a huge mental boost for the Bulls and one wonders if Wigan could have clawed

Stuart Fielden off loads in the tackle.

their way back. It became even more crucial when on 25 minutes Andy Lynch side stepped his way over near the sticks to give Deacon an easy conversion that made it 0–8—add the no try decision and you could see why the Bradford camp were frustrated. Not that Wigan were complaining; they hung on to regroup and sort out the defence problems and for once started to find space and get over the advantage line. The introduction of Palea'aesina once again revived Wigan and his strong bursts helped them gain good field position for the two half backs, Leuluai and Barrett, to start singing from the same hymn book.

Barrett again started the fight-back with some neat play that gave Hock and Fielden the chance to shine. From one of Hock's runs they positioned themselves to allow Leuluai to dart from dummy-half and race away to score near the posts giving Richards an easy conversion to

leave them just two points adrift at 6–8. Four minutes later the Warriors took the lead after Barrett had been held up near to the line but the Bulls couldn't halt Leuluai getting a short pass away to Hansen who burst over from close range. Richards obliged again with the extras and one wondered if the bubble had burst for Bradford who watched their scrum-half Paul Deacon limp away to the dressing room in agony.

The non appearance of Deacon for the restart was a huge blow; the Bulls needed a constructive player to lift their spirits and his absence gave Wigan the green light to go further in front courtesy of winger Calderwood, who appeared to save his best until last. Barrett's kick into the corner was inch perfect and the speedster had an easy job of picking up the ball and diving over, yet he slipped and came so close to the dead in goal line that it was referred to the video referee again. This time the try scorer got the nod but it was a close-run thing. Richards made it three from three and Wigan were coasting at 18–8.

Andy Lynch appeared to have pulled his side back into the game but again the video referee turned the try down, although it appeared he had got it right this time. It was yet another mental blow to the Bulls but instead of lowering their heads they bounced back with a

Iafeta Palea'aesina takes up the charge.

The Wigan team applaud their fans for supporting them at 'home' at Widnes.

Finnigan try that Harris goaled to make it 18–14 and game on with still 30 minutes remaining.

Nerves were jangling on both sides and it took the experience of Barrett to once again produce a fantastic kick into open space giving Calderwood a chance to pick up and off load to Joel Tomkins, a player who has come on in leaps and bounds of late, who scored. Richards again booted over to return the Warriors to a 10 point lead. Bradford looked jaded at this point and struggled to keep their defensive formation in shape and it came as no surprise when Hock dived between the sticks to ensure victory.

Bradford boss McNamara was furious over the Nero no try, 'I don't know how they can get a decision wrong, the ball went back before going forward. The only luck we have had this season is bad luck,' he added and left the stadium far from impressed by the officials. Brian Noble wouldn't be dragged into the issue but thanked the Wigan fans for their support, 'Credit goes to the fans for lifting the side, we thought the Bulls would hang their hat on a huge start and they had the quality to trouble us but we were patient and responded with energy

and vigour.' They must have watched with interest the clash the following day in the South of France where Warrington were taking on Catalans. Would it be a home tie or would they be booking flights to Perpignan?

Saturday 13 September 2008

Kick off: 18.30, Venue: Stade Gilbert Brutus, Att: 8,442,
Match official: S Ganson

Catalans (22) 46
T: C Greenshields 1, J Murphy 4,
D Pelo 1, T Bosc 1, C McGuire 1,
G Mounis 1 **G:** T Bosc 5

Warrington (2) 8
T: S Grix 1 **G:** C Hicks 2

Catalans squad
Greenshields, Murphy, Wilson, Raguin, Pelo, Mogg, Bosc, Chan, McGuire, Elima, Croker, Mounis, Carlaw
Replacements: Guisset, Casty, Fakir, Baile

Warrington squad
Hicks, Riley, Martin Gleeson, King, Penny, Briers, Monaghan, Morley, Clarke, Rauhihi, Westwood, Mitchell, Grix
Replacements: Wood, Bracek, Cooper, Blythe

It would be churlish to think Wigan officials had booked flights straight after that Friday night victory but considering Warrington's form of late it was hardly expected a troubled injury hit Wolves side would create major problems for Catalans. With the return of Briers and the amazing recovery by Adrian Morley from a bad rib injury one could never write them off.

One pities the poor bloke who has bet the odd shilling on Warrington over the years for they are without doubt the Jekyll and Hyde of rugby league. Surprisingly the sun wasn't shining down in Perpignan and a strong wind was sweeping a chill down from the mountains. The heat and humidity wouldn't help Catalans' cause, but would it bring out the best of Briers' kicking game? The answer took a while to emerge. A brave defence for the first quarter by Warrington frustrated the home side who were enjoying the strong gusts of wind in the first half but never really capitalised until Murphy went in for his first try out wide on 20 minutes. That erased the penalty goal from Chris Hicks just a few minutes into the game. Once the Catalans winger dived over it was all one way as the Wolves had no answer for the delightful combination of Bosc and Mogg who created chance after chance. It was little wonder that Murphy ended up scoring four tries, a club record that would not have been achieved if coach Mick Potter had not selected him late in the week after deciding to leave out Aaron Gorrell. To say he took his chances is an understatement but the forwards set the scene and the skills of the two halves guided them home.

Casey McGuire was another star who teased the Warrington defence with sharp runs from dummy-half and with

Thomas Bosc added a try and five goals in the victory over Warrington. © RLphotos.com

the likes of Chan, Mounis and Elima doing damage up front it was going to be tough for Warrington to get back into the match. Two Murphy tries and one each for Pelo and Bosc left Warrington facing a 22–2 deficit at the break. But even with the strong wind behind them in the second half one hardly expected a fight-back despite the efforts of Morley and Westwood who were the pick of a tired and lacklustre outfit.

Casey McGuire enjoyed a free run to the line soon after the restart and another four tries were to follow, interrupted by a Simon Grix try midway through the half. Three tries in as many minutes blasted Warrington away as the heads went down before Murphy finished his try scoring feat of four three minutes from the final hooter.

It was a great showing by the home side who entertained a big crowd of over

8,000 with some scintillating stuff ensuring another home tie against Wigan. Not surprisingly the club announced it expected a full house the following week after it decided to not take the game away to the Union Stadium one mile down the road for the Wigan clash. The Stade Aimé Giral holds just over 15,000 and whilst it would boost the coffers it was left to the players to make the decision of playing at 'home', a fact that pleased coach Mick Potter who accepted his side had played their best rugby football this year, 'It's up there with some of the best performances of the season. Our guys were determined and they executed well in the second half.'

James Lowes was upbeat despite this being the fifth loss on the trot to end a disappointing year, 'We had a few bumps and bruises, but they put their hands up to play. I'm proud of the boys for their effort,' he added. But Lowes no doubt left the South of France wondering what went wrong after experiencing a good start to his top flight coaching career. To his credit Lowes made himself unavailable to help out the England training staff for the upcoming World Cup stating he wanted to concentrate on preparing Warrington for next season instead. He certainly learned a lot in a short time and one wouldn't bet on him not making a few changes for next season's charge for a higher position in the league table.

Player of the Play-offs   Week 1

Thomas Bosc, Catalans
Creative and energetic, Bosc produced amazing patches of play that baffled Warrington.

Jason Croker charges through the Warrington tacklers. © RLphotos.com

engage
Mutual Assurance

Friday 19 September 2008

Kick off: 20.00, Venue: GPW Recruitment Stadium, Att: 11,407

St Helens (12) 38
T: A Gardner 1, M Gidley 1, F Meli 1, J Wilkin 2, J Roby 2 **G:** S Long 5

Leeds (4) 10
T: D McGuire 1, G Ellis 1 **G:** R Burrow 1

St Helens squad
Wellens, Gardner, Gidley, Talau, Meli, Pryce, Long, Graham, Cunningham, Hargreaves, Gilmour, Wilkin, Flannery
Replacements: Fozzard, Roby, Clough, Fa'asavalu

Leeds squad
Smith, Ablett, Senior, Donald, McGuire, Burrow, Leuluai, Diskin, Peacock, Jones-Buchanan, Ellis, Sinfield
Replacements: Lauitiiti, Bailey, Scruton, Tansey

Some were calling it the battle of the season and nobody expected anything but a tight game between the two best sides in the competition, so it came as a huge surprise to see Leeds fall apart in such a fashion and get walloped 38–10. After watching Saints rip Leeds apart with such ease one was left wondering who could stop Daniel Anderson's men wrapping up the treble once again.

Minutes after the hooter had sounded the bookies were slashing the odds and making St Helens odds on favourites to lift the engage Super League Trophy, such was the ease with which they took the visitors apart. Twelve months ago Leeds came with a battle plan to 'rough' up the Saints and whilst they didn't win they

knew they had the measure up front and battered the Saints pack. So much so that when it came to the Grand Final the men from Knowsley Road were a patched up bunch and were taken to the cleaners.

Not so this time, Saints knew to keep the ball alive and not get involved down the middle in an arm wrestle. It stunned the Rhinos so much they had no answer to the dash and flair from the entire St Helens squad. With the ball passing through so many hands it was hard to see how Leeds could stop them and it took just seven minutes before Francis Meli burst down the left flank on a 50 metre run that stretched the visitors' defence. From the ensuing play the ball the three quarter's slick handling sent Ade Gardner in over into the right hand corner for a sensational touchdown. Long missed the difficult conversion from out wide but you sensed the home side were in the mood.

Yet despite not having much early possession, Leeds struck back through a huge high bomb from Sinfield that Meli couldn't take cleanly leaving McGuire an easy task to snatch up the loose ball and score. Sinfield also missed the conversion to leave it at 4–4. Poor discipline allowed St Helens two penalties which applied the pressure. It was no surprise when Cunningham breached the defence but Ellis palmed down his long pass to Meli and prevented the wingman from scoring an easy try. From the resulting scrum they swept the ball to the right which ended in Gidley latching onto a short blind side pass from Cunningham to crash over on 26 minutes. Long didn't miss this time as they took a commanding

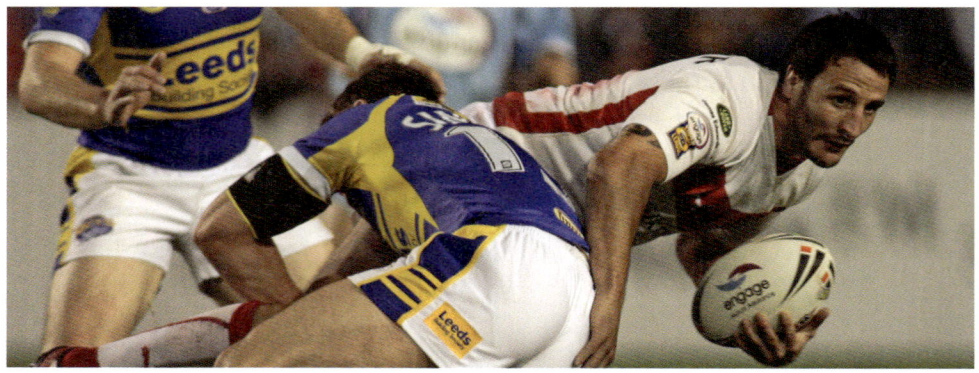

Lee Gilmour looks to off load in Saints' victory over the Rhinos.

lead of 10–4.

To their credit, Leeds were scrambling back in defence well but one wondered if they could drag themselves back into the match. They managed to do this on the back of two relieving penalties that allowed both Peacock and Senior chances to score but Saints were equal to the task. St Helens took advantage of a penalty for stealing just five minutes to the break giving Long an easy chance to score and he banged over a vital two pointer to stretch the lead to 12–4. Both sides battled bravely but Leeds had to do the most tackling and they were happy to go to the dressing rooms with just eight points adrift.

The half time talk from McClennan obviously lifted the Rhinos who surged forward time and time again in the hope of scoring but Saints' defence was solid as they denied Ryan Bailey close to the line. They then had a huge let off when Jordan Tansey put down a neat pass from Nick Scruton, an error that seemed to upset the visitors and offer a real boost to the home side, who soon afterwards supplied the combination of passes to see Francis Meli score out wide. Again Long missed the conversion but Saints were looking dangerous and full of confidence whilst Leeds appeared to be running out of steam. Leon Pryce was now running the

show as he produced some neat side stepping and constructive ball handling to get Saints over for another try barely four minutes after Meli had dived over in the corner. Cunningham's crafty off load sent James Roby in for his first of the game and he then scored a second just a few minutes later after another piece of magic from the veteran hooker created the gap. Long may have missed the first conversion but didn't fail with the second Roby try.

At 26–4 the game was over. Heads went down in the Rhinos ranks and the defence started to look ragged and struggled to keep Saints at bay. It didn't help matters when fullback Webb was helped from the field of play with what looked like a bad knee injury that could

Willie Talau drives for the line.

Daniel Anderson applauds the Saints fans.

leave him in doubt for the remaining play-off games. Jon Wilkin scored soon after Webb's injury by intercepting a lazy pass from Sinfield, giving Long an easy conversion. The home crowd were baying for more points, which they did get from the opposition however, with Gareth Ellis claiming some consolation for his hard work with a neat try that Burrows converted. It was all Saints soon after.

Wilkin yet again scored after chasing down a Pryce kick across the angle of the posts and touched down under the sticks. Long added more misery to the Rhinos' night by slotting over the extra two to bring up a massive 38–10 victory. Leeds boss Brian McClennan made no excuses, 'They were too good tonight...We'll take this on the chin. We're a very disappointed bunch at the moment...A bit of a reality check for us.' Daniel Anderson was over the moon at the way his players gelled together, 'I sat in awe of their performance in that second half especially.' Putting it mildly, the Rhinos disappointed their travelling fans and it will take something special from coach McClennan to get his players back up off the ground and back on the horse again for they were beaten both physically and mentally on the night.

One team had a place in the Grand Final but who would face them? Could Brian Noble produce the magic touch again, or would a French side grace Old Trafford? Would the Rhinos emulate last year's effort to come from behind yet again and have the chance to hold onto the trophy they picked up last year? The race was on.

Saturday 20 September 2008

Kick off: 18.00, Venue: Stade Gilbert Brutus, Att: 9,985
Match official: R Silverwood

Catalans (10) 26
T: J Murphy 1, J Wilson 1, D Pelo 2, O Elima 1 **G:** T Bosc 3

Wigan (14) 50
T: R Mathers 1, M Calderwood 2, G Carmont 1, P Richards 2, T Barrett 2, G Hock 1 **G:** P Richards 7

Catalans squad
Greenshields, Murphy, Wilson, Raguin, Pelo, Mogg, Bosc, Chan, McGuire, Elima, Croker, Fakir, Carlaw
Replacements: Guisset, Duport, Casty, Baile

Wigan squad
Mathers, Calderwood, Phelps, Carmont, Richards, Barrett, Leuluai, Fielden, Higham, Coley, Hansen, Bailey, J Tomkins
Replacements: Palea'aesina, Hock, O'Carroll, Smith

Wigan arrived in Perpignan full of confidence following their strong victory over Bradford and knowing they had snatched a draw at the Stade Gilbert Brutus a few weeks before. They also knew they would face a visit to Headingley if they could overturn the rampant French outfit. Headingley holds no fears for Noble due to his many wins there over the past few years so it was an added incentive for the Warriors to seek victory down on the South Coast of France.

The 26–50 final score bears no resemblance to how the game panned out for it was a hard solid slog for the first 55 minutes where neither side felt confident of winning. As for most games at home, the Catalans threw it all at Wigan. In the first 20 minutes they had all the possession and field position yet it wasn't until the 18th minute that the home side scored. Jerome Guisset made the break and found winger Pelo who rounded fullback Mathers with ease for a great try into the corner. Thomas Bosc kicked a superb touchline conversion to make it 6–0.

Wigan's defence was outstanding and Coach Brian Noble attributed this win to their efforts in that first stanza when they tackled like demons. 'The start of the game was really hard in relation to our defence and that desire set us up.' It was a remarkable showing because Catalans weaved plenty of magic but couldn't just get over the line and suffered for it later on. The drive was there for all to see but Wigan wouldn't give in and started to get back into the game after some fine tactical kicking from Trent Barrett, desperate to leave Wigan with some medal at least. On this showing they looked likely to upset Leeds.

Catalans made a mess of the restart kick from the Pelo try as they knocked on which allowed Wigan to put Carmont over from a great off load by Hock. Surprisingly the faithful boot of Pat Richards let him down when he sliced the ball wide of the posts. Wigan soon took

Iafeta Palea'aesina draws the Catalans defence.
© RLphotos.com

the lead when Phelps burst downfield before handing on to Barrett to cross near the posts. Richards didn't miss this time and the Warriors forged ahead 6–10. Catalans were bemused over the video referee's decision to turn down a try claim from McGuire who snapped up a dropped ball from Hock and raced away under the posts. But the video clearly showed Hock had been hit high in the tackle and the penalty went Wigan's way after the try was correctly disallowed.

Referee Ganson had to stop the game because his communication had broken down and it was a long wait before the decision was beamed onto the screen, much to the annoyance of the large record home crowd. The decision appeared to upset the home side who lost control and handed a penalty for a high shot which took them downfield for fullback Mathers to race over. Richards again missed the extras but at 6–14 Wigan were looking happy to go to the break with a nice lead.

Catalans were not to be outdone though and with just one minute remaining of the first half they struck back with another

Pelo try this time worked out from outstanding ball work from Fakir and Raguin. Bosc also missed the conversion but it was game on at 10–14 at the break. The home fans were somewhat confused when their side started the second half with a tentative approach and poor defence. Gone was the eagerness they had shown over the past two weeks and in its place was a more lethargic attitude that played into the hands of the Warriors.

Richards had a try turned down by the video referee soon after the kick off but two minutes later he was not going to be denied for it was a smart intercept of Wilson's pass that allowed him to race 80 metres and score. He added the extras to make it 10–20, and with Barrett pulling the strings it looked likely the French outfit were going to crumble but full credit to their fighting ability for they found some extra energy to bounce back. Winger Pelo started the run with a 35 metre break that gave Olivier Elima a try on 50 minutes, followed soon after by a touchdown from Wilson following a smart break from Mogg. Bosc couldn't add the extras but it was all square at 20–20. One would have

Gareth Hock looks for support. © RLphotos.com

expected the home side to take advantage as their loyal fans urged them on but some poor handling and bad options in the kicking stakes allowed Wigan back into the match.

Quick hands sent in Richards for his second try and he obliged with the extras, and from there on in it was all Wigan as the Catalans folded badly. Lack of discipline didn't help the Catalans cause as they gave away two penalties for dissent and referee Ganson made them pay. Richards kicked another penalty and soon after a Barrett try sealed the game. Hock and Calderwood added late touchdowns as did Wilson for the Catalans but it was all over well before this trio added to the scoreboard. It was an amazing effort from Wigan and Coach Noble was pleased with the way they played good open football saying, 'To come here and score 50 points is a massive effort.'

It was the end of the road for the Catalans but the record crowd stayed behind to cheer off their heroes, for it had been a great season for a club expected to be in the bottom half of the table. Their coach, Mick Potter, did a great job and it was no surprise when he announced at the press conference that it was a great place to live and he had enjoyed his time in the South of France. 'If I could take the weather with me back to England it would be great.' The prospect of finding the sunshine on a regular basis seemed far-fetched as he will take over St Helens—a far from easy job—stepping into the shoes of one Daniel Anderson. Wigan lived to fight another day and travel to Headingley with more than fingers crossed. In this game they played top rugby league football, especially in the second half.

Kick off: 20.00, Venue: Headingley Carnegie, Att: 13,112

Leeds (6) 18
T: L Smith 2, K Senior 1 **G:** K Sinfield 3

Wigan (2) 14
T: H Hansen 1, I Palea'aesina 1
G: P Richards 3

Leeds squad
Webb, Smith, Ablett, Senior, Donald, McGuire, Burrow, Leuluai, Diskin, Peacock, Jones-Buchanan, Ellis, Sinfield
Replacements: Lauitiiti, Bailey, Scruton, Kirke

Wigan squad
Mathers, Calderwood, Phelps, Carmont, Richards, Barrett, Leuluai, Fielden, Higham, Coley, Hansen, Bailey, J Tomkins
Replacements: Palea'aesina, Smith, Hock, Colbon

Both Leeds and Wigan knew they were just 80 minutes away from making the Grand Final and taking on the mighty St Helens for the richest prize in Super League. It was a repeat of last year's final eliminator and Brian Noble was hoping the momentum would carry them through against a side that had come back over the Pennines a week ago licking their wounds after a flogging by St Helens to the tune of 38–10.

The ground was a buzz of excitement as the fans waited to see if coach McClennan had found the right sort of magic to turn them back into champions. Or would Wigan use their new found momentum and leave the Headingley outfit in a fit of failure? To say it was a thriller was an understatement, as both sets of

Lee Smith added two tries to see Leeds through to Old Trafford.

forwards and backs alike charged into each other with so much venom it was obvious things could get out of hand. So it proved with skirmishes being the order of the day and at one point there was an all-in brawl.

It's very rare to find a man of the match going to a player from the losing side. Anyone watching Mark Calderwood's effort would have to agree that this flyer, not wanted at Wigan and set to play for Hull FC next season, became the hero for most of the game. He could have helped Wigan pull off an amazing victory that was still on the cards right up until the final seconds when sadly Stuart Fielden knocked on. Calderwood pulled off five sensational tackles to thwart a Leeds side that looked likely to win by a massive margin such was their advantage in possession and field position.

His first heroic tackle came after just 19 minutes when the big forward Jamie Jones-Buchanan made a sensational break of 50 metres before the Wigan winger cut him down. Calderwood predictably, was penalised for diving on the ball at the play the ball which resulted in a penalty and an all-in brawl. Tomkins and Barrett got involved and before you knew it the entire set of players came into the fray swirging rights and lefts that would have done Mike Tyson proud!

Referee Steve Ganson sent Senior and Calderwood to the sin-bin but he could have added a few more if he wanted. That scuffle perhaps did Leeds a favour for it appeared to fire them up more than Wigan. Although defences were tight, the game was exciting as both teams tried to gain space and the gap but it was left to a penalty goal each from Sinfield and Richards to get the scoreboard working.

Leeds should have got the first try when

Harrison Hansen picked up a try to make life difficult for the Rhinos.

The force of the tackle from Jamie Peacock on Phil Bailey denotes the tension in the game.

the big frame of Jones-Buchanan dived for the corner only to be bounced into touch by none other than that man again, Calderwood. With Jamie Peacock leading the forward rushes it was only going to be a matter of time until the Rhinos scored a try. It came from Lee Smith who latched onto a looping pass from McGuire who had supported the fine break from dummy-half by Burrow. Sinfield missed the goal but it was a surprise to see them go into the dressing rooms just with a 6–2 lead.

After the restart it was clear that Wigan were struggling to get going and when Lauitiiti dived in at the corner it was no surprise to see who had forced him into the corner flag—Calderwood! The video ref turned down Lauitiiti's effort and five minutes later he turned down Jamie Jones-Buchanan who looked to have got the ball down. Wigan were looking desperate in defence and Calderwood

again stopped Rob Burrow from diving under the posts, his ball-and-all tackle stunning not just Burrow but all the crowd. Soon after Leeds appeared to score a fair try but it was turned down yet again making a total of three tries disallowed in the space of 15 minutes. This made the home crowd nervous in case it was going to be one of those nights. It certainly looked that way when Jamie Peacock seemed to score a clear cut try that Ian Smith wiped out for what he saw as an obstruction. The fact it took nearly five minutes to make the decision did little to soothe the nerves of the crowd who were baying for blood. We went into the final quarter with Leeds hanging on to a four point lead at 6–2.

Wigan's defence finally broke when Donald interchanged with Senior who barged over to settle the nerves. Sinfield goaled and it looked like the Warriors were done at 12–2. Sinfield added another two points from a penalty to stretch it to 14–2 and it stayed that way until, with seven minutes to go, Wigan struck back against the run of play. Wigan looked towards something special from Trent Barrett and the former Australian test star didn't let them down, his kick created havoc amongst the Leeds defence before Hansen crossed and with Richards adding the two extra points the Warriors were just a converted try away from levelling the scores.

At 14–8, Skipper Sinfield went for a drop goal with four minutes remaining but it went wide which gave the visitors possession and they charged downfield looking dangerous. Palea'aesina dropped the ball allowing winger Lee Smith to kick forward and regather to score what surely would be the winning try but Wigan would not lie down. Again they regained possession from the kick off and with two minutes to go Palea'aesina crashed over under the posts to give Richards an easy conversion. This made it 18–14 and offered Wigan a slim chance with just seconds remaining.

The crowd were on their toes as Leeds slowly came back to the half way line to kick off. Ganson stopped the clock and when Sinfield restarted the game the tension was electric as they watched the long kick fly through the air towards Stuart Fielden who was standing under his own posts. What last throw of the dice would Wigan produce? A kick and chase downfield? Or a chip over the first line of defence? Or would they feed it wide and hope Calderwood could snatch the winner with his speed? Before one could take breath and make a decision Fielden knocked on! It was a tragic end to a fine match.

Wigan boss Brian Noble paid tribute to

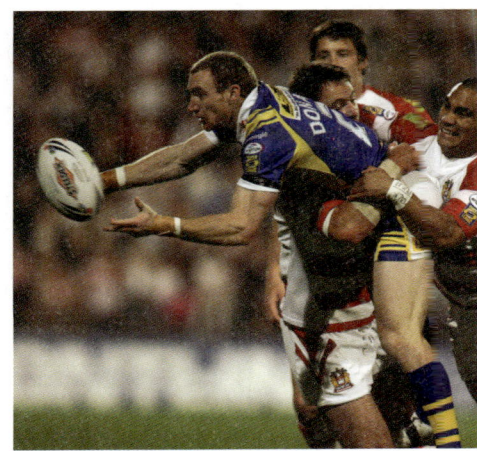
Scott Donald takes the tackle.

his players for a great effort and sticking in there, 'All 17 gave their all but we just couldn't find field position to post some points. I'm extremely proud of my players.' Rhinos' coach Brian McClennan was indeed a relieved man as they had so many chances to wrap up the game early and that he felt the referee failed to allow space at the ruck, 'The ruck was so sloppy. I was concerned that the players would get upset about how it was being policed that they would throw their hands up, they needed to show some fortitude and they did.'

And so we go to the big one, a repeat of the engage Super League Grand Final of 2007 where Leeds will once again go to Old Trafford as underdogs but the question was could Brian McClennan get the players back up onto the horse? The answer at Headingley was yes. Could he do it again at the Theatre of Dreams?

Player of the Play-off   Week 3
Mark Calderwood, Wigan
Tremendous speed and superb incisive tackling that kept Wigan in the game and almost saw them through to Old Trafford.

engage
Mutual Assurance

Kick off: 18.00, Venue: Old Trafford,
Att: 68,810, Match official: A Klein

St Helens (6) 16
T: A Gardner 1, M Gidley 1, J Graham 1
G: S Long 2

Leeds (12) 24
T: L Smith 1, R Hall 1, D McGuire 2
G: K Sinfield 4

St Helens squad
Wellens, Gardner, Gidley, Talau, Meli,
Pryce, Long, Graham, Cunningham,
Hargreaves, Gilmour, Wilkin, Flannery
Replacements: Roby, Fozzard, Clough,
Fa'asavalu

Leeds squad
Smith, Hall, Ablett, Senior, Donald,
McGuire, Burrow, Leuluai, Diskin,
Peacock, Jones-Buchanan, Ellis, Sinfield
Replacements: Lauitiiti, Bailey, Scruton,
Kirke

Harry Sunderland Trophy winner Lee Smith fends off the tackle.

St Helens started the day firm favourites despite an overcast morning, and when the news filtered through that Brent Webb was out of the Rhinos side, the punters started piling onto Daniel Anderson's men with gusto. To make matters worse for Leeds they had to switch Lee Smith from the wing to fullback and brought in Ryan Hall out on the right flank. Smith is no stranger to the number 1 position but the loss of Webb and his classic link up style and evasive running was going to be a huge blow to their chances. Add to that the fact Hall had not played since an injury in July, it was a huge gamble for Leeds coach Brian McClennan. All the pundits had Saints winning by a mile after they ripped Leeds apart in the major semi

final but as the day wore on the sky darkened and the chance of rain looked highly likely—the Saints fans hoped the rain would stay away.

Leeds on the other hand were doing a rain dance all around the Old Trafford ground for they knew a wild and wet night could swing things in their favour. Was this the same side who won the World Club Challenge against the Melbourne Storm at the start of the year in shocking wet conditions? Of course it was and the players and fans were milking this fully. The Challenge Cup holders and League Leaders made no bones over the fact they wanted a dry track and their hearts must have dipped somewhat when just one hour before

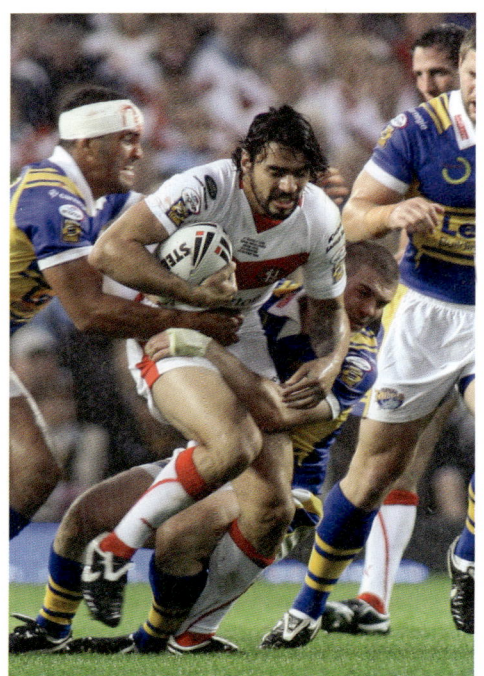

Ade Gardner is hauled down by the Leeds defenders.

kick off the heavens opened. The atmosphere was electric and so was the sky as both sides walked out into the pouring rain and you sensed a buzz going around the ground at what tactics would be used from both teams.

Full credit to St Helens, they opted to play dry weather stuff and kept the ball alive with amazing handling. Within five minutes they broke the Leeds defence with a superb inside pass from Sean Long from the play the ball area to the rampaging second rower Lee Gilmour. He raced away 30 metres before interchanging with fullback Wellens and sending in the supporting prop James Graham under the posts. Long slotted over the extras and one sensed a nervous flutter amongst the supporters from both sides who were no doubt thinking this could be another easy win for the red and whites.

Soon after, Gilmour again charged through the confused Rhinos defence and it took a great tackle from Lee Smith to stop them scoring again. Leeds had all sorts of problems down the middle and seemed incapable of stopping the hard running from the Saints pack but somehow they hung in there with desperate cover defending. It was only when fullback Smith returned a deep kick that the Rhinos showed any form. Smith's weaving run took him over the half way line and only a solid tackle from Wellens prevented him going all the way. Yet the momentum had changed—Leeds were applying the pressure this time and it was Saints' turn to defend for their life.

For 15 minutes the game settled down into a battle royal with some fierce exchanges and the odd error. This was no surprise considering the conditions, yet Leeds drove into the red zone of Saints and scrum-half Rob Burrow scooted away from dummy-half to set up a strong run from Jamie Jones-Buchanan who appeared to be lunging for the line. Instead he slipped out a superb pass to the supporting Smith who dived over near the sticks. Sinfield tagged on the easy conversion to square it all up. It looked to stay that way to the break but Leeds mounted one last surge. With only seconds remaining of the first stanza, a neat three quarter line link found Senior who under pressure from Meli decided to tap it onto his winger Hall, who amazingly accepted the pass and then kicked forward towards the line where he lunged out with his arm to touch down. The try was referred to the video referee who took his time before giving the nod of approval sending Leeds into the break with a handy lead.

To say Saints coach Daniel Anderson was none too pleased with his side was an understatement as the Sky TV cameras showed a normally composed coach ranting and raving like a mad man. Needless to say that all the players got the message! It was amazing television and the look on some player's faces told its own story, but did it work? In the short term, yes, because within two minutes of the restart a kick into the corner created problems for Rhinos winger Donald who couldn't prevent Gardner from palming down the ball backwards into the path of Gidley who made no mistake in crossing out wide. Sean Long banged over a tremendous pressure conversion and it was game on. Instead of the try lifting Saints, they appeared confused and tried to score on each play the ball rather than obtaining good field position before trying something fancy.

Sinfield's kicking game was outstanding and repeatedly forced the Saints back. It was no surprise when Saints coughed up possession close to their own line and that Sinfield's kick enabled McGuire to race onto the ball and touch down. The try creator made no mistake with the extras. Again, Saints tried to rally but dropped the ball or sent out poor passes that stifled and frustrated their attack. Not surprisingly they reverted to the kicking game that had proved so successful for Leeds. From a deep kick they obtained possession which enabled Roby to send out a long looping pass on the overlap for Gardner to race in with ease out wide. Sadly Long couldn't add the two extra points but Saints were back in the hunt.

With 18 minutes to go it was anyone's match but you sensed Leeds were getting on top with Peacock leading the way and Sinfield's near perfect kicking game ensuring Saints got more tired as the game wore on. It was no coincidence when the Leeds skipper hoisted a huge bomb towards winger Meli who couldn't take it cleanly and the bouncing ball shot into the supporting hands of McGuire who executed some magic steps and swerved to score a fine solo try.

Kylie Leuluai hauls down Paul Wellens.

As the minutes ticked by the game was becoming tighter and Leeds were not going to let St Helens back into the game. Solid defence was a major factor in those final moments and Brian McClennan's men knew they would retain the trophy, the first time a Leeds outfit had won back-to-back titles. It was a win Leeds fully deserved, especially coach McClennan who had the difficult job of stepping into the shoes of Tony Smith, the now England coach, but his quiet laid back style had helped his players regroup and overcome adversity over the past fortnight since Saints ripped their hearts and minds out at Knowsley Road.

It was a nice touch when the two coaches embraced and shook hands with about 30 seconds of the match remaining; Anderson knew a better team and better coaching tactics had beaten him on the night. Anderson openly admitted they were outplayed and in some ways it was a shame that he couldn't have finished his stint here in England with a treble but he's been a great boost to our game and his style of play has excited fans from all over the country and of course France. 'I'm very proud of my time at St Helens, they are a great club and the fans are fantastic,' he added. For Leeds the scenes of joy were there for all to see, especially for Lee Smith who rightly won the Harry Sunderland Trophy for being man of the match—his all round effort was superb. McGuire and Sinfield were also heroes displaying enough skills and brain power to earn a trip down under for the World Cup.

McGuire would have been more pleased than most as two weeks ago he was completely outplayed by his opposite Leon Pryce; the same couldn't be said on this wet Saturday night where he weaved his magic that left Pryce struggling to make any impact on the game at all. It now remains to be seen if McGuire has done enough to prize away the England number 6 shirt for the opening game in Australia. Only time will tell.

The Rhinos celebrate winning the engage Super League Grand Final.

The squad are interviewed for the fans at Headingley.

For Brian McClennan it was a dream come true, 'We were a bit down when Saints flogged us but we have a great spirit here and the boys did well and made the club and the City of Leeds proud.' When asked if it was a huge gamble to select Ryan Hall on the wing after being out for so long with an injury he just smiled and said, 'He did great, it's the first time I have ever seen him kick a ball.' It may be the first time but it probably won't be the last as he came up trumps with a vital try just before half time. A sustained team effort got them over the line along with a defence that worked like demons on fire.

The lap of honour was a pleasure to watch as the Leeds faithful embraced their heroes with songs and cheers that would have gone on until way past midnight. It was a fitting end to a fantastic engage Super League season, why even the referee Ashley Klein had a fine game and you can't really ask for much more than that!

Player of the Grand Final

Lee Smith, Leeds
Smith justifiably won the Harry Sunderland Trophy with a tremendous all round display and some superb tackling.

Coach and captain proudly display the Grand Final Trophy.

	Team	P	W	D	L	PF	PA	DIF	PTS
1	Leeds	1	1	0	0	30	10	+20	2
2	Wigan	1	1	0	0	47	28	+19	2
3	Warrington	1	1	0	0	32	20	+12	2
4	Catalans	1	1	0	0	21	14	+7	2
5	Hull KR	1	1	0	0	24	22	+2	2
6	Wakefield	1	1	0	0	26	24	+2	2
7	St Helens	1	0	0	1	22	24	-2	0
8	Bradford	1	0	0	1	24	26	-2	0
9	Castleford	1	0	0	1	14	21	-7	0
10	Hull FC	1	0	0	1	20	32	-12	0
11	Harlequins	1	0	0	1	28	47	-19	0
12	Huddersfield	1	0	0	1	10	30	-20	0

	Team	P	W	D	L	PF	PA	DIF	PTS
1	Leeds	2	2	0	0	74	18	+55	4
2	Wigan	2	2	0	0	75	44	+31	4
3	Hull KR	2	2	0	0	48	42	+6	4
4	Bradford	2	1	0	1	62	38	+24	2
5	St Helens	2	1	0	1	52	46	+6	2
6	Warrington	2	1	0	1	54	50	+4	2
7	Catalans	2	1	0	1	41	38	+3	2
8	Harlequins	2	1	0	1	52	53	-1	2
9	Wakefield	2	1	0	1	34	68	-34	2
10	Castleford	2	0	0	2	30	49	-19	0
11	Hull FC	2	0	0	2	26	56	-30	0
12	Huddersfield	2	0	0	2	22	68	-46	0

	Team	P	W	D	L	PF	PA	DIF	PTS
1	Leeds	3	3	0	0	108	24	+84	6
2	Wigan	3	2	0	1	97	68	+29	4
3	Harlequins	3	2	0	1	86	71	+15	4
4	St Helens	3	2	0	1	74	62	+12	4
5	Hull KR	3	2	0	1	76	71	+5	4
6	Warrington	3	2	0	1	83	78	+5	4
7	Bradford	3	1	0	2	78	60	+18	2
8	Huddersfield	3	1	0	2	86	80	+6	2
9	Catalans	3	1	0	2	47	72	-25	2
10	Hull FC	3	1	0	2	50	78	-28	2
11	Wakefield	3	1	0	2	52	102	-50	2
12	Castleford	3	0	0	3	42	113	-71	0

	Team	P	W	D	L	PF	PA	DIF	PTS
1	Leeds	4	4	0	0	128	36	+92	8
2	Wigan	4	3	0	1	125	82	+43	6
3	Warrington	4	3	0	1	121	96	+25	6
4	Harlequins	4	3	0	1	108	87	+21	6
5	St Helens	4	3	0	1	108	92	+16	6
6	Huddersfield	4	2	0	2	114	88	+26	4
7	Hull KR	4	2	0	2	88	91	-3	4
8	Bradford	4	1	0	3	92	88	+4	2
9	Catalans	4	1	0	3	65	110	-45	2
10	Hull FC	4	1	0	3	58	106	-48	2
11	Wakefield	4	1	0	3	82	136	-54	2
12	Castleford	4	0	0	4	58	135	-77	0

	Team	P	W	D	L	PF	PA	DIF	PTS
1	Leeds	5	4	0	1	148	74	+74	8
2	Harlequins	5	4	0	1	132	87	+45	8
3	Warrington	5	4	0	1	153	116	+37	8
4	St Helens	5	4	0	1	138	121	+17	8
5	Wigan	5	3	0	2	145	114	+31	6
6	Bradford	5	2	0	3	112	106	+6	4
7	Huddersfield	5	2	0	3	114	112	+2	4
8	Hull KR	5	2	0	3	108	113	-5	4
9	Wakefield	5	2	0	3	104	156	-52	4
10	Catalans	5	1	0	4	83	130	-47	2
11	Hull FC	5	1	0	4	87	136	-49	2
12	Castleford	5	1	0	4	96	155	-59	2

	Team	P	W	D	L	PF	PA	DIF	PTS
1	Leeds	6	5	0	1	196	74	+122	10
2	Wigan	6	4	0	2	165	133	+32	8
3	Warrington	6	4	0	2	163	139	+24	8
4	St Helens	6	4	0	2	148	145	+3	8
5	Harlequins	6	4	0	2	132	135	-3	8
6	Bradford	6	3	0	3	135	116	+19	6
7	Hull KR	6	3	0	3	128	117	+11	6
8	Huddersfield	6	2	0	4	133	132	+1	4
9	Catalans	6	2	0	4	107	140	-33	4
10	Hull FC	6	2	0	4	105	144	-39	4
11	Wakefield	6	2	0	4	112	174	-62	4
12	Castleford	6	1	0	5	100	175	-75	2

	Team	P	W	D	L	PF	PA	DIF	PTS
1	Leeds	7	6	0	1	240	76	+164	12
2	Warrington	7	5	0	2	193	153	+40	10
3	St Helens	7	5	0	2	194	155	+39	10
4	Hull KR	7	4	0	3	139	127	+12	8
5	Wigan	7	4	0	3	175	179	-4	8
6	Harlequins	7	4	0	3	154	159	-5	8
7	Bradford	7	3	0	4	137	160	-23	6
8	Catalans	7	3	0	4	131	162	-31	6
9	Wakefield	7	3	0	4	140	188	-48	6
10	Huddersfield	7	2	0	5	147	162	-15	4
11	Hull FC	7	2	0	5	115	155	-40	4
12	Castleford	7	1	0	6	114	203	-89	2

	Team	P	W	D	L	PF	PA	DIF	PTS
1	Leeds	8	7	0	1	270	80	+190	14
2	Warrington	8	6	0	2	227	184	+43	12
3	St Helens	8	5	0	3	220	183	+37	10
4	Wigan	8	5	0	3	193	191	+2	10
5	Hull KR	8	4	0	4	151	145	+6	8
6	Harlequins	8	4	0	4	178	191	-13	8
7	Bradford	8	4	0	4	169	184	-15	8
8	Catalans	8	4	0	4	159	182	-23	8
9	Huddersfield	8	3	0	5	175	188	-13	6
10	Wakefield	8	3	0	5	160	216	-56	6
11	Hull FC	8	2	0	6	119	185	-66	4
12	Castleford	8	1	0	7	145	237	-92	2

	Team	P	W	D	L	PF	PA	DIF	PTS
1	Leeds	9	8	0	1	284	90	+194	16
2	Warrington	9	6	0	3	233	192	+41	12
3	Wigan	9	6	0	3	201	195	+6	12
4	St Helens	9	5	0	4	230	197	+33	10
5	Bradford	9	5	0	4	219	188	+31	10
6	Harlequins	9	5	0	4	186	197	-11	10
7	Hull KR	9	4	1	4	175	169	+6	9
8	Catalans	9	4	1	4	187	210	-23	9
9	Huddersfield	9	3	1	5	199	212	-13	7
10	Wakefield	9	3	0	6	164	224	-60	6
11	Hull FC	9	2	1	6	147	213	-66	5
12	Castleford	9	1	0	8	149	287	-138	2

	Team	P	W	D	L	PF	PA	DIF	PTS
1	Leeds	10	8	0	2	294	104	+190	16
2	Wigan	10	7	0	3	215	205	+10	14
3	Bradford	10	6	0	4	243	196	+47	12
4	Warrington	10	6	0	4	235	208	+27	12
5	Harlequins	10	6	0	4	221	213	+8	12
6	Catalans	10	5	1	4	207	226	-19	11
7	St Helens	10	5	0	5	254	227	+27	10
8	Hull KR	10	4	1	5	191	204	-13	9
9	Wakefield	10	4	0	6	180	226	-46	8
10	Huddersfield	10	3	1	6	215	232	-17	7
11	Hull FC	10	2	1	7	155	237	-82	5
12	Castleford	10	2	0	8	179	311	-132	4

	Team	P	W	D	L	PF	PA	DIF	PTS
1	Leeds	11	9	0	2	326	116	+210	18
2	Wigan	11	7	0	4	239	231	+8	14
3	Catalans	11	6	1	4	233	250	-17	13
4	St Helens	11	6	0	5	312	239	+73	12
5	Bradford	11	6	0	5	261	216	+45	12
6	Warrington	11	6	0	5	247	240	+7	12
7	Harlequins	11	6	0	5	233	271	-38	12
8	Hull KR	11	5	1	5	211	222	-11	11
9	Wakefield	11	5	0	6	198	242	-44	10
10	Huddersfield	11	3	1	7	231	250	-19	7
11	Hull FC	11	3	1	7	187	249	-62	7
12	Castleford	11	2	0	9	191	343	-152	4

	Team	P	W	D	L	PF	PA	DIF	PTS
1	Leeds	12	10	0	2	362	138	+224	20
2	Catalans	12	7	1	4	271	280	-9	15
3	St Helens	12	7	0	5	342	261	+81	14
4	Bradford	12	7	0	5	287	228	+59	14
5	Wigan	12	7	0	5	251	257	-6	14
6	Warrington	12	6	0	6	269	270	-1	12
7	Wakefield	12	6	0	6	222	262	-40	12
8	Harlequins	12	6	0	6	253	295	-42	12
9	Hull KR	12	5	1	6	233	258	-25	11
10	Hull FC	12	4	1	7	215	269	-54	9
11	Huddersfield	12	3	1	8	251	278	-27	7
12	Castleford	12	2	0	10	221	381	-160	4

	Team	P	W	D	L	PF	PA	DIF	PTS
1	Leeds	13	11	0	2	402	164	+238	22
2	Catalans	13	8	1	4	289	296	-7	17
3	St Helens	13	8	0	5	399	277	+122	16
4	Bradford	13	7	0	6	313	268	+45	14
5	Warrington	13	7	0	6	305	304	+1	14
6	Wakefield	13	7	0	6	276	278	-2	14
7	Wigan	13	7	0	6	267	314	-47	14
8	Hull KR	13	6	1	6	255	275	-20	13
9	Harlequins	13	6	0	7	269	313	-44	12
10	Hull FC	13	4	1	8	232	291	-59	9
11	Huddersfield	13	3	1	9	285	314	-29	7
12	Castleford	13	2	0	11	237	435	-198	4

	Team	P	W	D	L	PF	PA	DIF	PTS
1	Leeds	14	12	0	2	460	176	+284	24
2	St Helens	14	9	0	5	427	287	+140	18
3	Catalans	14	8	1	5	299	324	-25	17
4	Bradford	14	8	0	6	359	292	+67	16
5	Wigan	14	8	0	6	305	328	-23	16
6	Warrington	14	7	0	7	319	342	-23	14
7	Harlequins	14	7	0	7	303	339	-36	14
8	Wakefield	14	7	0	7	288	336	-48	14
9	Hull KR	14	6	1	7	271	325	-54	13
10	Huddersfield	14	4	1	9	335	330	+5	9
11	Hull FC	14	4	1	9	258	325	-67	9
12	Castleford	14	2	0	12	261	481	-220	4

	Team	P	W	D	L	PF	PA	DIF	PTS
1	Leeds	15	13	0	2	490	190	+300	26
2	St Helens	15	10	0	5	443	295	+148	20
3	Catalans	15	9	1	5	347	324	+23	19
4	Wigan	15	9	0	6	343	358	-15	18
5	Bradford	15	8	0	7	373	322	+51	16
6	Hull KR	15	7	1	7	293	333	-40	15
7	Warrington	15	7	0	8	347	378	-31	14
8	Harlequins	15	7	0	8	311	361	-50	14
9	Wakefield	15	7	0	8	318	374	-56	14
10	Huddersfield	15	4	1	10	335	378	-43	9
11	Hull FC	15	4	1	10	266	341	-75	9
12	Castleford	15	3	0	12	297	509	-212	6

	Team	P	W	D	L	PF	PA	DIF	PTS
1	Leeds	16	14	0	2	528	212	+316	28
2	St Helens	16	11	0	5	495	305	+190	22
3	Catalans	16	10	1	5	371	340	+31	21
4	Wigan	16	9	0	7	347	392	-45	18
5	Bradford	16	8	0	8	389	346	+43	16
6	Warrington	16	8	0	8	387	402	-15	16
7	Wakefield	16	8	0	8	350	390	-40	16
8	Hull KR	16	7	1	8	303	385	-82	15
9	Harlequins	16	7	0	9	335	401	-66	14
10	Huddersfield	16	5	1	10	369	382	-13	11
11	Hull FC	16	4	1	11	288	379	-91	9
12	Castleford	16	3	0	13	313	541	-228	6

	Team	P	W	D	L	PF	PA	DIF	PTS
1	Leeds	17	14	0	3	552	240	+312	28
2	St Helens	17	12	0	5	553	325	+228	24
3	Catalans	17	11	1	5	416	378	+38	23
4	Warrington	17	9	0	8	425	422	+3	18
5	Wakefield	17	9	0	8	378	416	-38	18
6	Wigan	17	9	0	8	385	437	-52	18
7	Bradford	17	8	0	9	409	404	+5	16
8	Harlequins	17	8	0	9	363	425	-62	16
9	Hull KR	17	7	1	9	323	423	-100	15
10	Huddersfield	17	5	1	11	395	410	-15	11
11	Hull FC	17	5	1	11	328	393	-65	11
12	Castleford	17	3	0	14	327	581	-254	6

	Team	P	W	D	L	PF	PA	DIF	PTS
1	Leeds	18	14	0	4	564	266	+298	28
2	St Helens	18	13	0	5	579	337	+242	26
3	Catalans	18	12	1	5	468	392	+76	25
4	Wakefield	18	10	0	8	404	434	-30	20
5	Wigan	18	9	1	8	407	459	-52	19
6	Bradford	18	9	0	9	445	426	+19	18
7	Warrington	18	9	0	9	439	474	-35	18
8	Harlequins	18	8	0	10	379	451	-72	16
9	Hull KR	18	7	1	10	341	449	-108	15
10	Huddersfield	18	6	1	11	421	426	-5	13
11	Hull FC	18	5	1	12	350	429	-79	11
12	Castleford	18	3	1	14	349	603	-254	7

	Team	P	W	D	L	PF	PA	DIF	PTS
1	Leeds	19	15	0	4	582	278	+304	30
2	St Helens	19	14	0	5	625	353	+272	28
3	Catalans	19	13	1	5	498	406	+92	27
4	Wigan	19	10	1	8	445	479	-34	21
5	Bradford	19	10	0	9	485	446	+39	20
6	Warrington	19	10	0	9	463	496	-33	20
7	Wakefield	19	10	0	9	418	464	-46	20
8	Harlequins	19	8	0	11	399	489	-90	16
9	Hull KR	19	7	1	11	361	489	-128	15
10	Huddersfield	19	6	1	12	437	472	-35	13
11	Hull FC	19	5	1	13	372	453	-81	11
12	Castleford	19	3	1	15	361	621	-260	7

	Team	P	W	D	L	PF	PA	DIF	PTS
1	St Helens	20	15	0	5	679	353	+326	30
2	Leeds	20	15	0	5	604	301	+303	30
3	Catalans	20	14	1	5	528	424	+104	29
4	Wigan	20	11	1	8	468	501	-33	23
5	Warrington	20	11	0	9	523	520	+3	22
6	Bradford	20	10	0	10	509	471	+38	20
7	Wakefield	20	10	0	10	442	524	-82	20
8	Harlequins	20	8	0	12	399	543	-144	16
9	Huddersfield	20	7	1	12	462	496	-34	15
10	Hull KR	20	7	1	12	371	507	-136	15
11	Hull FC	20	5	1	14	390	483	-93	11
12	Castleford	20	4	1	15	379	631	-252	9

	Team	P	W	D	L	PF	PA	DIF	PTS
1	St Helens	21	16	0	5	747	365	+382	32
2	Leeds	21	16	0	5	650	309	+341	32
3	Catalans	21	15	1	5	560	450	+110	31
4	Warrington	21	12	0	9	555	548	+7	24
5	Wigan	21	11	1	9	490	540	-50	23
6	Bradford	21	10	0	11	537	503	+34	20
7	Wakefield	21	10	0	11	460	550	-90	20
8	Hull KR	21	8	1	12	410	529	-119	17
9	Harlequins	21	8	0	13	425	575	-150	16
10	Huddersfield	21	7	1	13	470	542	-72	15
11	Hull FC	21	6	1	14	416	501	-85	13
12	Castleford	21	4	1	16	391	699	-308	9

	Team	P	W	D	L	PF	PA	DIF	PTS
1	St Helens	22	17	0	5	793	377	+416	34
2	Leeds	22	17	0	5	687	333	+354	34
3	Catalans	22	15	1	6	584	487	+97	31
4	Warrington	22	13	0	9	574	566	+8	26
5	Wigan	22	11	1	10	502	586	-84	23
6	Bradford	22	11	0	11	561	513	+48	22
7	Wakefield	22	10	0	12	470	574	-104	20
8	Hull KR	22	8	1	13	428	573	-145	17
9	Harlequins	22	8	0	14	437	641	-204	16
10	Hull FC	22	7	1	14	460	519	-59	15
11	Huddersfield	22	7	1	14	488	561	-73	15
12	Castleford	22	5	1	16	457	711	-254	11

	Team	P	W	D	L	PF	PA	DIF	PTS
1	St Helens	23	18	0	5	835	387	+448	36
2	Leeds	23	17	0	6	699	355	+344	34
3	Catalans	23	15	1	7	600	517	+83	31
4	Warrington	23	14	0	9	596	578	+18	28
5	Wigan	23	12	1	10	568	592	-24	25
6	Bradford	23	11	0	12	585	549	+36	22
7	Wakefield	23	10	0	13	480	616	-136	20
8	Hull KR	23	9	1	13	458	589	-131	19
9	Harlequins	23	9	0	14	473	665	-192	18
10	Huddersfield	23	8	1	14	528	575	-47	17
11	Hull FC	23	7	1	15	466	585	-119	15
12	Castleford	23	5	1	17	471	751	-280	11

	Team	P	W	D	L	PF	PA	DIF	PTS
1	St Helens	24	19	0	5	852	403	+449	38
2	Leeds	24	18	0	6	727	373	+354	36
3	Catalans	24	15	2	7	616	533	+83	32
4	Warrington	24	14	0	10	612	595	+17	28
5	Wigan	24	12	2	10	584	608	-24	26
6	Bradford	24	11	0	13	603	577	+26	22
7	Wakefield	24	10	0	14	502	664	-162	20
8	Harlequins	24	10	0	14	513	681	-168	20
9	Huddersfield	24	9	1	14	558	599	-41	19
10	Hull KR	24	9	1	14	474	629	-155	19
11	Hull FC	24	7	1	16	490	615	-125	15
12	Castleford	24	6	1	17	519	773	-254	13

	Team	P	W	D	L	PF	PA	DIF	PTS
1	St Helens	25	20	0	5	884	419	+465	40
2	Leeds	25	19	0	6	781	385	+396	38
3	Catalans	25	16	2	7	638	553	+85	34
4	Warrington	25	14	0	11	646	631	−15	28
5	Wigan	25	13	2	10	616	630	-14	28
6	Bradford	25	12	0	13	645	591	+54	24
7	Hull KR	25	10	1	14	510	663	-153	21
8	Wakefield	25	10	0	15	524	696	-172	20
9	Harlequins	25	10	0	15	529	713	-184	20
10	Huddersfield	25	9	1	15	578	621	-43	19
11	Hull FC	25	7	1	17	504	657	-153	15
12	Castleford	25	6	1	18	531	827	-296	13

	Team	P	W	D	L	PF	PA	DIF	PTS
1	St Helens	26	21	0	5	924	441	+483	42
2	Leeds	26	20	0	6	833	401	+432	40
3	Catalans	26	16	2	8	670	591	+79	34
4	Warrington	26	14	0	12	670	675	-5	28
5	Wigan	26	13	2	11	632	682	-50	28
6	Bradford	26	13	0	13	687	609	+78	26
7	Wakefield	26	11	0	15	562	728	-166	22
8	Hull KR	26	10	1	15	528	705	-177	21
9	Harlequins	26	10	0	16	535	739	-204	20
10	Huddersfield	26	9	1	16	600	661	-61	19
11	Hull FC	26	8	1	17	530	663	-133	17
12	Castleford	26	7	1	18	575	851	-276	15

	Team	P	W	D	L	PF	PA	DIF	PTS
1	St Helens	27	21	1	5	940	457	+483	43
2	Leeds	27	21	0	6	863	413	+450	42
3	Catalans	27	16	2	9	694	625	+69	34
4	Wigan	27	13	3	11	648	698	-50	29
5	Bradford	27	14	0	13	705	625	+80	28
6	Warrington	27	14	0	13	690	713	-23	28
7	Hull KR	27	11	1	15	564	713	-149	23
8	Wakefield	27	11	0	16	574	758	-184	22
9	Harlequins	27	11	0	16	569	763	-194	22
10	Huddersfield	27	10	1	16	638	681	-43	21
11	Hull FC	27	8	1	18	538	699	-161	17
12	Castleford	27	7	1	19	591	869	-278	15